INTRODUCTION
OF THE
STUDY OF HISTORY

INTRODUCTION
OF THE
STUDY OF HISTORY

By

CH. V. LANGLOIS & CH. SEIGNOBOS
of the Sorbonne

Translated by

G. G. Berry

With a Preface
by
F. York Powell

GYAN

Published by

Gyan Publishing House
5, Ansari Road
Daryaganj, New Delhi-110002
Phone: 011-47034999, 9811692060
E-mail: books@gyanbooks.com

Distribution Network
gyanbooks.com
India, USA, Canada, UK, Australia, France

ISBN : 978-81-212-6514-0 (PB)
First Published, 1897

2nd Impression 2022

Printed at: Gyan Press, Delhi.

INTRODUCTION OF THE STUDY OF HISTORY
Authors: CH. V. LANGLOIS & CH. SEIGNOBOS

INTRODUCTION

TO THE

STUDY OF HISTORY

BY

CH. V. LANGLOIS & CH. SEIGNOBOS

OF THE SORBONNE

TRANSLATED BY G. G. BERRY

WITH A PREFACE BY F. YORK POWELL

TO THE READER

It is a pleasure to recommend this useful and well-written little book to English readers. It will both interest and help. There are, for instance, a few pages devoted to the question of evidence that will be an aid to every one desirous of getting at the truth respecting any series of facts, as well as to the student of history. No one can read it without finding out that to the historian history is not merely a pretty but rather difficult branch of literature, and that a history book is not necessarily good if it appears to the literary critic 'readable and interesting,' nor bad because it seems to him 'hard or heavy reading.' The literary critic, in fact, is beginning to find out that he reads a history as he might read a treatise on mathematics or linguistics, at his peril, and that he is no judge of its value or lack of value. Only the expert can judge that. It will probably surprise some people to find that in the opinion of our authors (who agree with Mr. Morse Stephens and with the majority of scholars here) the formation and expression of ethical judgments, the approval or condemnation of Caius Julius Cæsar, or of Cæsar Borgia, is not a thing within the historian's province. His business is to find out what can be known about the characters and situations with which he is engaged, to put what he can ascertain before his readers in a clear form, and lastly to consider and attempt to ascertain what scientific use can be made of these facts he has ascertained. Ethic on its didactic side is outside his business altogether. In fact MM. Langlois and Seignobos write for those "who propose to deal with documents [especially written documents] with a view to preparing or accomplishing historic work in a scientific way." They have the temerity to view history as a scientific pursuit, and they are endeavouring to explain to the student who intends to pursue this branch of anthropologic science the best and safest methods of observation open to him, hence they modestly term their little book "an essay on the method of historic sciences." They are bold enough to look forward to a day, as not far distant, when a sensible or honest man will no more dare to write history unscientifically than he would to-day be willing to waste his time and that of others on observing the heavens unscientifically, and registering as trustworthy his unchecked and untimed observations.

Whether we like it or not, history has got to be scientifically studied, and it is not a question of style but of accuracy, of fulness of observation, and correctness of reasoning, that is before the student. Huxley and Darwin and Clifford have shown that a book may be good science and yet good reading. Truth has not always been found repulsive although she was not bedizened with rhetorical adornments; indeed, the very pursuit of her has long been recognised as arduous but extremely fascinating. *Toute trouvaille*, as our authors aptly remark, *procure une jouissance.*

It will be a positive gain to have the road cleared of a mass of rubbish, that has hindered the advance of knowledge. History must be worked at in a scientific spirit, as biology or chemistry is worked at. As M. Seignobos says, "On ne s'arrête plus guère aujourd'hui à discuter, sous sa forme théologique la théorie de la Providence dans l'Histoire. Mais la tendence à expliquer les faits historiques par les causes transcendantes persiste dans des théories plus modernes où la metaphysique se déguise sous des formes scientifiques." We should certainly get rid in time of those curious Hegelianisms "under which in lay disguise lurks the old theologic theory of final causes"; or the pseudo-patriotic supposition of the "historic mission (Beruf) attributed to certain people or persons." The study of historic facts does not even make for the popular newspaper theory of the continuous and necessary progress of humanity, it shows only "partial and intermittent advances, and gives us no reason to attribute them to a permanent cause inherent in collective humanity rather than to a series of local accidents." But the historian's path is still like that of Bunyan's hero, bordered by pitfalls and haunted by hobgoblins, though certain of his giant adversaries are crippled and one or two slain. He has also his own faults to master, or at least to check, as MM. Langlois and Seignobos not infrequently hint, *e.g.* "Nearly all beginners have a vexatious tendency to go off into superfluous digressions, heaping up reflexion and information that have no bearing on the main subject. They will recognise, if they think over it, that the causes of this leaning are bad taste, a kind of naïve vanity, sometimes a disordered mind." Again: "The faults of historic works intended for the general public . . . are the results of the insufficient preparation of the bad literary training of the popularisers." What an admirable criticism there is too of that peculiarly German shortcoming (one not, however, unknown elsewhere), which results in men "whose learning is ample, whose monographs destined for scholars are highly praiseworthy, showing themselves capable, when they write for the public, of sinning heavily against scientific methods," so that, in their determination to stir their public, "they who are so scrupulous and particular when it is a question of dealing with minutiæ, abandon themselves like the mass of mankind to their natural inclinations when they come to set forth general questions. They take sides, they blame, they praise, they colour, they embellish, they allow themselves to take account of personal, patriotic, ethical, or metaphysical considerations. Above all, they apply themselves with what talent has fallen to their lot to the task of creating a work of art, and, so applying themselves, those of them who lack talent become ridiculous, and the talent of those who possess it is spoilt by their anxiety for effect."

On the other hand, while the student is rejoicing at the smart raps bestowed upon the Teutonic offender, he is warned against the error of thinking that "provided he can make himself understood, the historian has the right to use a faulty, low, careless, or clogged style. . . . Seeing the extreme complexity of the phenomena he must endeavour to describe, he has not the privilege of writing badly. But he ought *always* to write well, and not to bedizen his prose with extra finery once a week."

Of course much that is said in this book has been said before, but I do not know any book wherein the student of history will find such an organised collection of practical and helpful instructions. There are several points on which one is unable to find oneself in agreement with MM. Langlois and Seignobos, but these occur mainly where they are dealing with theory; as far as practical work goes, one finds oneself in almost perfect concurrence with them. That they know little of the way in which history is taught and studied in England or Canada or the United States is not at all an hindrance to the use of their book. The student may enjoy the pleasure of making his own examples out of English books to the rules they lay down. He may compare their cautions against false reasoning and instances of fallacy with those set forth in that excellent and concise essay of Bentham's, which is apparently unknown to them. He will not fail to see that we in England have much to learn in this subject of history from the French. The French archives are not so fine as ours, but they take care to preserve their local and provincial documents, as well as their national and central records; they give their archivists a regular training, they calendar and make accessible all that time and fate have spared of pre-revolutionary documents. We have not got farther than the provision of a fine central Record Office furnished with very inadequate means for calendaring the masses of documents already stored and monthly accumulating there, though we have lately set up at Oxford, Cambridge, and London the regular courses of palæography, diplomatic, and bibliography, that constitute the preliminary training of the archivist or historical researcher. We want more: we must have county archives, kept by trained archivists. We must have more trained archivists at the disposal of the Deputy Keeper of the Rolls, we must have such means as the *Bibliotéque de l'École des Chartes* for full reports of special and minute investigations and discoveries, for hand-lists and the like, before we can be considered as doing as much for history as the heavily taxed French nation does cheerfully, and with a sound confidence that the money it spends wisely in science is in the truest sense money saved.

For those interested in the teaching of history, this book is one of the most suggestive helps that has yet appeared. With a blackboard, a text (such as are now cheap), or a text-book (such as Stubbs or Prothero or Gardiner), an atlas, and access to a decent public library and an average local museum, the teacher who has mastered its intent should never be at a loss for an interesting catechetical lecture or exposition to a class, whether of adults or of younger folk.

Not the least practical part of the work of MM. Langlois and Seignobos has been the consideration they have given to such every-day issues as the teacher is constantly called upon to face. History cannot safely be neglected in schools, though it is by no means necessary that the Universities should turn out large bodies of trained historians. It is possible indeed that the serious study of history might gain were there fewer external inducements at the Universities to lead to the popularity of the History Schools. But in this very popularity there lies a great opportunity for concerted efforts, not only to better the processes of study, but also to clear off the vast arrears of classification and examination of the erroneous historic material at our disposition in this country.

The historian has been (as our authors hint) too much the ally of the politician; he has used his knowledge as material for preaching democracy in the United States, absolutism in Prussia, Orleanist opposition in France, and so on (English readers will easily recall examples from their own countrymen's work): in the century to come he will have to ally himself with the students of physical science, with whose methods his own have so much in common. It is not patriotism, nor religion, nor art, but the attainment of truth that is and must be the historian's single aim.

But it is also to be borne in mind that history is an excellent instrument of culture, for, as our authors point out, "the practice and method of historic investigation is a pursuit extremely healthful for the mind, freeing it from the disease of credulity," and fortifying it in other ways as a discipline, though precisely how to best use history for this purpose is still in some ways uncertain, and after all it is a matter which concerns Pædagogic and Ethic more than the student of history, though it is plain that MM. Langlois and Seignobos have not neglected to consider it.

One can hardly help thinking, too, that, in schools and places where the young are trained, something might be gained by treating such books as Plutarch's Lives not as history (for which they were never intended) but as text-books of ethic, as examples of conduct, public or private. The historian very properly furnishes the ethical student with material, though it is not right to reckon the ethical student's judgment upon the historian's facts as history in any sense. It is not an historian's question, for instance, whether Napoleon was right or wrong in his conduct at Jaffa, or Nelson in his behaviour at Naples; that is a matter for the student of ethic or the religious dogmatist to decide: all that the historian has to do is to get what conclusion he can out of the conflict of evidence, and to decide whether Napoleon or Nelson actually did that of which their enemies accused them, or, if he cannot arrive at fact, to state probability, and the reasons that incline him to lean to the affirmative or negative.

As to the possibility of a "philosophy of history," a real one, not the mockeries that have long been discredited by scientific students, the reader will find some pregnant remarks here in the epilogue and the chapters that precede it. There is an absence of unreasonable optimism in our authors' views. "It is probable that hereditary differences have contributed to determine events; so that in part historic evolution is produced by physiological and anthropologic causes. But history furnishes no trustworthy process by which it may be possible to determine the action of those hereditary differences between man and man," *i.e.* she starts with races 'endowed' each with peculiarities that make them 'disposed to act' somewhat differently under similar pressure. "History is only able to grasp the conditions of their existence." And what M. Seignobos calls the final problem—*Is evolution produced merely by changed conditions?*—must according to him remain insoluble by the legitimate processes of history. The student may accept or reject this view as his notions of evidence prompt him to do. M. Seignobos has at all events laid down a basis for discussion in sufficiently clear terms.

As to the composition of the joint work we are told that M. Seignobos has been especially concerned with the chapters that touch theory, and M. Langlois with those that deal with practice. Both authors have already proved their competence—M. Seignobos' labours on Modern History have been widely appreciated, while M. Langlois' "Hand-book of Historic Bibliography" is already a standard text-book, and bids fair to remain so. We are grateful to both of them for the pains they have taken to be clear and definite, and for their determination to shirk none of the difficulties that have met them. They have produced a hand-book that students will use and value in proportion to their use of it, a book that will save much muddle of thought and much loss of time, a book written in the right spirit to inspire its readers. We are not bound to agree with all M. Seignobos' dogmas, and can hardly accept, for instance, M. Langlois' apology for the brutal methods of controversy that are an evil legacy from the theologian and the grammarian, and are apt to darken truth and to cripple the powers of those who engage in them. For though it is possible that the secondary effect of these barbarous scuffles may sometimes have been salutary in deterring impostors from 'taking up' history, I am not aware of any positive examples to justify this opinion. There is this, however, to be said, that fully conscious of their own fallibility, M. Langlois and his excellent collaborator have supplied in their canons of criticism and maxims the best corrections of any mistakes into which they may have fallen by the way. Is not the House of Fame, as the poet tells us, a more wonderful and quaintly wrought habitation than *Domus Dedali* itself? And may not honest historians be pardoned if they are sometimes confused for a brief moment by the never-ending noise and marvellous motion of that deceptive mint and treasury, and fatigued by the continual trial and examination of the material that issues therefrom? The student will, at least, learn from MM. Langlois and Seignobos to have no mercy on his own shortcomings, to spare no pains, to grudge no expenditure of time or energy in the investigation of a carefully chosen and important historical problem, to aim at doing the bit of work in hand so thoroughly that it will not need to be done again.

It would be unjust to omit here to mention Dr. Bernheim's "Exposition of Historic Method," or *Lehrbuch der historischen Methode*, so justly praised and used by our authors, but I believe that as an introduction to the subject, intended for the use of English or North American students, this little volume will be found the handier and more practical work. Of its value to English workers I can speak from experience, and I know many teachers to whom it will be welcome in its present form.

It would have been easy to 'adapt' this book by altering its examples, by modifying its excellent plan, by cutting here and carving there to the supposed convenience of an imaginary public, but the better part has been chosen of giving English readers this manual precisely as it appeared in French. And surely one would rather read what M. Langlois, an experienced teacher and a tried scholar, thought on a moot point, than be presented with the views of some English 'adaptor' who had read his book, as to what he would have said had he been an Englishman lecturing to English students. That the present translator has taken much pains to faithfully report his authors, I know (though I have not compared English and French throughout every page), so that I can commend his honest work to the reader as I have already commended the excellent matter that he has been concerned in preparing for a wider public than the French original could command.

F. YORK POWELL.

ORIEL COLLEGE, OXFORD, *July* 1898.

CONTENTS

Contents

CHAPTER II

"AUXILIARY SCIENCES"

BOOK II

ANALYTICAL OPERATIONS

CHAPTER I

GENERAL CONDITIONS OF HISTORICAL KNOWLEDGE

SECTION I.—EXTERNAL CRITICISM

CHAPTER II

TEXTUAL CRITICISM

CHAPTER III

CRITICAL INVESTIGATION OF AUTHORSHIP

CHAPTER IV

CRITICAL CLASSIFICATION OF SOURCES

CHAPTER V

CRITICAL SCHOLARSHIP AND SCHOLARS

SECTION II.—INTERNAL CRITICISM

CHAPTER VI

INTERPRETATIVE CRITICISM (HERMENEUTIC)

CHAPTER VII

THE NEGATIVE INTERNAL CRITICISM OF THE GOOD FAITH AND ACCURACY OF AUTHORS

CHAPTER VIII

THE DETERMINATION OF PARTICULAR FACTS

BOOK III

SYNTHETIC OPERATIONS

CHAPTER I

GENERAL CONDITIONS OF HISTORICAL CONSTRUCTION

CHAPTER II

THE GROUPING OF FACTS

CHAPTER III

CONSTRUCTIVE REASONING

CHAPTER IV

THE CONSTRUCTION OF GENERAL FORMULÆ

CHAPTER V

EXPOSITION

CONCLUSION

APPENDIX I

THE SECONDARY TEACHING OF HISTORY IN FRANCE

APPENDIX II

THE HIGHER TEACHING OF HISTORY IN FRANCE

AUTHORS' PREFACE

THE title of this work is clear. However, it is necessary to state succinctly both what our intention has, and what it has not been; for under this same title, "Introduction to the Study of History," very different books have already been published.

It has not been our intention to give, as Mr. W. B. Boyce[1] has done, a summary of universal history for the use of beginners and readers of scanty leisure.

Nor has it been our intention to add a new item to the abundant literature of what is ordinarily called the "Philosophy of History." Thinkers, for the most part not professed historians, have made history the subject of their meditations; they have sought for its "analogies" and its "laws." Some have supposed themselves to have discovered "the laws which have governed the development of humanity," and thus to have "raised history to the rank of a positive science."[2] These vast abstract constructions inspire with an invincible *a priori* mistrust, not the general public only, but superior minds as well. Fustel de Coulanges, as his latest biographer tells us, was severe

[1] W. B. Boyce, "Introduction to the Study of History, Civil, Ecclesiastical, and Literary," London, 1894, 8vo.

[2] For example, P. J. B. Buchez, in his *Introduction à la science de l'histoire*, Paris, 1842, 2 vols. 8vo.

on the Philosophy of History; these systems were as repugnant to him as metaphysics to the positivists. Rightly or wrongly (without doubt wrongly), the Philosophy of History, not having been cultivated exclusively by well-informed, cautious men of vigorous and sound judgment, has fallen into disrepute. The reader will be reassured—or disappointed, as the case may be—to learn that this subject will find no place in the present work.[1]

We propose to examine the conditions and the methods, to indicate the character and the limits, of historical knowledge. How do we ascertain, in respect of the past, what part of it it is possible, what part of it it is important, to know? What is a document? How are documents to be treated with a view to historical work? What are historical facts? How are they to be grouped to make history? Whoever occupies himself with history performs, more or less unconsciously, complicated operations of criticism and construction, of analysis and synthesis. But beginners, and the majority of those who have never reflected on the principles of historical methodology,

[1] The history of the attempts which have been made to understand and explain philosophically the history of humanity has been undertaken, as is well known, by Robert Flint. Mr. Flint has already given the history of the Philosophy of History in French-speaking countries: "Historical Philosophy in France and French Belgium and Switzerland," Edinburgh and London, 1893, 8vo. It is the first volume of the expanded re-edition of his "History of the Philosophy of History in Europe," published twenty-five years ago. Compare the retrospective (or historical) part of the work of N. Marselli, *La scienza della storia*, i., Torino, 1873.

The most important original work which has appeared in France since the publication of the analytical repertory of R. Flint is that of P. Lacombe, *De l'histoire considérée comme science*, Paris, 1894, 8vo. Cf. *Revue Critique*, 1895, i. p. 132.

make use, in the performance of these operations, of instinctive methods which, not being, in general, rational methods, do not usually lead to scientific truth. It is, therefore, useful to make known and logically justify the theory of the truly rational methods—a theory which is now settled in some parts, though still incomplete in some points of capital importance.

The present "Introduction to the Study of History" is thus intended, not as a summary of ascertained facts or a system of general ideas on universal history, but as an essay on the method of the historical sciences.

We proceed to state the reasons why we have thought such a work opportune, and to explain the spirit in which we have undertaken to write it.

I

The books which treat of the methodology of the historical sciences are scarcely less numerous, and at the same time not in much better favour, than the books on the Philosophy of History. Specialists despise them. A widespread opinion is expressed in the words attributed to a certain scholar: "You wish to write a book on philology; you will do much better to produce a book with some good philology in it. When I am asked to define philology, I always answer that it is what I work at."[1] Again, in reference to J. G. Droysen's *Précis of the Science of History*, a certain critic expressed an opinion which was meant to be, and was, a commonplace: "Generally speaking, treatises of this kind

[1] *Revue Critique d'histoire et de littérature*. 1892. i. p. 164.

are of necessity both obscure and useless: obscure, because there is nothing more vague than their object; useless, because it is possible to be an historian without troubling oneself about the principles of historical methodology which they claim to exhibit."[1] The arguments used by these despisers of methodology are strong enough in all appearance. They reduce to the following. As a matter of fact, there are men who manifestly follow good methods, and are universally recognised as scholars or historians of the first order, without having ever studied the principles of method; conversely, it does not appear that those who have written on historical method from the logical point of view have in consequence attained any marked superiority as scholars or historians: some, indeed, have been known for their incompetence or mediocrity in these capacities. In this there is nothing that need surprise us. Who would think of postponing original research in chemistry, mathematics, the sciences proper, until he had studied the methods employed in those sciences? Historical criticism! Yes, but the best way to learn it is to apply it; practice teaches all that is wanted.[2] Take, too, the

[1] *Revue Critique d'histoire et de littérature*, 1888, ii. p. 295. Cf. *Le Moyen Age*, x. (1897), p. 91: "These books [treatises on historical method] are seldom read by those to whom they might be useful, amateurs who devote their leisure to historical research; and as to professed scholars, it is from their masters' lessons that they have learnt to know and handle the tools of their trade, leaving out of consideration the fact that the method of history is the same as that of the other sciences of observation, the gist of which can be stated in a few words.

[2] In accordance with the principle that historical method can only be taught by example, L. Mariani has given the humorous

extant works on historical method, even the most recent of them, those of J. G. Droysen, E. A. Freeman, A. Tardif, U. Chevalier, and others; the utmost diligence will extract from them nothing in the way of clear ideas beyond the most obvious and commonplace truisms.[1]

We willingly recognise that this manner of thinking is not entirely wrong. The great majority of works on the method of pursuing historical investigations and of writing history—what is called *Historic* in Germany and England—are superficial, insipid, unreadable, sometimes ridiculous.[2] To begin

title *Corso pratico di metodologia della storia* to a dissertation on a detail in the history of Fermo. See the *Archivio della Società romana di storia patria*, xiii. (1890), p. 211.

[1] See an account of Freeman's work, "The Methods of Historical Study," in the *Revue Critique*, 1887, i. p. 376. This work, says the critic, is empty and commonplace. We learn from it "that history is not so easy a study as many fondly imagine, that it has points of contact with all the sciences, and that the historian truly worthy of the name ought to know everything; that historical certitude is unattainable, and that, in order to make the nearest approach to it, it is necessary to have constant recourse to the original sources; that it is necessary to know and use the best modern historians, but never to take their word for gospel. That is all." He concludes: Freeman "without a doubt taught historical method far better by example than he ever succeeded in doing by precept."

Compare *Bouvard et Pécuchet*, by G. Flaubert. Here we have two simpletons who, among other projects, propose to write history. In order to help them, one of their friends sends them (p. 156) "rules of criticism taken from the *Cours* of Daunou," such as: "It is no proof to appeal to rumour and common opinion; the witnesses cannot appear. Reject impossibilities: Pausanias was shown the stone swallowed by Saturn. Keep in mind the skill of forgers, the interest of apologists and calumniators." Daunou's work contains a number of truisms quite as obvious, and still more comic than the above.

[2] Flint (ibid. p. 15) congratulates himself on not having to study the literature of *Historic*, for "a very large portion of it is so trivial and superficial that it can hardly ever have been of use even to persons

with, those prior to the nineteenth century, a full analysis of which is given by P. C. F. Daunou in the seventh volume of his *Cours d'études historiques*,[1] are nearly all of them mere treatises on rhetoric, in which the rhetoric is antiquated, and the problems discussed are the oddest imaginable.[2] Daunou makes merry over them, but he himself has shown good sense and nothing more in his monumental work, which at the present time seems little better, and certainly not more useful, than the earlier treatises.[3] As to the modern ones, it is true

of the humblest capacity, and may certainly now be safely confined to kindly oblivion." Nevertheless, Flint has given in his book a summary list of the principal works of this kind published in French-speaking countries from the earliest times. A more general and complete account (though still a summary one) of the literature of this subject in all countries is furnished by the *Lehrbuch der historischen Methode* of E. Bernheim (Leipzig, 1894, 8vo), pp. 143 *sqq.* Flint (who was acquainted with several works unknown to Bernheim) stops at 1893, Bernheim at 1894. Since 1889 the *Jahresberichte der Geschichtswissenschaft* have contained a periodical account of recent works on historical methodology.

1 This seventh volume was published in 1844. But Daunou's celebrated *Cours* was delivered at the Collège de France in the years 1819–30.

2 The Italians of the Renaissance (Mylæus, Francesco Patrizzi, and others), and after them the writers of the last two centuries, ask what is the relation of history to dialectic and rhetoric; to how many laws the historical branch of literature is subject; whether it is right for the historian to relate treasons, acts of cowardice, crimes, disorders; whether history is entitled to use any style other than the sublime; and so on. The only books on *Historic*, published before the nineteenth century, which give evidence of any original effort to attack the real difficulties, are those of Lenglet de Fresnoy (*Méthode pour étudier l'histoire*, Paris, 1713), and of J. M. Chladenius (*Allgemeine Geschichtswissenschaft*, Leipzig, 1752). The work of Chladenius has been noticed by Bernheim (ibid. p. 166).

3 He has not always shown even good sense, for, in the *Cours d'études historiques* (vii. p. 105), where he treats of a work, *De*

that not all have been able to escape the two dangers to which works of this character are exposed—that of being obscure on the one hand, or commonplace on the other. J. G. Droysen's *Grundriss der Historik* is heavy, pedantic, and confused beyond all imagination.[1] Freeman, Tardif, and Chevalier tell us nothing but what is elementary and obvious. Their followers may still be observed discussing at interminable length idle questions, such as: whether history is a science or an art; what are the duties of history; what is the use of history; and so on. On the other hand, there is incontestable truth in the remark that nearly all the specialists and historians of to-day are, as far as method goes, self-taught, with no training except what they have gained by practice, or by imitating and associating with the older masters of the craft.

But though many works on the principles of method justify the distrust with which such works are generally regarded, and though most professed historians have been able, apparently with no ill results, to dispense with reflection upon historical method, it would, in our opinion, be a strained inference to conclude that specialists and historians (especially

l'histoire, published in 1670 by Père Le Moyne, a feeble production, to say the least, bearing evident traces of senility, he expresses himself as follows: "I cannot adopt all the maxims and precepts contained in this treatise; but I believe that, after that of Lucian, it is the best we have yet seen, and I greatly doubt whether any of those whose acquaintance we have still to make has risen to the same height of philosophy and originality." Père H. Chérot has given a sounder estimate of the treatise *De l'histoire* in his *Étude sur la vie et les œuvres du P. Le Moyne* (Paris, 1887, 8vo), pp. 406 *sqq.*

[1] Bernheim declares, however (ibid. p. 177), that this little work is, in his opinion, the only one which stands at the present level of science.

those of the future) have no need to make themselves acquainted with the processes of historical work. The literature of methodology is, in fact, not without its value: gradually there has been formed a treasury of subtle observations and precise rules, suggested by experience, which are something more than mere common sense.[1] And, admitting the existence of those who, without having ever learnt to reason, always reason well, by a gift of nature, it would be easy to set against these exceptions innumerable cases in which ignorance of logic, the use of irrational methods, want of reflection on the conditions of historical analysis and synthesis, have robbed the work of specialists and historians of much of its value.

The truth is, that, of all branches of study, history is without a doubt the one in which it is most necessary for students to have a clear consciousness of the methods they use. The reason is, that in history instinctive methods are, as we cannot too often repeat, irrational methods; some preparation is therefore required to counteract the first impulse. Besides, the rational methods of obtaining historical knowledge differ so widely from the methods of all other sciences, that some perception of their distinctive features is necessary to avoid the temptation of applying to history the methods of those sciences which have already been systematised. This explains why mathematicians and chemists can, more easily than historians, dispense with an "introduction" to

[1] Flint says very well (ibid. p. 15): "The course of Historic has been, on the whole, one of advance from commonplace reflection on history towards a philosophical comprehension of the conditions and processes on which the formation of historical science depends.

their subject. There is no need to insist at greater length on the utility of historical methodology, for there is evidently nothing very serious in the attacks which have been made on it. But it behoves us to explain the reasons which have led to the composition of the present work. For the last fifty years a great number of intelligent and open-minded men have meditated on the methods of the historical sciences. Naturally we find among them many historians, university professors, whose position enables them to understand better than others the intellectual needs of the young; but at the same time professed logicians, and even novelists. In this connection, Fustel de Coulanges left a tradition behind him at the University of Paris. "He endeavoured," we are told,[1] "to reduce the rules of method to very precise formulæ . . .; in his view no task was more urgent than that of teaching students how to attain truth." Among these men, some, like Renan,[2] have been content to insert scattered observations in their general works or their occasional writings;[3] others, as Fustel de

[1] By P. Guiraud, in the *Revue des Deux Mondes*, March 1896, p. 75.

[2] Renan has said some of the truest and best things that have ever been said on the historical sciences in *L'Avenir de la science* (Paris, 1890, 8vo), written in 1848.

[3] Some of the most ingenious, some of the most logical, and some of the most widely applicable observations, on the method of the historical sciences, have so far appeared, not in books on methodology, but in the reviews—of which the *Revue Critique d'histoire et de littérature* is the type—devoted to the criticism of new works of history and erudition. It is a very useful exercise to run through the file of the *Revue Critique*, founded, at Paris, in 1867, "to enforce respect for method, to execute justice upon bad books, to check misdirected and superfluous work."

Coulanges, Freeman, Droysen, Laurence, Stubbs, De Smedt, Von Pflugk-Harttung, and so on, have taken the trouble to express their thoughts on the subject in special treatises. There are many books, "inaugural lectures," "academic orations," and review-articles, published in all countries, but especially in France, Germany, England, the United States, and Italy, both on the whole subject of methodology and on the different parts of it. It will occur to the reader that it would be a far from useless labour to collect and arrange the observations which are scattered, and, one might say, lost, in these numerous books and minor writings. But it is too late to undertake this pleasant task; it has been recently performed, and in the most painstaking manner. Professor Ernst Bernheim, of the University of Greifswald, has worked through nearly all the modern works on historical method, and the fruit of his labours is an arrangement under appropriate headings, most of them invented by himself, of a great number of reflections and selected references. His *Lehrbuch der historischen Methode*[1] (Leipzig, 1894, 8vo) condenses, in the manner of German *Lehrbücher*, the special literature of the subject of which it treats. It is not our intention to do over again what has already been done so well. But we are of opinion that even after this laborious and well-planned compilation something still remains to be said. In the first place, Professor Bernheim deals largely with metaphysical problems which we consider devoid of interest; while, conversely, he entirely ignores certain considerations which appear to us to

[1] The first edition of the *Lehrbuch* is dated 1889.

be, both theoretically and practically, of the greatest importance. In the second place, the teaching of the *Lehrbuch* is sound enough, but lacks vigour and originality. Lastly, the *Lehrbuch* is not addressed to the general public; both the language in which it is written and the form in which it is composed render it inaccessible to the great majority of French readers. This is enough to justify our undertaking to write a book of our own, instead of simply recommending the book of Professor Bernheim.[1]

II

This "Introduction to the Study of History" does not claim, like the *Lehrbuch der historischen Methode*, to be a treatise on historical methodology.[2] It is a sketch in outline. We undertook its composition, at the beginning of the scholastic year 1896–97, in order that the new students at the Sorbonne might be warned what the study of history is and ought to be.

Long experience has taught us the necessity of such warnings. The greater part of those who enter upon a career of historical study do so, as a matter of fact, without knowing why, without having ever asked themselves whether they are fitted for historical work, of the true nature of which they are

[1] The best work that has hitherto been published (in French) on historical method is a pamphlet by MM. Ch. and V. Mortet, *La Science de l'histoire* (Paris, 1894, 8vo), 88 pp., extracted from vol. xx. of the *Grande Encyclopédie*.

[2] One of us, M. Seignobos, proposes to publish later on a complete treatise of Historical Methodology, if there appears to be a public for this class of work.

often ignorant. Generally their motives for choosing an historical career are of the most futile character. One has been successful in history at college;[1] another feels himself drawn towards the past by the same kind of romantic attraction which, we are told, determined the vocation of Augustin Thierry; some are misled by the fancy that history is a comparatively easy subject. It is certainly important that these irrational votaries should be enlightened and put to the test as soon as possible.

Having given a course of lectures, to novices, by way of "Introduction to the Study of History," we thought that, with a little revision, these lectures might be made useful to others besides novices. Scholars and professed historians will doubtless have nothing to learn from this work; but if they should find in it a stimulus to personal reflection on the craft which some of them practise in a mechanical fashion, that would be something gained.

[1] It cannot be too often stated that the study of history, as it is prosecuted at school, does not presuppose the same aptitudes as the same study when prosecuted at the university or in after life. Julien Havet, who afterwards devoted himself to the (critical) study of history, found history wearisome at school. "I believe," says M. L. Havet, "that the teaching of history [in schools] is not organised in such a manner as to provide sufficient nourishment for the scientific spirit. . . . Of all the studies comprised in our school curricula, history is the only one in which the pupil is not being continually called upon to verify something. When he is learning Latin or German, every sentence in a translation requires him to verify a dozen different rules. In the various branches of mathematics the results are never divorced from their proofs; the *problems*, too, compel the pupil to think through the whole for himself. Where are the *problems* in history, and what schoolboy is ever trained to gain by independent effort an insight into the interconnection of events?" (*Bibliothèque de l'École des chartes*, 1896, p. 84).

As for the public, which reads the works of historians, is it not desirable that it should know how these works are produced, in order to be able to judge them better?

We do not, therefore, like Professor Bernheim, write exclusively for present and future specialists, but also for the public interested in history. We thus lay ourselves under an obligation to be as concise, as clear, and as little technical as possible. But to be concise and clear on subjects of this kind often means to appear superficial. Commonplace on the one hand, obscurity on the other: these, as we have already seen, are the evils between which we have the sorry privilege of choosing. We admit the difficulty. But we do not think it insurmountable, and our endeavour has been to say what we had to say in the clearest possible manner.

The first half of the book has been written by M. Langlois, the second by M. Seignobos; but the two collaborators have constantly aided, consulted, and checked each other.[1]

PARIS, *August* 1897.

[1] M. Langlois wrote Book I., Book II. as far as Chapter VI., the second Appendix, and this Preface; M. Seignobos the end of Book II., Book III., and the first Appendix. Chapter I. in the second book, Chapter V. of the third book, and the Conclusion, were written in common.

BOOK I

PRELIMINARY STUDIES

INTRODUCTION TO THE STUDY OF HISTORY

BOOK I

PRELIMINARY STUDIES

CHAPTER I

THE SEARCH FOR DOCUMENTS (HEURISTIC)

THE historian works with documents. Documents are the traces which have been left by the thoughts and actions of men of former times. Of these thoughts and actions, however, very few leave any visible traces, and these traces, when there are any, are seldom durable; an accident is enough to efface them. Now every thought and every action that has left no visible traces, or none but what have since disappeared, is lost for history; is as though it had never been. For want of documents the history of immense periods in the past of humanity is destined to remain for ever unknown. For there is no substitute for documents: no documents, no history.

In order to draw legitimate inferences from a document to the fact of which it is the trace, numerous precautions are requisite which will be indicated in the sequel. But it is clear that, prior to any critical examination or interpretation of documents, the question presents itself whether there are any documents at all, how many there are, and where they are. If I undertake to deal with a point of history,[1] of whatever nature, my first step will be to ascertain the place or places where the documents necessary for its treatment, if any such exist, are to be found. The search for and the collection of documents is thus a part, logically the first and most important part, of the historian's craft. In Germany it has received the convenient, because short, name of *Heuristik*. Is there any need to prove the capital importance of Heuristic? Assuredly not. It is obvious that if it is neglected, if the student does not, before he sets to work on a point of history, place himself in a position to command all accessible sources of information, his risk (no small one at the best) of working upon insufficient data is quite unnecessarily increased: works of erudition or history constructed in accordance with the rules of the most exact method have been vitiated, or even rendered worthless, by the accidental circumstance that the author was unacquainted with the documents by which those which he had within reach, and with which he was content, might have been illustrated, supplemented, or discredited. The scholars and historians of to-day, standing, as they

[1] In practice one does not as a rule resolve to treat a point of history before knowing whether there are or are not documents in existence which enable it to be studied. On the contrary, it is the accidental discovery of a document which suggests the idea of thoroughly elucidating the point of history to which it relates, and thus leads to the collection, for this purpose, of other documents of the same class.

do, in other respects on an equality with their predecessors of the last few centuries, are only enabled to surpass them by their possession of more abundant means of information.[1] Heuristic is, in fact, easier to-day than it used to be, although the honest Wagner has still good grounds for saying:

> "Wie schwer sind nicht die Mittel zu erwerben,
> Durch die man zu den Quellen steigt!"[2]

Let us endeavour to explain why the collection of documents, once so laborious, is still no easy matter, in spite of the progress made in the last century; and how this essential operation may, in the course of continued progress, be still further simplified.

I. Those who first endeavoured to write history from the sources found themselves in an embarrassing situation. Were the events they proposed to relate recent, so that all the witnesses of them were not yet dead? They had the resource of interviewing the witnesses who survived. Thucydides, Froissart, and many others have followed this procedure. When Mr. H. H. Bancroft, the historian of the Pacific Coast of California, resolved to collect materials for the history of events many of the actors in which were still alive, he mobilised a whole army of reporters charged to extract conversations from them.[3] But

[1] It is pitiable to see how the best of the early scholars struggled bravely, but vainly, to solve problems which would not even have existed for them if their collections had not been so incomplete. This lack of material was a disadvantage for which the most brilliant ingenuity could not compensate.

[2] "How hard it is to gain the means whereby we mount to the sources" (Goethe, *Faust*, i. 3).

[3] See C. V. Langlois, *H. H. Bancroft et Cie.*, in the *Revue universitaire*, 1894, i. p. 233.

when the events to be related were ancient, so that no man then living could have witnessed them, and no account of them had been preserved by oral tradition, what then? Nothing was left but to collect documents of every kind, principally written ones, relating to the distant past which was to be studied. This was a difficult task at a time when libraries were rare, archives secret, and documents scattered. About the year 1860, Mr. Bancroft, in California, was in a situation analogous to that of the earlier researchers in our part of the world. His plan was as follows: He was rich; he cleared the market of all documents, printed or manuscript; he negotiated with financially embarrassed families and corporations for the purchase of their archives, or the permission to have them copied by his paid agents. This done, he housed his collection in premises built for the purpose, and classified it. Theoretically there could not be a more rational procedure. But this rapid, American method has only once been employed with sufficient resources and sufficient consistency to ensure its success; at any other time, and in any other place, it would have been out of the question. Nowhere else have the circumstances been so favourable for it.

At the epoch of the Renaissance the documents of ancient and modern history were scattered in innumerable private libraries and in innumerable depositories of archives, almost all of them inaccessible, not to mention those which lay hidden beneath the soil, their very existence as yet unsuspected. It was at that time a physical impossibility to procure a list of all the documents serving for the elucidation of a question (for example, a list of all the manuscripts still preserved of an ancient work); and if, by a miracle, such a list was to be had, it was another impossibility to consult all these documents except at the cost of journeys, expenses, and negotiations without end. Consequences easy to foresee did, as a matter of fact, ensue. Firstly, the difficulties of Heuristic being insurmountable, the earliest scholars and historians—employing, as they did, not all the documents, nor the best documents, but those documents on which they could lay their hands—were nearly always ill-informed; and their works are now without interest except so far as they are founded on documents which have since been lost. Secondly, the first scholars and historians to be relatively well-informed were those who, in virtue of their profession, had access to rich storehouses of documents—librarians, keepers of archives, monks, magistrates, whose order or whose corporation possessed libraries or archives of considerable extent.[1]

It is true that collectors soon arose who, by money payments, or by more questionable expedients, such as theft, formed, with more or less regard for the interests of scientific study, "cabinets" of collections of original documents, and of copies. But these

[1] The earlier scholars were conscious of the unfavourable character of the conditions under which they worked. They suffered keenly from the insufficiency of the instruments of research and the means of comparison. Most of them made great efforts to obtain information. Hence these voluminous correspondences between scholars of the last few centuries, of which our libraries preserve so many precious fragments, and these accounts of scientific searches, of journeys undertaken for the discovery of historical documents, which, under the name of *Iter* (*Iter Italicum*, *Iter Germanicum*, &c.), were formerly fashionable.

European collectors, of whom there has been a great number since the fifteenth century, differ very noticeably from Mr. Bancroft. The Californian, in fact, only collected documents relating to a particular subject (the history of certain Pacific states), and his ambition was to make his collection complete; most European collectors have acquired waifs and strays and fragments of every description, forming, when combined, totals which appear insignificant by the side of the huge mass of historical documents which existed at the time. Besides, it was not, in general, with any purpose of making them generally accessible that collectors like Peiresc, Gaignières, Clairambault, Colbert, and many others, withdrew from circulation documents which were in danger of being lost; they were content (and it was creditable to do as much as this) to share them, more or less freely, with their friends. But collectors (and their heirs) are fickle people, and sometimes eccentric in their notions. Certainly it is better that documents should be preserved in private collections, than that they should be entirely unprotected and absolutely inaccessible to the scientific worker; but in order that Heuristic should be made really easier, the first condition is that all collections of documents should be *public*.[1]

[1] We may remark, in passing, a delusion which is childish enough but very natural, and very common among collectors: they all tend to exaggerate the intrinsic value of the documents they possess, simply because they themselves are the possessors. Documents have been published with a sumptuous array of commentaries by persons who had accidentally acquired them, and who would, quite rightly, have attached no importance to them if they had met with them in public collections. This is, we may add, merely a manifestation, in a somewhat crude form, of a general tendency against which it is always necessary to guard: a man readily exaggerates the

Now the finest private collections of documents—libraries and museums combined—were naturally, in the Europe of the Renaissance, those possessed by kings. And while other private collections were often dispersed upon the death of their founders, these, on the contrary, never ceased to grow; they were enriched, indeed, by the wreckage of all the others. The *Cabinet des manuscrits de France*, for example, formed by the French kings, and by them thrown open to the public, had, at the end of the eighteenth century, absorbed the best part of the collections which had been the personal work of the amateurs and scholars of the two preceding centuries.[1] Similarly in other countries. The concentration of a great number of historical documents in vast public (or semi-public) establishments was the fortunate result of this spontaneous evolution.

The arbitrary proceedings of the Revolution were still more favourable, and still more effective in securing the amelioration of the material conditions of historical research. The Revolution of 1789 in France, analogous movements in other countries, led to the violent confiscation, for the profit of the state (that is, of everybody), of a host of private archives and collections—the archives, libraries, and museums of the crown, the archives and libraries of monasteries and suppressed corporations, and so on. In

importance of the documents he possesses, the documents he has discovered, the texts he has edited, the persons and the questions he has studied.

[1] See L. Delisle, *Le Cabinet des manuscrits de la Bibliothèque nationale*, Paris, 1868-81, 3 vols. 4to. The histories of ancient depositories of documents, which have been recently published in considerable number, have been modelled on this admirable work.

France, in 1790, the Constituent Assembly thus placed the state in possession of a great number of depositories of historical documents, previously scattered, and guarded more or less jealously from the curiosity of scholars; these treasures have since been divided among four different national institutions. The same phenomenon has been more recently observed, on a smaller scale, in Germany, Spain, and Italy.

The confiscations of the revolutionary period, as well as the collections of the period which preceded it, have both been productive of serious damage. The collector is, or rather often was, a barbarian who did not hesitate, when he saw a chance of adding to his collection of specimens and rare remains, to mutilate monuments, to dissect manuscripts, to break up whole archives, in order to possess himself of the fragments. On this score many acts of vandalism were perpetrated before the Revolution. Naturally, the revolutionary procedure of confiscation and transference was also productive of lamentable consequences; besides the destruction which was the result of negligence and that which was due to the mere pleasure of destroying, the unfortunate idea arose that collections might be systematically *weeded*, those documents only to be preserved which were "interesting" or "useful," the rest to be got rid of. The task of weeding was entrusted to well-meaning but incompetent and overworked men, who were thus led to commit irreparable havoc in our ancient archives. At the present day there are workers engaged in the task, one requiring an extraordinary amount of time, patience, and care, of restoring the dismembered collections, and replacing the fragments which were then isolated in so brutal a manner by these zealous but unreflecting manipulators of historical documents. It must be recognised, moreover, that the mutilations due to revolutionary activity and the pre-revolutionary collectors are insignificant in comparison with those which are the result of accident and the destructive work of time. But had they been ten times as serious, they would have been amply compensated by two advantages of the first importance, on which we cannot lay too much stress: (1) the concentration, in a relatively small number of depositories, of documents which were formerly scattered, and, as it were, lost, in a hundred different places; (2) the opening of these depositories to the public. The remnant of historical documents which has survived the destructive effects of accident and vandalism is now at last safely housed, classified, made accessible, and treated as public property.

Ancient historical documents are now, as we have seen, collected and preserved chiefly in those public institutions which are called archives, libraries, and museums. It is true that this does not apply to *all* existing documents; in spite of the unceasing acquisitions by purchase and gift which archives, libraries, and museums all over the world have been making every year for a long time past, there still exist private collections, dealers who supply them, and documents in circulation. But the exceptions, which in this case are negligeable, do not affect the general rule. Besides, all the ancient documents which, in limited quantity, still range at large, are destined sooner or later to find their way into the state institutions, whose doors are always open to let in, but never to let out.[1]

It is to be desired, as a matter of principle, that the depositories of documents (archives, libraries, and museums) should not be too numerous; and we have pointed out that, fortunately, they are now beyond comparison less numerous than they were a hundred years ago. Could not the centralisation of documents, with its evident advantages for researchers, be carried still further? Are there not still collections of documents of which it would be hard to justify the separate existence? Perhaps;[2] but the problem of the centralisation of documents is no longer urgent, now that the processes of re-

[1] Many of the ancient documents still in circulation are the proceeds of ancient thefts from state institutions. The precautions now taken against a recurrence of such depredations are stringent, and, in nearly every instance, as effective as could be desired.

As to modern (printed) documents, the rule of legal deposit [compulsory presentation of copies to specified libraries], which has now been adopted by nearly all civilised countries, guarantees their preservation in public institutions.

[2] It is known that Napoleon I. entertained the chimerical design of concentrating at Paris the archives of the whole of Europe, and that, for a beginning, he conveyed to that city the archives of the Vatican, the Holy Roman Empire, the crown of Castile, and others, which later on the French were compelled to restore. Confiscation is now out of the question. But the ancient archives of the notaries might be centralised everywhere, as in some countries they are already, in public institutions. It is not easy to explain why at Paris the departments of Foreign Affairs, of War, and of Marine preserve ancient papers whose natural place would be at the Archives Nationales. A great many more anomalies of this kind might be mentioned, which in certain cases impede, where they do not altogether preclude, research; for the small collections, whose existence is not required, are precisely those whose regulations are the most oppressive.

production have been perfected, especially as the inconveniences arising from a multitude of depositories are met by the expedient, now in general use, of allowing the documents to travel: it is now possible for the student to consult, without expense, in the public library of the city where he resides, documents belonging, say, to the libraries of St. Petersburg, Brussels, and Florence; we now rarely meet with institutions like the Archives Nationales at Paris, the British Museum at London, and the Méjanes Library at Aix-en-Provence, whose statutes absolutely prohibit all lending-out of their contents.[1]

II. It being granted that the majority of historical documents are now preserved in public institutions (archives, libraries, and museums), Heuristic would be very easy if only good descriptive catalogues had been drawn up of all the existing collections of documents, if these catalogues were furnished with indexes, or if general repertories (alphabetical, systematic, &c.) had been made relating to them; lastly, if there were some place where it was possible to consult the complete collection of all these catalogues and their indexes. But Heuristic is still difficult, because these conditions are, unfortunately, still very far from being adequately realised.

[1] The international exchange of documents is worked in Europe (without charge to the public) by the agency of the various Foreign Offices. Besides this, most of the great institutions have agreements with each other for mutual loans; this system is as sure and sometimes more rapid in its operation than the diplomatic system. The question of lending original documents for use outside the institution where they are preserved has of late years been frequently mooted at congresses of historians and librarians. The results so far obtained are eminently satisfactory.

Firstly, there are depositories of documents (archives, libraries, and museums) whose contents have never been even partially catalogued, so that no one knows what is in them. The depositories of which we possess complete descriptive catalogues are rare; there are many collections preserved in celebrated institutions which have only been catalogued in part, and the bulk of which still remains to be described.[1] In the second place, what a variety there is among existing catalogues! There are some old ones which do not now correspond to the present classification of documents, and which cannot be used without reference-tables; there are new ones which are equally based on obsolete systems, too detailed or too summary; some are printed, others in manuscript, on registers or slips; some are carefully executed and clear, many are scamped, inadequate, and provisional. Taking printed catalogues alone, it requires a whole apprenticeship to learn to distinguish, in this enormous mass of confusion, between what is trustworthy and what is not; in other words, to make any use of them at all. Lastly, where are the existing catalogues to be consulted? Most of the great libraries only possess incomplete collections of them; there is no general guide to them anywhere.

This is a deplorable state of things. In fact, the documents contained in uncatalogued depositories

[1] These are sometimes large collections of formidable bulk; it is more natural to undertake the cataloguing of small accumulations which demand less labour. It is for the same reason that many insignificant but short cartularies have been published, while several cartularies of the highest importance, being voluminous, have still to be edited.

and collections are practically non-existent for researchers who have no leisure to work through the whole of their contents for themselves. We have said before: no documents, no history. But to have no good descriptive catalogues of collections of documents means, in practice, to be unable to ascertain the existence of documents otherwise than by chance. We infer that the progress of history depends in great measure on the progress of the general catalogue of historical documents which is still fragmentary and imperfect. On this point there is general agreement. Père Bernard de Montfaucon considered his *Bibliotheca bibliothecarum manuscriptarum nova*, a collection of library catalogues, as "the most useful and most interesting work he had produced in his whole life."[1] "In the present state of science," wrote Renan in 1848,[2] "nothing is wanted more urgently than a critical catalogue of the manuscripts in the different libraries . . . a humble task to all appearance; . . . and yet the researches of scholars are hampered and incomplete pending its definitive completion." "We should have better books on our ancient literature" says M. P. Meyer,[3] "if the predecessors of M. Delisle [in his capacity of administrator of the Bibliothèque Nationale at Paris] had applied themselves with equal ardour and diligence to the cataloguing of the treasures committed to their care."

It will be well to indicate briefly the causes and state the exact consequences of a state of things

[1] See his autobibliography, published by E. de Broglie, *Bernard de Montfaucon et les Bernardins*, ii. (Paris, 1891, 8vo), p. 323

[2] E. Renan, *L'Avenir de la science*, p. 217.

[3] *Romania*, xxi. (1892), p. 625.

which has been deplored as long as scholars have existed, and which is improving, though slowly. "I assure you," said Renan,[1] "that the few hundred thousand francs a Minister of Public Instruction might apply to the purpose [of preparing catalogues] would be better employed than three-quarters of the sum now devoted to literature." It is rare to find a minister, in France or elsewhere, convinced of this truth, and resolute enough to act accordingly. Besides, it has not always been true that, in order to obtain good catalogues, it is sufficient, as well as necessary, to make a pecuniary sacrifice: it is only recently that the best methods of describing documents have been authoritatively fixed; the task of recruiting competent workers—no great difficulty nowadays—would have been neither easy nor free from anxiety at an epoch when competent workers were rarer than they are now. So much for the material obstacles—want of money and want of men. A cause of another kind has not been without its influence. The functionaries charged with the administration of depositories of documents have not always displayed the zeal which they now display for making their collections accessible by means of accurate catalogues. To prepare a catalogue (in the exact and at the same time summary form which is now used) is a laborious task, a task without joy and without reward. It has often happened that such a functionary, living, in virtue of his office, in the midst of documents which he is at liberty to consult at any moment, and placed in a much more favourable position than the general

[1] In the passage quoted above.

public for utilising the collection without the aid of a catalogue, and making discoveries in the process, has preferred to work for himself rather than for others, and made the tedious construction of a catalogue a secondary matter compared with his personal researches.

Who are the persons that in our own day have discovered, published, and annotated the greatest number of documents? The functionaries attached to the depositories of documents. Without a doubt this circumstance has retarded the progress of the general catalogue of historical documents. The situation has been this: the persons who were the best able to dispense with catalogues were precisely the persons whose duty it was to make them.

The imperfection of descriptive catalogues has consequences which deserve our attention. On the one hand, we can never be sure that we have exhausted all the sources of information; who knows what may be held in reserve by the uncatalogued collections?[1]

[1] Mr. H. H. Bancroft, in his Memoirs, entitled "Literary Industries" (New York, 1891, 16mo), analyses with sufficient minuteness some practical consequences of the imperfection of the methods of research. He considers the case of an industrious writer proposing to write the history of California. He easily procures a few books, reads them, takes notes; these books refer him to others, which he consults in the public libraries of the city where he resides. Several years are passed in this manner, at the end of which he perceives that he has not a tenth part of the resources in his hands; he travels, maintains correspondences, but, finally despairing of exhausting the subject, he comforts his conscience and pride with the reflection that he has done much, and that many of the works he has not seen, like many of those he has, are probably of very slight historic value. As to newspapers and the myriads of United States government reports, all of them containing facts bearing on Californian history; being a sane man, he has never dreamed of searching them from beginning to end: he has turned over a few

On the other hand, in order to obtain the maximum amount of information, it is necessary to be thoroughly acquainted with the resources furnished by the existing literature of Heuristic, and to devote a great deal of time to preliminary researches. In point of fact, every one who proposes to collect documents for the treatment of a point of history begins by consulting indexes and catalogues.[1] Novices set about this important operation so slowly, with so little skill, and with so much effort, as to move more experienced workers to mirth or pity, according to their disposition. Those who find amusement in watching novices stumble and strain and waste their time in the labyrinth of catalogues, neglecting those which are valuable, and thoroughly exploring those which are useless, remember that they also have passed

of them, that is all; he knows that each of these fields of research would afford a labour of several years, and that all of them would fill the better part of his life with drudgery. As for oral testimony and manuscripts, he will gather a few unpublished anecdotes in chance conversations; he will obtain access to a few family papers; all this will appear in his book as notes and authorities. Now and again he will get hold of a few documentary curiosities among the state archives, but as it would take fifteen years to master the whole collection, he will naturally be content to glean a little here and there. Then he begins to write. He does not feel called upon to inform the public that he has not seen *all* the documents; on the contrary, he makes the most of what he has been able to procure in the course of twenty-five years of industrious research.

[1] Some dispense with personal search by invoking the assistance of the functionaries charged with the administration of depositories of documents; the indispensable search is, in these cases, conducted by the functionaries instead of by the public. Cf. *Bouvard et Pécuchet*, p. 158. Bouvard and Pécuchet resolve to write the life of the Duke of Angoulême; for this purpose "they determined to spend several days at the municipal library of Caen to make researches. The librarian placed general histories and pamphlets at their disposal. . . ."

through similar experiences: let every one have his turn. Those who observe with regret this waste of time and strength consider that, while inevitable up to a certain point, it serves no good purpose; they ask whether something might not be done to mitigate the severity of this apprenticeship to Heuristic, which at one time cost them so dear. Besides, is not research, in the present condition of its material aids, difficult enough whatever the experience of the researcher? There are scholars and historians who devote the best part of their powers to material searches. Certain branches of historical work, relating chiefly to mediæval and modern subjects (the documents of ancient history are fewer, have been more studied, and are better catalogued than the others), imply not merely the assiduous use of catalogues, not all furnished with indexes, but also the personal inspection of the whole contents of immense collections which are either badly catalogued or not catalogued at all. Experience proves beyond a doubt that the prospect of these long searches, which must be performed before the more intellectual part of the work can be begun, has deterred, and continues to deter, men of excellent abilities from undertaking historical work. They are, in fact, confronted with a dilemma: either they must work on a supply of documents which is in all probability incomplete, or they must spend themselves in unlimited searches, often fruitless, the results of which seldom appear worth the time they have cost. It goes against the grain to spend a great part of one's life in turning over catalogues without indexes, or in passing under review, one after another, all the items which go to form accumulations of uncatalogued *miscellanea,* in order to obtain information (positive or negative) which might have been obtained easily and instantaneously if the collections had been catalogued and if the catalogues had been indexed. The most serious consequence of the present imperfection of the material aids to Heuristic is the discouragement which is sure to be felt by many able men who know their worth, and have some sense of the due proportion of effort and reward.[1]

If it lay in the nature of things that the search for historical documents, in public depositories, must necessarily be as laborious as it still is, we might resign ourselves to the inconvenience: no one thinks of regretting the inevitable expenditure of time and labour which is demanded by archæological research, whatever the results may prove to be. But the imperfection of the modern instruments of Heuristic is quite unnecessary. The state of things which existed for some centuries has now been reformed indifferently; there is no valid reason why it should not some day be reformed altogether. We are thus led, after treating of the causes and the effects, to say a few words about the remedies.

The instruments of Heuristic are being continually perfected, before our eyes, in two ways. Every year witnesses an increase in the number of descriptive catalogues of archives, libraries, and museums, prepared by the functionaries attached to these institutions. In addition to this, powerful

[1] These considerations have already been presented and developed in the *Revue universitaire*, 1894, i. p. 321 *sqq.*

learned societies employ experts to pass from one depository to another cataloguing the documents there, in order to pick out all the documents of a particular class, or relating to a special subject: thus the society of Bollandists caused a general catalogue of hagiographical documents to be prepared by its emissaries, and the Imperial Academy of Vienna catalogued in a similar manner the monuments of patristic literature. The society of the *Monumenta Germaniæ Historica* has for a long time been conducting vast searches of the same kind; and it was by the same process of exploring the museums and libraries of the whole of Europe that the construction of the *Corpus Inscriptionum Latinarum* was lately rendered possible. Lastly, several governments have taken the initiative in sending abroad persons charged to catalogue, on their behalf, documents in which they are interested: thus England, the Netherlands, Switzerland, the United States, and other governments, grant regular subsidies to agents of theirs occupied in cataloguing and transcribing, in the great depositories of Europe, the documents which relate to the history of England, the Netherlands, Switzerland, the United States, and the rest.[1] With what rapidity and with what

[1] It is well known that, since the opening of the Papal Archives, several governments and learned societies have established Institutes at Rome, the members of which are, for the most part, occupied in cataloguing and making known the documents of these archives, in co-operation with the functionaries of the Vatican. The French School at Rome, the Austrian Institute, the Prussian Institute, the Polish Mission, the Institute of the "Goerresgesellschaft," Belgian, Danish, Spanish, Portuguese, Russian, and other scholars, have performed, and are performing, cataloguing work of considerable extent in the archives of the Vatican.

perfection these useful labours can be conducted, provided that a competent staff, suitably directed, can be had as well as the money to pay it, is shown by the history of the *general catalogue of the manuscripts in the public libraries of France.* This excellent descriptive catalogue was begun in 1885, and now, in 1897, it extends to nearly fifty volumes, and will soon be completed. The *Corpus Inscriptionum Latinarum* will have been produced in less than fifty years. The results obtained by the Bollandists and the Imperial Academy of Vienna are not less conclusive. Assuredly nothing is now lacking, except funds, to secure the speedy endowment of historical study with the indispensable instruments of research. The methods employed in the construction of these instruments are now permanently fixed, and it is an easy matter to recruit a trained staff. Such a staff must evidently be largely composed of keepers of archives and professional librarians, but it would also contain unattached workers with a decided vocation for the construction of catalogues and indexes. Such workers are more numerous than one would at first be inclined to think. Not that cataloguing is easy: it requires patience, the most scrupulous attention, and the most varied learning; but many minds are attracted by tasks which, like this, are at once determinate, capable of being definitely completed, and of manifest utility. In the large and heterogeneous family of those who labour to promote the progress of historical study, the makers of descriptive catalogues and indexes form a section to themselves. When they devote themselves exclusively to their art they acquire by practice, as one might expect, a high degree of dexterity.

While waiting for the fact to be clearly recognised that the time is opportune for pushing vigorously in every country the construction of a general catalogue of historical documents, we may indicate a palliative: it is important that scholars and historians, especially novices, should be accurately informed of the state of the instruments of research which are at their disposal, and be regularly apprised of any improvements that from time to time may be made in them. Experience and accident have been for a long time trusted to supply this information; but empirical knowledge, besides being costly, as we have already pointed out, is almost always imperfect. Recently the task has been undertaken of constructing catalogues of catalogues—critical and systematic lists of all the catalogues in existence. There can be no doubt that few bibliographical enterprises have possessed, in so great a degree, the character of general utility.

But scholars and historians often need, in respect of documents, information not usually supplied by descriptive catalogues; they wish, for example, to know whether such and such a document is known or not, whether it has already been critically dealt with, annotated, or utilised.[1] This information can only be found in the works of former scholars and

[1] Catalogues of documents sometimes, but not always, mention the fact that such and such a document has been edited, dealt with critically, utilised. The generally received rule is that the compiler mentions circumstances of this kind when he is aware of them, without imposing on himself the enormous task of ascertaining the truth on this head in every instance where he is ignorant of it.

historians. In order to become acquainted with these works, recourse must be had to those "bibliographical repertories," properly so called, of all kinds, compiled from very different points of view, which have already been published. Among the indispensable instruments of Heuristic must thus be reckoned bibliographical repertories of historical literature, as well as repertories of catalogues of original documents.

To supply the classified list of all those repertories (repertories of catalogues, bibliographical repertories, properly so called), together with other appropriate information, in order to save students from mistakes and waste of time, is the object of what we are at liberty to call the "science of repertories," or "historical bibliography." Professor Bernheim has published a preliminary sketch[1] of it, which we have endeavoured to expand.[2] The expanded sketch bears date April 1896: numerous additions, not to speak of revision, would already be necessary, for the bibliographical apparatus of the historical sciences is being renewed, at the present time, with astonishing rapidity. A book on the repertories for the use of scholars and historians is, as a general rule, out of date the day after it has been completed.

III. The knowledge of repertories is useful to all; the preliminary search for documents is laborious to all; but not in the same degree. Certain parts of history, which have been long cultivated, now enjoy

[1] E. Bernheim, *Lehrbuch der historischen Methode*, 2nd ed., pp. 196–202.

[2] C. V. Langlois, *Manuel de Bibliographie historique: I. Instruments bibliographiques*, Paris, 1896, 16mo.

the advantage of having all their documents described, collected, and classified in large publications devoted to the purpose, so that, in dealing with these subjects, the historian can do all that need be done at his desk. The study of local history does not generally require more than local search. Some important monographs are based on a small number of documents, all belonging to the same collection, and of such a nature that it would be superfluous to look for others elsewhere. On the other hand, a humble piece of work, such as a modest edition of a text of which the ancient copies are not rare, and are to be found scattered in several libraries of Europe, may have involved inquiries, negotiations, and journeys without end. Since the majority of the documents of mediæval and modern history are still unedited, or badly edited, it may be laid down as a general principle that, in order to write a really new chapter of mediæval or modern history, it is necessary to have long haunted the great depositories of original documents, and to have, if we may use the expression, worried their catalogues.

It is thus incumbent on every one to choose the subject of his labours with the greatest care, instead of leaving it to be determined by pure chance. There are some subjects which, in the present state of the instruments of research, cannot be treated except at the cost of enormous searches in which life and intellect are consumed without profit. These subjects are not necessarily more interesting than others, and some day, perhaps to-morrow, improvements in the aids to research will make them easily manageable. It is necessary for the student consciously and deliberately to make his choice between different historical subjects depend on the existence or non-existence of particular catalogues of documents and bibliographical repertories; on his relative inclination for desk work on the one hand, and the labour of exploring depositories on the other; even on the facilities he has for making use of particular collections. "Is it possible to do work in the provinces?" Renan asked at the congress of learned societies at the Sorbonne in 1889; and gave a very good answer to his own question: "At least half one's scientific work can be done at one's own desk. . . . Take comparative philology, for example: with an initial outlay of some thousands of francs, and subscriptions to three or four special publications, a student would command all the tools of his trade. . . . The same applies to universal philosophy. . . . Many branches of study can thus be prosecuted quite privately, and in the closest retirement."[1] Doubtless, but there are "rarities, specialities, researches which require the aid of powerful machinery." One half of historical work may now be done in private, with limited resources, but only half; the other half still presupposes the employment of such resources, in the way of repertories and documents, as can only be found in the great centres of study; often, indeed, it is necessary to visit several of these centres in succession. In short, the case stands with history much as it does with geography: in respect of some portions of the globe, we possess documents published in manageable form sufficiently complete and

[1] E. Renan, *Feuilles détachées* (Paris, 1892, 8vo), pp. 96 *sqq.*

sufficiently well classified to enable us to reason about them to good purpose without leaving our fireside; while in the case of an unexplored or badly explored region, the slightest monograph implies a considerable expenditure of time and physical strength. It is dangerous to choose a subject of study, as many do, without having first realised the nature and extent of the preliminary researches which it demands; there are instances of men struggling for years with such researches, who might have been occupied to better advantage in work of another character. As precautions against this danger, which is the more formidable to novices the more active and zealous they are, an examination of the present conditions of Heuristic in general, and positive notions of Historical Bibliography, are certainly to be warmly recommended.

CHAPTER II

"AUXILIARY SCIENCES"

LET us suppose that the preliminary searches, treated of in the preceding chapter, have been made methodically and successfully; the greater part, if not the whole, of the documents bearing on a given subject have been discovered and made available. Of two things one: either these documents have been already subjected to critical elaboration, or they are in the condition of raw material; this is a point which must be settled by "bibliographical" researches, which also, as we have already observed, form part of the inquiries which precede the logical part of the work. In the first case, where the documents have already gone through a process of elaboration, it is necessary to be in a position to verify the accuracy of the critical work; in the second case, where the documents are still raw material, the student must do the critical work himself. In both cases certain antecedent and auxiliary knowledge of a positive kind, *Vor- und Hülfskenntnisse*, as they are called, are every whit as indispensable as the habit of accurate reasoning; for if, in the course of critical work, it is possible to go wrong through reasoning badly, it is also possible to go wrong out of pure ignorance.

The profession of a scholar or historian is, moreover, similar in this respect to all other professions; it is impossible to follow it without possessing a certain equipment of technical notions, whose absence neither natural aptitude nor even method can make good. In what, then, does the technical *apprenticeship* of the scholar or the historian consist? Or, to employ language which, though inappropriate, as we shall endeavour to show, is in more common use: what, in addition to the knowledge of repertories, are the "auxiliary sciences" of history?

Daunou, in his *Cours d'études historiques*,[1] has proposed a question of the same kind. "What studies," says he, "will the intending historian need to have gone through, what kinds of knowledge ought he to have acquired, in order to begin writing a work with any hope of success?" Before him, Mably, in his *Traité de l'étude de l'histoire*, had also recognised that "there are preparatory studies with which no historian can dispense." But on this subject Mably and Daunou entertained views which nowadays seem singular enough. It is instructive to mark the exact distance which separates their point of view from ours. "First of all," said Mably, "study the law of nature, public law, moral and political science." Daunou, a man of great judgment, permanent secretary to the Academy of Inscriptions and Belles-Lettres, writing about 1820, divides the studies which, in his opinion, constitute "the apprenticeship of the historian," into three classes—literary, philosophical, historical. On the "literary" studies he expatiates at great length: to begin with, the

[1] vii. p. 228 *sqq.*

historian must "have read with attention the great models." Which great models? Daunou "does not hesitate" to place in the front rank "the masterpieces of epic poetry;" for "it is the poets who have created the art of narrative, and whoever has not learnt it from them cannot have more than an imperfect knowledge of it." He further recommends the reading of modern novels; "they will teach the method of giving an artistic pose to persons and events, of distributing details, of skilfully carrying on the thread of the narrative, of interrupting it, of resuming it, of sustaining the attention and provoking the curiosity of the reader." Finally, good historical works should be read: "Herodotus, Thucydides, Xenophon, Polybius, and Plutarch among the Greeks; Cæsar, Sallust, Livy, and Tacitus among the Latins; and among the moderns, Macchiavelli, Guicciardini, Giannone, Hume, Robertson, Gibbon, the Cardinal de Retz, Vertot, Voltaire, Raynal, and Rulhière. Not that I would exclude the others, but these will suffice to provide all the styles which are suitable for history; for a great diversity of form is to be met with in the works of these writers." In the second place come philosophical studies; a thorough mastery of "ideology, morals, and politics" is required. "As to the works from which knowledge of this kind is to be obtained, Daguesseau has instanced Aristotle, Cicero, Grotius: I should add the best ancient and modern moralists, treatises on political economy published since the middle of the last century, the writings on political science in general, and on its details and application, of Macchiavelli, Bodin, Locke, Montesquieu, Rousseau, Mably, and the most enlightened of their disciples and commentators." In the third place, before writing history, "it is evidently necessary to know it." "A writer will not give the world new information on a subject like this unless he begins by making himself master of what is already known of it." The future historian has already made the acquaintance of the best historical works, and studied them as models of style; "it will be to his advantage to read them a second time, but endeavouring more particularly to grasp all the facts which they contain, and to let them make so deep an impression on his mind that they may be permanently fixed in his memory."

These are the "positive" notions which, eighty years ago, were considered indispensable to the general historian. At the same time there was a confused idea that "in order to acquire a profound knowledge of particular subjects" there were yet other useful branches of study. "The subjects of which historians treat," says Daunou, "the details which they occasionally light upon, require very extensive and varied attainments." He goes on to particularise, observe in what terms: "very often a knowledge of several languages, sometimes too some notion of physics and mathematics." And he adds: "On these subjects, however, the general education which we may assume to be common to all men of letters is sufficient for the writer who devotes himself to historical composition. . . ."

All the authors who, like Daunou, have attempted to enumerate the preliminary attainments, as well as the moral or intellectual aptitudes, necessary for "writing history," have either fallen into commonplace or pitched their requirements ridiculously high. According to Freeman, the historian ought to know everything—philosophy, law, finance, ethnography, geography, anthropology, natural science, and what not; is not an historian, in point of fact, likely enough in the course of his study of the past to meet with questions of philosophy, law, finance, and the rest of the series? And if financial science, for example, is necessary to a writer who treats of contemporary finance, is it less so to the writer who claims to express an opinion on the financial questions of the past? "The historian," Freeman declares, "may have incidentally to deal with any subject whatever, and the more branches of knowledge he is master of, the better prepared he is for his own work." True, all branches of human knowledge are not equally useful; some of them are only serviceable on rare occasions, and accidentally: "We could hardly make it even a counsel of perfection to the historian to make himself an accomplished chemist, on the chance of an occasion in which chemistry might be of use to him in his study;" but other special subjects are more closely related to history: "for example, geology and a whole group of sciences which have a close connection with geology . . . The historian will clearly do his own regular work better for being master of them . . ." [1] The question has

[1] E. A. Freeman, *The Methods of Historical Study* (London, 1885, 8vo), p. 45.

In France geography has long been regarded as a science closely related to history. An *Agrégation*, which combines history and geography, exists at the present day, and in the *lycées* history and geography are taught by the same professors. Many people persist in asserting the legitimacy of this combination, and even take

also been asked whether "history is one of those studies anciently called *umbratiles*, for which all that is wanted is a quiet mind and habits of industry;" or whether it is a good thing for the historian to have mingled in the turmoil of active life, and to have helped to make the history of his own time before sitting down to write that of the past. Indeed, what questions have not been asked? Floods of ink have been poured out over these uninteresting and unanswerable questions, the long and fruitless debating of which has done not a little to discredit works on methodology. Our opinion is that nothing relevant can be added to the dictates of mere common sense on the subject of the apprenticeship to the "art of writing history," unless perhaps that this apprenticeship should consist, above everything, in the study, hitherto so generally neglected, of the principles of historical method.

Besides, it is not the "literary historian," the moralising and quill-driving "historians," as conceived by Daunou and his school, that we have had in view; we are here only concerned with

umbrage when it is proposed to separate two branches of knowledge united, as they say, by many essential connecting links. But it would be hard to find any good reason, or any facts of experience, to prove that a professor of history, or an historian, is so much the better the more he knows of geology, oceanography, climatology, and the whole group of geographical sciences. In fact, it is with some impatience, and to no immediate advantage, that students of history work through the courses of geography which their curricula force upon them; and those students who have a real taste for geography would be very glad to throw history overboard. The artificial union of history with geography dates back, in France, to an epoch when geography was an ill-defined and ill-arranged subject, regarded by all as a negligeable branch of study. It is a relic of antiquity that we ought to get rid of at once.

those scholars and historians who intend to deal with documents in order to facilitate or actually perform the scientific work of history. These stand in need of a *technical apprenticeship.* What meaning are we to attach to this term?

Let us suppose we have before us a written document. What use can we make of it if we cannot read it? Up to the time of François Champollion, Egyptian documents, being written in hieroglyphics, were, without metaphor, a dead-letter. It will be readily admitted that in order to deal with ancient Assyrian history it is necessary to have learnt to decipher cuneiform inscriptions. Similarly, whoever desires to do original work from the sources, in ancient or mediæval history, will, if he is prudent, learn to decipher inscriptions and manuscripts. We thus see why Greek and Latin epigraphy and mediæval palæography—that is, the sum of the various kinds of knowledge required for the deciphering of ancient and mediæval manuscripts and inscriptions—are considered as "auxiliary sciences" to history, or rather, the historical study of antiquity and the middle ages. It is evident that mediæval Latin palæography forms part of the necessary outfit of the mediævalist, just as the palæography of hieroglyphics is essential to the Egyptologist. There is, however, a difference to be observed. No one will ever think of devoting himself to Egyptology without having first studied the appropriate palæography. On the other hand, it is not very rare for a man to undertake the study of local documents of the middle ages without having learnt to date their forms approximately, and to decipher their abbreviations correctly. The resemblance which most mediæval writing bears to modern writing is sufficiently close to foster the illusion that ingenuity and practice will be enough to carry him through. This illusion is dangerous. Scholars who have received no regular palæographical initiation can almost always be recognised by the gross errors which they commit from time to time in deciphering—errors which are sometimes enough to completely ruin the subsequent operations of criticism and interpretation. As for the self-taught experts who acquire their skill by dint of practice, the orthodox palæographic initiation which they have missed would at least have saved them much groping in the dark, long hours of labour, and many a disappointment.

Suppose a document has been deciphered. How is it to be turned to account, unless it be first understood? Inscriptions in Etruscan and the ancient language of Cambodia have been read, but no one understands them. As long as this is the case they must remain useless. It is clear that in order to deal with Greek history it is necessary to consult documents in the Greek language, and therefore necessary to know Greek. Rank truism, the reader will say. Yes, but many proceed as if it had never occurred to them. Young students attack ancient history with only a superficial tincture of Greek and Latin. Many who have never studied mediæval French and Latin think they know them because they understand classical Latin and modern French, and they attempt the interpretation of texts whose literal meaning escapes them, or appears to be obscure when in reality perfectly plain. Innumerable historical errors owe their origin to false or inexact interpretations of quite straightforward texts, perpetrated by men who were insufficiently acquainted with the grammar, the vocabulary, or the niceties of ancient languages. Solid philological study ought logically to precede historical research in every instance where the documents to be employed are not to be had in a modern language, and in a form in which they can be easily understood.

Suppose a document is intelligible. It would not be legitimate to take it into consideration without having verified its authenticity, if its authenticity has not been already settled beyond a doubt. Now in order to verify the authenticity or ascertain the origin of a document two things are required—reasoning power and knowledge. In other words, it is necessary to reason from certain positive data which represent the condensed results of previous research, which cannot be improvised, and must, therefore, be learnt. To distinguish a genuine from a spurious charter would, in fact, be often an impossible task for the best trained logician, if he were unacquainted with the practice of such and such a chancery, at such and such a date, or with the features common to all the admittedly genuine charters of a particular class. He would be obliged to do what the first scholars did—ascertain for himself, by the comparison of a great number of similar documents, what features distinguish the admittedly genuine documents from the others, before allowing himself to pronounce judgment in any special instance. Will not his task be enormously simplified if there is in existence a body of doctrine, a treasury of accumulated observations, a system of results obtained by workers who have already made, repeated, and checked the minute comparisons he would otherwise have been obliged to make for himself? This body of doctrines, observations, and results, calculated to assist the criticism of diplomas and charters, does exist; it is called Diplomatic. We shall, therefore, assign to Diplomatic, along with Epigraphy, Palæography, and Philology, the character of a subject auxiliary to historical research.

Epigraphy and Palæography, Philology, and Diplomatic with its adjuncts (technical Chronology and Sphragistic) are not the only subjects of study which subserve historical research. It would be extremely injudicious to undertake to deal critically with literary documents on which no critical work has as yet been done without making oneself familiar with the results obtained by those who have already dealt critically with documents of the same class: the sum of these results forms a department to itself, which has a name—the History of Literature.[1] The critical treatment of illustrative documents, such as the productions of architecture, sculpture, and painting, objects of all kinds (arms, dress, utensils, coins, medals, armorial bearings, and so forth), presupposes a thorough acquaintance with the rules and observations which constitute Archæology properly so

[1] "Historiography" is a branch of the "History of Literature;" it is the sum of the results obtained by the critics who have hitherto studied ancient historical writings, such as annals, memoirs, chronicles, biographies, and so forth.

called and its detached branches—Numismatic and Heraldry.

We are now in a position to examine to some purpose the hazy notion expressed by the phrase, "the sciences auxiliary to history." We also read of "ancillary sciences," and, in French, "sciences satellites." None of these expressions is really satisfactory.

First of all, the so-called "auxiliary sciences" are not all of them *sciences*. Diplomatic, for example, and the History of Literature are only systematised accumulations of facts, acquired by criticism, which are of a nature to facilitate the application of critical methods to documents hitherto untouched. On the other hand, Philology is an organised science, and has its own laws.

In the second place, among the branches of knowledge auxiliary—properly speaking, not to history, but to historical research—we must distinguish between those which every worker in the field ought to master, and those in respect of which he needs only to know where to look when he has occasion to make use of them; between knowledge which ought to become part of a man's self, and information which he may be content to possess only in potentiality. A mediævalist should *know* how to read and understand mediæval texts; he would gain no advantage by accumulating in his memory the mass of particular facts pertaining to the History of Literature and Diplomatic which are to be found, in their proper place, in well-constructed works of reference.

Lastly, there are no branches of knowledge which

are auxiliary to History (or even historical research) in general—that is, which are useful to all students irrespectively of the particular part of history on which they are engaged.[1] It appears, then, that there is no general answer possible to the question raised at the beginning of this chapter: in what should the technical apprenticeship of the scholar or historian consist? In what does it consist? That depends. It depends on the part of history he proposes to study. A knowledge of palæography is quite useless for the purpose of investi-

[1] This is only true under reservation; there is an instrument of research which is indispensable to all historians, to all students, whatever be the subject of their special study. History, moreover, is here in the same situation as the majority of the other sciences: all who prosecute original research, of whatever kind, need to know several living languages, those of countries where men think and work, of countries which, from the point of view of science, stand in the forefront of contemporary civilisation.

In our days the cultivation of the sciences is not confined to any single country, or even to Europe. It is international. All problems, the same problems, are being studied everywhere simultaneously. It is difficult to-day, and to-morrow it will be impossible, to find a subject which can be treated without taking cognisance of works in a foreign language. Henceforth, for ancient history, Greek and Roman, a knowledge of German will be as imperative as a knowledge of Greek and Latin. Questions of strictly local history are the only ones still accessible to those who do not possess the key to foreign literatures. The great problems are beyond their reach, for the wretched and ridiculous reason that works on these problems in any language but their own are sealed books to them.

Total ignorance of the languages which have hitherto been the ordinary vehicles of science (German, English, French, Italian) is a disease which age renders incurable. It would not be exacting too much to require every candidate for a scientific profession to be at least *trilinguis*—that is, to be able to understand, fairly easily, two languages besides his mother-tongue. This is a requirement to which scholars were not subject formerly, when Latin was still the common language of learned men, but which the conditions of

gating the history of the French Revolution, and a knowledge of Greek is equally useless for the treatment of a question in mediæval French history.[1] But wé may go so far as to say that the preliminary outfit of every one who wishes to do original work in history should consist (in addition to the "common education," that is, general culture, of which Daunou writes) in the knowledge calculated to aid in the

modern scientific work will henceforth cause to press with increasing weight upon the scholars of every country.*

The French scholars who are unable to read German and English are thereby placed in a position of permanent inferiority as compared with their better instructed colleagues in France and abroad; whatever their merit, they are condemned to work with insufficient means of information, to work badly. They know it. They do their best to hide their infirmity, as something to be ashamed of, except when they make a cynical parade of it and boast of it; but this boasting, as we can easily see, is only shame showing itself in a different way. Too much stress cannot be laid upon the fact that a practical knowledge of foreign languages is auxiliary in the first degree to all historical work, as indeed it is to scientific work in general.

[1] When the "auxiliary sciences" were first inserted in the curricula of French universities, it was observed that some students whose special subject was the French Revolution, and who had no interest whatever in the middle ages, took up palæography as an "auxiliary science," and that some students of geography, who were in no way interested in antiquity, took up epigraphy. Evidently they had failed to understand that the study of the "auxiliary sciences" is recommended, not as an end in itself, but because it is of practical utility to those who devote themselves to certain special subjects. See the *Revue universitaire*, 1895, ii. p. 123.

---

* Perhaps a day will come when it will be necessary to know the most important Slavonic language; there are already scholars who are setting themselves to learn Russian. The idea of restoring Latin to its old position of universal language is chimerical. See the file of the *Phœnix, seu nuntius latinus universalis* (London, 1891, 4to).

discovery, the understanding, and the criticism of documents. The exact nature of this knowledge varies from case to case according as the student specialises in one or another part of universal history. The technical apprenticeship is relatively short and easy for those who occupy themselves with modern or contemporary history, long and laborious for those who occupy themselves with ancient and mediæval history.

This reform of the historian's technical apprenticeship, which consists in substituting the acquisition of positive knowledge, truly auxiliary to historical research, for the study of the "great models," literary and philosophical, is of quite recent date. In France, for the greater part of the present century, students of history received none but a literary education, after Daunou's pattern. Almost all of them were contented with such a preparation, and did not look beyond it; some few perceived and regretted, when it was too late for a remedy, the insufficiency of their early training; with a few illustrious exceptions, the best of them never rose to be more than distinguished men of letters, incapable of scientific work. There was at that time no organisation for teaching the "auxiliary sciences" and the technique of research except in the case of French mediæval history, and that in a special school, the École des chartes. This simple fact, moreover, secured for this school during a period of fifty years a marked superiority over all the other French (or even foreign) institutions of higher education; excellent workers were there trained who contributed many new results, while elsewhere people were idly discussing problems.[1] To-day it is still at the École des chartes that the mediævalist has the opportunity of going through his technical apprenticeship in the best and most complete manner, thanks to the combined and progressive three-years courses of Romance philology, palæography, archæology, historiography, and mediæval law. But the "auxiliary sciences" are now taught everywhere more or less adequately; they have been introduced into the university curricula. On the other hand, students' handbooks of epigraphy, palæography, diplomatic, and so forth, have multiplied during the last twenty-five years. Twenty-five years ago it would have been vain to look for a good book which should supply the want of oral instruction on these subjects; since the establishment of professorships "manuals" have appeared [2] which

[1] On this point note the opinions of T. von Sickel and J. Havet, quoted in the *Bibliothèque de l'École des chartes*, 1896, p. 87. In 1854 the Austrian Institute "für österreichische Geschichtsforschung" was organised on the model of the French École des chartes. Another institution of the same type has lately been created in the "Istituto di studi superiori" at Florence. "We are accustomed," we read in England, "to hear the complaint that there is not in this country any institution resembling the École des chartes" (*Quarterly Review*, July 1896, p. 122).

[2] This is a suitable place to enumerate the principal "manuals" published in the last twenty-five years. But a list of them, ending at 1894, will be found in Bernheim's *Lehrbuch*, pp. 206 *sqq*. We will only refer to the great "manuals" of "Philology" (in the comprehensive sense of the German "Philologie," which includes the history of language and literature, epigraphy, palæography, and all that pertains to textual criticism) now in course of publication: the *Grundriss der indo-arischen Philologie und Altertumskunde*, edited by G. Bühler; the *Grundriss der iranischen Philologie*, edited by W. Geiger and E. Kuhn; the *Handbuch der classischen Altertumswissenschaft*, edited by I. von Müller; the *Grundriss der germanischen Philologie*, edited by H. Paul, the second edition of which began to appear in 1896; the *Grundriss der romanischen Philologie*, edited

would almost make them superfluous were it not that oral instruction, based on practical exercises, has here an exceptional value. Whether a student does or does not enjoy the advantage of a regular drilling in an institution for higher education, he has henceforth no excuse for remaining in ignorance of those things which he ought to know before entering upon historical work. There is, in fact, less of this kind of neglect than there used to be. On this head, the success of the above-mentioned "manuals," with their rapid succession of editions, is very significant.[1]

Here, then, we have the future historian armed with the preliminary knowledge, the neglect of which would have condemned him to powerlessness or to continual mistakes. We suppose him protected from the errors without number which have their origin in an imperfect knowledge of the writing and the language of documents, in ignorance of previous work and the results obtained by textual criticism; he has an irreproachable *cognitio cogniti et cognoscendi*. A very optimistic supposition, by the way, as we are bound to admit. We know but too well that to have gone through a regular course of "auxiliary sciences," or to have read attentively the best treatises on

by G. Gröber. In these vast repertories there will be found, along with a short presentment of the subject, complete bibliographical references, direct as well as indirect.

[1] The French "manuals" of MM. Prou (Palæography), Giry (Diplomatic), Cagnat (Latin Epigraphy), and others, have diffused among the public the idea and knowledge of the auxiliary subjects of study. New editions have enabled, and will enable, them to be kept up to date—a very necessary operation, for most of these subjects, though now settled in the main, are being enriched and made more precise every day. Cf. *supra*, p. 38.

bibliography, palæography, philology, and so on, or even to have acquired some personal experience by practical exercises, is not enough to ensure that a man shall always be well informed, still less to make him infallible. In the first place, those who have for a long time studied documents of a given class or of a given period possess, in regard to these, incommunicable knowledge in virtue of which they are able to deal better than others with new documents which they may meet with of the same class or period; nothing can replace the "special erudition" which is the specialist's reward for hard work.[1] And secondly, specialists themselves make mistakes: palæographers must be perpetually on their guard not to decipher falsely; is there a philologist who has not some faults of construing on his conscience? Scholars usually well informed have printed as unedited texts which had already been published, and have neglected documents it was their business to know. Scholars spend their lives in incessantly perfecting their "auxiliary" knowledge, which they rightly regard as never perfect. But all this does

[1] What exactly are we to understand by this "incommunicable knowledge," of which we speak? When a specialist is very familiar with the documents of a given class or period, associations of ideas are formed in his brain; and when he examines a new document of the same class or species, analogies suddenly dawn upon him which would escape any one of less experience, however well furnished he might be with the most perfect repertories. The fact is, that not all the peculiarities of documents can be isolated; there are some which cannot be classified under any intelligible head, and which, therefore, cannot be found in any tabulated list. But the human memory, when it is good, retains the impression of these peculiarities, and even a faint and distant stimulus suffices to revive the apprehension of them.

not prevent us from maintaining our hypothesis. Only let it be understood that in practice we do not postpone work upon documents till we shall have gained a serene and absolute mastery over all the "auxiliary branches of knowledge:" we should never dare to begin.

It remains to know how to treat documents supposing one has successfully passed through the preliminary apprenticeship.

BOOK II

ANALYTICAL OPERATIONS

BOOK II

ANALYTICAL OPERATIONS

CHAPTER I

GENERAL CONDITIONS OF HISTORICAL KNOWLEDGE

WE have already stated that history is studied from documents, and that documents are the traces of past events.[1] This is the place to indicate the consequences involved in this statement and this definition.

Events can be empirically known in two ways only: by direct observation while they are in progress; and indirectly, by the study of the traces which they leave behind them. Take an earthquake, for example. I have a direct knowledge of it if I am present when the phenomenon occurs; an indirect knowledge if, without having been thus present, I observe its physical effects (crevices, ruins), or if, after these effects have disappeared, I read a description written by some one who has himself witnessed the phenomenon or its effects. Now, the peculiarity of "historical facts"[2] is this,

[1] *Supra*, p. 17.

[2] This expression, which frequently occurs, needs explanation. It is not to be taken to apply to a *species* of facts. There are no

that they are only known indirectly by the help of their traces. Historical knowledge is essentially indirect knowledge. The methods of historical science ought, therefore, to be radically different from those of the direct sciences; that is to say, of all the other sciences, except geology, which are founded on direct observation. Historical science, whatever may be said,[1] is not a science of observation at all.

The facts of the past are only known to us by the traces of them which have been preserved. These traces, it is true, are directly observed by the historian, but, after that, he has nothing more to observe; what remains is the work of reasoning, in which he endeavours to infer, with the greatest possible exactness, the facts from the traces. The document is his starting-point, the fact his goal.[2] Between this starting-point and this goal he has to pass through a complicated series of inferences, closely interwoven with each other, in which there are innumerable chances of error; while the least error, whether committed at the beginning, middle, or end of the work, may vitiate all his conclusions.

historical facts in the sense in which we speak of chemical facts. The same fact is or is not historical according to the manner in which it is known. It is only the mode of acquiring knowledge that is historical. A sitting of the Senate is a fact of direct observation for one who takes part in it; it becomes historical for the man who reads about it in a report. The eruption of Vesuvius in the time of Pliny is a geological fact which is known historically. The historical character is not in the facts, but in the manner of knowing them.

[1] Fustel de Coulanges has said it. Cf. *supra*, p. 4, note 1.

[2] In the sciences of observation it is the fact itself, observed directly, which is the starting-point.

The "historical," or indirect, method is thus obviously inferior to the method of direct observation; but historians have no choice: it is the *only* method of arriving at past facts, and we shall see later on[1] how, in spite of these disadvantages, it is possible for this method to lead to scientific knowledge.

The detailed analysis of the reasonings which lead from the inspection of documents to the knowledge of facts is one of the chief parts of Historical Methodology. It is the domain of criticism. The seven following chapters will be devoted to it. We shall endeavour, first of all, to give a very summary sketch of the general lines and main divisions of the subject.

I. We may distinguish two species of documents. Sometimes the past event has left a material trace (a monument, a fabricated article). Sometimes, and more commonly, the trace is of the psychological order—a written description or narrative. The first case is much simpler than the second. For there is a fixed relation between certain physical appearances and the causes which produced them; and this relation, governed by physical laws, is known to us.[2] But a psychological trace, on the other hand, is purely symbolic: it is not the fact itself; it is not even the immediate impression made by the fact upon the witness's mind, but only a conventional symbol of that impression. Written documents, then, are not, as material documents

[1] *Infra*, ch. vii.

[2] We shall not treat specially of the criticism of material documents (objects, monuments, &c.) where it differs from the criticism of written documents.

are, valuable by themselves; they are only valuable as signs of psychological operations, which are often complicated and hard to unravel. The immense majority of the documents which furnish the historian with starting-points for his reasonings are nothing else than traces of psychological operations.

This granted, in order to conclude from a written document to the fact which was its remote cause—that is, in order to ascertain the relation which connects the document with the fact—it is necessary to reproduce the whole series of intermediate causes which have given rise to the document. It is necessary to revive in imagination the whole of that series of acts performed by the author of the document which begins with the fact observed by him and ends with the manuscript (or printed volume), in order to arrive at the original event. Such is the aim and such the process of critical analysis.[1]

First of all we observe the document. Is it now in the same state as when it was produced? Has it deteriorated since? We endeavour to find out how it was made in order to restore it, if need be, to its original form, and to ascertain its origin. The first group of preliminary investigations, bearing upon the writing, the language, the form, the source, constitutes the special domain of EXTERNAL CRITICISM, or critical scholarship. Next comes INTERNAL CRITICISM: it endeavours, by the help of

[1] For the details and the logical justification of this method see Seignobos, *Les Conditions psychologiques de la connaissance en histoire*, in the *Revue philosophique*, 1887, ii. pp. 1, 168.

analogies mostly borrowed from general psychology, to reproduce the mental states through which the author of the document passed. Knowing what the author of the document has said, we ask (1) What did he mean? (2) Did he believe what he said? (3) Was he justified in believing whatever he did believe? This last step brings the document to a point where it resembles the data of the objective sciences: it becomes an observation; it only remains to treat it by the methods of the objective sciences. Every document is valuable precisely to the extent to which, by the study of its origin, it has been reduced to a well-made observation.

II. Two conclusions may be drawn from what we have just said: the extreme complexity and the absolute necessity of Historical Criticism.

Compared with other students the historian is in a very disagreeable situation. It is not merely that he cannot, as the chemist does, observe his facts directly; it very rarely happens that the documents which he is obliged to use represent precise observations. He has at his disposal none of those systematic records of observations which, in the established sciences, can and do replace direct observation. He is in the situation of a chemist who should know a series of experiments only from the report of his laboratory-boy. The historian is compelled to turn to account rough and ready reports, such as no man of science would be content with.[1] All the more

[1] The most favourable case, that in which the document has been drawn up by what is called an ocular "witness," is still far short of the ideal required for scientific knowledge. The notion

necessary are the precautions to be taken in utilising these documents, the only materials of historical science. It is evidently most important to eliminate those which are worthless, and to ascertain the amount of correct observation represented by those which are left.

All the more necessary, too, are cautions on this subject, because the natural inclination of the human mind is to take no precautions at all, and to treat these matters, which really demand the utmost obtainable precision, with careless laxity. It is true that every one admits the utility of criticism in theory; but this is just one of those principles which are more easily admitted than put into practice. Many centuries and whole eras of brilliant civilisation had to pass away before the first dawn of criticism was visible among the most intellectual peoples in the world. Neither the orientals nor the middle ages ever formed a definite conception of it.[1] Up to our own day there have been enlightened men who, in employing documents for the purpose of writing history, have neglected the most elementary precautions, and unconsciously assumed false

of *witness* has been borrowed from the procedure of the law-courts; reduced to scientific terms, it becomes that of an *observer*. A testimony is an observation. But, in point of fact, historical testimony differs materially from scientific observation. The observer proceeds by fixed rules, and clothes his report in language of rigorous precision. On the other hand, the "witness" observes without method, and reports in unprecise language; it is not known whether he has taken the necessary precautions. It is an essential attribute of historical documents that they come before us as the result of work which has been done without method and without guarantee.

[1] See B. Lasch, *Das Erwachen und die Entwickelung der historischen Kritik im Mittelalter* (Breslau, 1887, 8vo).

generalisations. Even now most young students would, if left to themselves, fall into the old errors. For criticism is antagonistic to the normal bent of the mind. The spontaneous tendency of man is to yield assent to affirmations, and to reproduce them, without even clearly distinguishing them from the results of his own observation. In everyday life do we not accept indiscriminately, without any kind of verification, hearsay reports, anonymous and unguaranteed statements, "documents" of indifferent or inferior authority? It takes a special reason to induce us to take the trouble to examine into the origin and value of a document on the history of yesterday; otherwise, if there is no outrageous improbability in it, and as long as it is not contradicted, we swallow it whole, we pin our faith to it, we hawk it about, and, if need be, embellish it in the process. Every candid man must admit that it requires a violent effort to shake off *ignavia critica*, that common form of intellectual sloth, that this effort must be continually repeated, and is often accompanied by real pain.

The natural instinct of a man in the water is to do precisely that which will infallibly cause him to be drowned; learning to swim means acquiring the habit of suppressing spontaneous movements and performing others instead. Similarly, criticism is not a natural habit; it must be inculcated, and only becomes organic by dint of continued practice.

Historical work is, then, pre-eminently critical; whoever enters upon it without having first been put on his guard against his instinct is sure to be drowned in it. In order to appreciate the danger it is well to examine one's conscience and analyse the causes of that *ignavia* which must be fought against till it is replaced by a critical attitude of mind.[1] It is also very salutary to familiarise oneself with the principles of historical method, and to analyse the theory of them, one by one, as we propose to do in the present volume. "History, like every other study, is chiefly subject to errors of fact arising from inattention, but it is more exposed than any other study to errors due to that mental confusion which produces incomplete analyses and fallacious reasonings. . . . Historians would advance fewer affirmations without proof if they had to analyse each one of their affirmations; they would commit themselves to fewer false principles if they made it a rule to formulate all their principles; they would be guilty of fewer fallacies if they were obliged to set out all their arguments in logical form."[2]

[1] Natural credulity is deeply rooted in indolence. It is easier to believe than to discuss, to admit than to criticise, to accumulate documents than to weigh them. It is also pleasanter; he who criticises documents must sacrifice some of them, and such a sacrifice seems a dead loss to the man who has discovered or acquired the document.

[2] *Revue philosophique*, l.c., p. 178.

SECTION I.—EXTERNAL CRITICISM

CHAPTER II

TEXTUAL CRITICISM

Let us suppose that an author of our own day has written a book: he sends his manuscript to the printer; with his own hand he corrects the proofs, and marks them "Press." A book which is printed under these conditions comes into our hands in what is, for a document, a very good condition. Whoever the author may be, and whatever his sentiments and intentions, we can be certain—and this is the only point that concerns us at present—that we have before us a fairly accurate reproduction of the text which he wrote. We are obliged to say "fairly accurate," for if the author has corrected his proofs badly, or if the printers have not paid proper attention to his corrections, the reproduction of the original text is imperfect, even in this specially favourable case. Printers not unfrequently make a man say something which he never meant to say, and which he does not notice till too late.

Sometimes it is required to reproduce a work the author of which is dead, and the autograph manuscript of which cannot be sent to the printer. This was the case with the *Mémoires d'outre-tombe* of

Chateaubriand, for example; it is of daily occurrence in regard to the familiar correspondence of well-known persons which is printed in haste to satisfy the curiosity of the public, and of which the original manuscript is very fragile. First the text is copied; it is then set up by the compositor from the copy, which comes to the same thing as copying it again; this second copy is lastly, or ought to be, collated (in the proofs) with the first copy, or, better still, with the original, by some one who takes the place of the deceased author. The guarantees of accuracy are fewer in this case than in the first; for between the original and the ultimate reproduction there is one intermediary the more (the manuscript copy), and it may be that the original is hard for anybody but the author to decipher. And, in fact, the text of memoirs and posthumous correspondence is often disfigured by errors of transcription and punctuation occurring in editions which at first sight give the impression of having been carefully executed.[1]

Turning now to ancient documents, let us ask in what state they have been preserved. In nearly every case the originals have been lost, and we have nothing but copies. Have these copies been made directly from the originals? No; they are copies of copies. The scribes who executed them were not by any means all of them capable and conscientious

[1] A member of the *Société des humanistes français* (founded at Paris in 1894) amused himself by pointing out, in the *Bulletin* of this society, certain errors amenable to verbal criticism which occur in various editions of posthumous works, especially the *Mémoires d'outre-tombe.* He showed that it is possible to remove obscurities in the most modern documents by the same methods which are used in restoring ancient texts.

men; they often transcribed texts which they did not understand at all, or which they understood incorrectly, and it was not always the fashion, as it was in the time of the Carlovingian Renaissance, to compare the copies with the originals.[1]

If our printed books, after the successive revisions of author and printer's reader, are still but imperfect reproductions, it is only to be expected that ancient documents, copied and recopied as they have been for centuries with very little care, and exposed at every fresh transcription to new risk of alteration, should have reached us full of inaccuracies.

There is thus an obvious precaution to be taken. Before using a document we must find out whether its text is "sound"—that is, in as close agreement as possible with the original manuscript of the author; and when the text is "corrupt" we must emend it. In using a text which has been corrupted in transmission, we run the risk of attributing to the author what really comes from the copyists. There are actual cases of theories which were based on passages falsified in transmission, and which collapsed as soon as the true readings were discovered or restored. Printers' errors and mistakes in copying are not always innocuous or merely diverting; they are sometimes insidious and capable of misleading the reader.[2]

One would naturally suppose that historians of

[1] On the habits of the mediæval copyists, by whose intermediate agency most of the literary works of antiquity have come down to us, see the notices collected by W. Wattenbach, *Das Schriftwesen im Mittelalter*, 3rd ed. (Berlin, 1896, 8vo).

[2] See, for example, the *Coquilles lexicographiques* which have been collected by A. Thomas, in *Romania*, xx. (1891), pp. 464 *sqq*.

repute would always make it a rule to procure "sound" texts, properly emended and restored, of the texts they have to consult. That is a mistake. For a long time historians simply used the texts which they had within easy reach, without verifying their accuracy. And, what is more, the very scholars whose business it is to edit texts did not discover the art of restoring them all at once; not so very long ago, documents were commonly edited from the first copies, good or bad, that came to hand, combined and corrected at random. Editions of ancient texts are nowadays mostly "critical;" but it is not yet thirty years since the publication of the first "critical editions" of the great works of the middle ages, and the critical text of some ancient classics (Pausanias, for example) has still to be constructed.

Not all historical documents have as yet been published in a form calculated to give historians the security they need, and some historians still act as if they had not realised that an unsettled text, as such, requires cautious handling. Still, considerable progress has been made. From the experience accumulated by several generations of scholars there has been evolved a recognised method of purifying and restoring texts. No part of historical method has a more solid foundation, or is more generally known. It is clearly explained in several works of popular philology.[1] For this reason we shall here be content to give a general view of its essential principles, and to indicate its results.

[1] See E. Bernheim, *Lehrbuch der historischen Methode*, 2nd ed., pp. 341–54. Also consult F. Blass, in the *Handbuch der klassischen Altertumswissenschaft*, edited by I. von Müller, I., 2nd ed. (1892), pp.

I. We will suppose a document has not been edited in conformity with critical rules. How are we to proceed in order to construct the best possible text? Three cases present themselves.

(*a*) The most simple case is that in which we possess the original, the author's autograph itself. There is then nothing to do but to reproduce the text of it with absolute fidelity.[1] Theoretically nothing can be easier; in practice this elementary operation demands a sustained attention of which not every one is capable. If any one doubts it, let him try. Copyists who never make mistakes and never allow their attention to be distracted are rare even among scholars.

(*b*) Second case. The original has been lost; only

249-89 (with a detailed bibliography); A. Tobler, in the *Grundriss der romanischen Philologie*, I. (1888), pp. 253-63; H. Paul, in the *Grundriss der germanischen Philologie*, I., 2nd ed. (1896), pp. 184-96.

In French read the section *Critique des textes*, in *Minerva*, *Introduction à l'étude des classiques scolaires grecs et latins*, by J. Gow and S. Reinach (Paris, 1890, 16mo), pp. 50-65.

The work of J. Taylor, "History of the Transmission of Ancient Books to Modern Times" (Liverpool, 1889, 16mo), is of no value.

[1] This rule is not absolute. The editor is generally accorded the right of unifying the spelling of an autograph document—provided that he informs the public of the fact—wherever, as in most modern documents, the orthographical vagaries of the author possess no philological interest. See the *Instructions pour la publication des textes historiques*, in the *Bulletin de la Commission royale d'histoire de Belgique*, 5th series, vi. (1896); and the *Grundsätze für die Herausgabe von Actenstücken zur neueren Geschichte*, laboriously discussed by the second and third Congresses of German historians, in 1894 and 1895, in the Deutsche *Zeitschrift für Geschichtswissenschaft*, xi. p. 200, xii. p. 364. The last Congresses of Italian historians, held at Genoa (1893) and at Rome (1895), have also debated this question, but without result. What are the liberties which it is legitimate to take in reproducing autograph texts? The question is more difficult than is imagined by those who are not professionally concerned with it.

a single copy of it is known. It is necessary to be cautious, for the probability is that this copy contains errors.

Texts degenerate in accordance with certain laws. A great deal of pains has been taken to discover and classify the causes and the ordinary forms of the differences which are observed between originals and copies; and hence rules have been deduced which may be applied to the conjectural restoration of those passages in a unique copy of a lost original which are certainly corrupt (because unintelligible), or are so in all probability.

Alterations of an original occurring in a copy—"traditional variants," as they are called—are due either to fraud or to error. Some copyists have deliberately modified or suppressed passages.[1] Nearly all copyists have committed errors of judgment or accidental errors. Errors of judgment when half-educated and not wholly intelligent copyists have thought it their duty to correct passages and words in the original which they could not understand.[2] Accidental errors when they misread while copying, or misheard while writing from dictation, or when they involuntarily made slips of the pen.

Modifications arising from fraud or errors of judgment are often very difficult to rectify, or even to discover. Some accidental errors (the omission of several lines, for example) are irreparable in the

[1] Interpolations will be treated of in chapter iii. p. 92.

[2] The scribes of the Carlovingian Renaissance and of the Renaissance proper of the fifteenth century endeavoured to furnish intelligible texts. They therefore corrected everything they did not understand. Several ancient works have been in this manner irretrievably ruined.

case we are considering, that of a unique copy. But most accidental errors can be detected by any one who knows the ordinary forms: confusions of sense, letters, and words, transpositions of words, letters, and syllables, dittography (unmeaning repetition of letters or syllables), haplography (syllables or words written once only where they should have been written twice), false divisions between words, badly punctuated sentences, and other mistakes of the same kind. Errors of these various types have been made by the scribes of every country and every age, irrespectively of the handwriting and language of the originals. But some confusions of letters occur frequently in copies of uncial originals, and others in copies of minuscule originals. Confusions of sense and of words are explained by analogies of vocabulary or pronunciation, which naturally vary from language to language and from epoch to epoch. The general theory of conjectural emendation reduces to the sketch we have just given; there is no general apprenticeship to the art. What a man learns is not to restore any text that may be put before him, but Greek texts, Latin texts, French texts, and so on, as the case may be; for the conjectural emendation of a text presupposes, besides general notions on the processes by which texts degenerate, a profound knowledge of (1) a special language; (2) a special handwriting; (3) *the confusions (of sense, letters, and words) which were habitual to those who copied texts of that language written in that style of handwriting.* To aid in the apprenticeship to the conjectural emendation of Greek and Latin texts, tabulated lists (alphabetical and systematic) of various readings, frequent confusions, and probable corrections, have been drawn up.[1] It is true that they cannot take the place of practical work, done under the guidance of experts, but they are of very great use to the experts themselves.[2]

It would be easy to give a list of happy emendations. The most satisfactory are those whose correctness is obvious palæographically, as is the case with the classical emendation by Madvig of the text of Seneca's Letters (89, 4). The old reading was: "Philosophia unde dicta sit, apparet; ipso enim nomine fatetur. Quidam et sapientiam ita quidam finierunt, ut dicerent divinorum et humanorum sapientiam . . ."—which does not make sense. It used to be supposed that words had dropped out between *ita* and *quidam*. Madvig pictured to himself the text of the lost archetype, which was written in capitals, and in which, as was usual before the eighth century, the words were not separated (*scriptio continua*), nor the sentences punctuated; he asked himself whether the copyist, with such an archetype before him, had not divided the words at random, and he had no difficulty

[1] The principal of these are, for the classical languages, besides the above-mentioned work of Blass (*supra*, p. 74, note), the *Adversaria critica* of Madvig (Copenhagen, 1871–74, 3 vols. 8vo). For Greek, the celebrated *Commentatio palæographica* of F. J. Bast, published as an appendix to an edition of the grammarian Gregory of Corinth (Leipzig, 1811, 8vo), and the *Variæ lectiones* of Cobet (Leiden, 1873, 8vo). For Latin, H. Hagen, *Gradus ad criticen* (Leipzig, 1879, 8vo), and W. M. Lindsay, "An Introduction to Latin Textual Emendation based on the Text of Plautus" (London, 1896, 16mo). A contributor to the *Bulletin de la Société des humanistes français* has expressed, in this publication, a wish that a similar collection might be compiled for modern French.

[2] Cf. *Revue Critique*, 1895, ii. p. 358.

in reading: "... ipso enim nomine fatetur quid amet. Sapientiam ita quidam finierunt ..." Blass, Reinach, and Lindsay, in the works referred to in the note, mention several other masterly and elegant emendations. Nor have the Hellenists and Latinists any monopoly; equally brilliant emendations might be culled from the works of Orientalists, Romancists, and Germanists, now that texts of Oriental, Romance, and Germanic languages have been subjected to verbal criticism. We have already stated that scholarly corrections are possible even in the text of quite modern documents, reproduced typographically under the most favourable conditions.

Perhaps no one, in our day, has equalled Madvig in the art of conjectural emendation. But Madvig himself had no high opinion of the work of modern scholarship. He thought that the humanists of the sixteenth and seventeenth centuries were, in this respect, better trained than modern scholars. The conjectural emendation of Greek and Latin texts is, in fact, a branch of sport success in which is proportionate not only to a man's ingenuity and palæographical instinct, but also to the corrrectness, rapidity, and delicacy of his appreciation of the niceties of the classical languages. Now, the early scholars were undoubtedly too bold, but they were more intimately familiar with the classical languages than our modern scholars are.

However that may be, there can be no doubt that numerous texts which have been preserved, in corrupt form, in unique copies, have resisted, and will continue to resist, the efforts of criticism. Very often criticism ascertains the fact of the text having been altered, states what the sense requires, and then prudently stops, every trace of the original reading having been obscured by a confused tangle of successive corrections and errors which it is hopeless to attempt to unravel. The scholars who devote themselves to the fascinating pursuit of conjectural criticism are liable, in their ardour, to suspect perfectly innocent readings, and, in desperate passages, to propose adventurous hypotheses. They are well aware of this, and therefore make it a rule to draw a very clear distinction, in their editions, between readings found in manuscripts and their own restorations of the text.

(*c*) Third case. We possess several copies, which differ from each other, of a document whose original is lost. Here modern scholars have a marked advantage over their predecessors: besides being better informed, they set about the comparison of copies more methodically. The object is, as in the preceding case, to reconstruct the archetype as exactly as possible.

The scholars of earlier days had to struggle, as novices have to struggle now, in a case of this kind, against a very natural and a very reprehensible impulse—to use the first copy that comes to hand, whatever its character may happen to be. The second impulse is not much better—to use the oldest copy out of several of different date. In theory, and very often in practice, the relative age of the copies is of no importance; a sixteenth-century manuscript which reproduces a good lost copy of the eleventh century is much more valuable than a faulty and retouched copy made in the twelfth or thirteenth century. The third impulse is still far from being good; it is to count the attested readings and decide by the majority. Suppose there are twenty copies of a text; the reading A is attested eighteen times, the reading B twice. To make this a reason for choosing A is to make the gratuitous assumption that all the manuscripts have the same authority. This is an error of judgment; for if seventeen of the eighteen manuscripts which give the reading A have been copied from the eighteenth, the reading A is in reality attested only once; and the only question is whether it is intrinsically better or worse than the reading B.

It has been recognised that the only rational procedure is to begin by determining in what relation the copies stand to each other. For this purpose we adopt as our starting-point the incontrovertible axiom that all the copies which contain the same mistakes in the same passages must have been either copied from each other or all derived from a copy containing those mistakes. It is inconceivable that several copyists, independently reproducing an original free from errors, should all introduce exactly the same errors; identity of errors attests community of origin. We shall cast aside without scruple all the copies derived from a single manuscript which has been preserved. Evidently they can have no value beyond what is possessed by their common source; if they differ from it, it can only be in virtue of new errors; it would be waste of time to study their variations. Having eliminated these, we have before us none but independent copies, which have been made directly from the archetype, or secondary copies whose source (a copy taken directly from the archetype) has been lost. In order to group the secondary copies into *families*, each of which shall represent what is substantially the same tradition, we again have recourse to the comparison of errors. By this method we can generally draw up without too much trouble a complete genealogical table (*stemma codicum*) of the preserved copies, which will bring out very clearly their relative importance. This is not the place to discuss the difficult cases where, in consequence of too great a number of intermediaries having been lost, or from ancient copyists having arbitrarily blended the texts of different traditions, the operation becomes extremely laborious or impracticable. Besides, in these extreme cases there is no new method involved: the comparison of corresponding passages is a powerful instrument, but it is the only one which criticism has at its disposal for this task.

When the genealogical tree of the manuscripts has been drawn up, we endeavour to restore the text of the archetype by comparing the different traditions. If these agree and give a satisfactory text, there is no difficulty. If they differ, we decide between them. If they accidentally agree in giving a defective text, we have recourse to conjectural emendation, as if there were only one copy.

It is, theoretically, much more advantageous to have several independent copies of a lost original than to have only one, for the mere mechanical comparison of the different readings is often enough to remove obscurities which the uncertain light of conjectural criticism would never have illuminated.

However, an abundance of manuscripts is an embarrassment rather than a help when the work of grouping them has been left undone or done badly; nothing can be more unsatisfactory than the arbitrary and hybrid restorations which are founded on copies whose relations to each other and to the archetype have not been ascertained beforehand. On the other hand, the application of rational methods requires, in some cases, a formidable expenditure of time and labour. Some works are preserved in hundreds of copies all differing from each other; sometimes (as in the case of the Gospels) the variants of a text of quite moderate extent are to be counted by thousands; several years of assiduous labour are necessary for the preparation of a critical edition of some mediæval romances. And after all this labour, all these collations and comparisons, can we be sure that the text of the romance is sensibly better than it would have been if there had been only two or three manuscripts to work upon? No. Some critical editions, owing to the apparent wealth of material applicable to the work, demand a mechanical effort which is altogether out of proportion to the positive results which are its reward.

"Critical editions" founded on several copies of a lost original ought to supply the public with the means of verifying the "*stemma codicum*" which the editor has drawn up, and should give the rejected variants in the notes. By this means competent readers are, at the worst, put in possession, if not of the best possible text, at least of the materials for constructing it.[1]

[1] Quite recently our scholars used to neglect this elementary precaution, in order, as they said, to avoid an "air of pedantry."

II. The results of textual criticism—a kind of cleaning and mending—are purely negative. By the aid of conjecture, or by the aid of conjecture and comparison combined, we are enabled to construct, not necessarily a good text, but the best text possible, of documents whose original is lost. What we thus effect is the elimination of corrupt and adventitious readings likely to cause error, and the recognition of suspected passages as such. But it is obvious that no new information is supplied by this process. The text of a document which has been restored at the cost of infinite pains is not worth more than that of a document whose original has been preserved; on the contrary, it is worth less. If the autograph manuscript of the Æneid had not been destroyed, centuries of collation and conjecture would have been saved, and the text of the Æneid would have been better than it is. This is intended for those who excel at the "emendation game,"[1] who are in consequence fond of it, and would really be sorry to have no occasion to play it.

III. There will, however, be abundant scope for textual criticism as long as we do not possess the

M. B. Hauréau has published, in his *Notices et extraits de quelques manuscrits latins de la Bibliothèque nationale* (vi. p. 310), a piece of rhythmic verse, "De presbytero et logico." "It is not unedited," says he; "Thomas Wright has already published it. . . . But this edition is very defective; the text is occasionally quite unintelligible. We have, therefore, considerably amended it, making use, for this purpose, of two copies, which, it must be conceded, are neither of them faultless. . . ." The edition follows, with no variants. Verification is impossible.

[1] "Textual emendation too often misses the mark through want of knowledge of what may be called *the rules of the game*" (W. M. Lindsay, p.v. in the work referred to above).

exact text of every historical document. In the present state of science few labours are more useful than those which bring new texts to light or improve texts already known. It is a real service to the study of history to publish unedited or badly edited texts in a manner conformable to the rules of criticism. In every country learned societies without number are devoting the greater part of their resources and activity to this important work. But the immense number of the texts to be criticised,[1] and the minute care required by the operations of verbal criticism,[2] prevent the work of

[1] It has often been asked whether *all* texts are worth the trouble of "establishing" and publishing them. "Among our ancient texts," says M. J. Bédier, referring to French mediæval literature, "which ought we to publish? Every one. But, it will be asked, are we not already staggering under the weight of documents? . . . The following is the reason why publication should be exhaustive. As long as we are confronted by this mass of sealed and mysterious manuscripts, they will appeal to us as if they contained the answer to every riddle; every candid mind will be hampered by them in its flights of induction. It is desirable to publish them, if only to get rid of them and to be able, for the future, to work as if they did not exist. . . ." (*Revue des Deux Mondes*, February 15, 1894, p. 910). All documents ought to be catalogued, as we have already pointed out (p. 31), in order that researchers may be relieved of the fear that there may be documents, useful for their purposes, of which they know nothing. But in every case where a summary analysis of a document can give a sufficient idea of its contents, and its form is of no special interest, there is nothing gained by publishing it *in extenso*. We need not overburden ourselves. Every document will be analysed some day, but many documents will never be published.

[2] Editors of texts often render their task still longer and more difficult than it need be by undertaking the additional duty of commentators, under the pretext of explaining the text. It would be to their advantage to spare themselves this labour, and to dispense with all annotation which does not belong to the "apparatus criticus" proper. See, on this point, T. Lindner, *Ueber die Heraus-*

publication and restoration from advancing at any but a slow pace. Before all the texts which are of interest for mediæval and modern history shall have been edited or re-edited *secundum artem*, a long period must elapse, even supposing that the relatively rapid pace of the last few years should be still further accelerated.[1]

gabe von geschichtlichen Quellen, in the *Mittheilungen des Instituts für österreichische Geschichtsforschung*, xvi., 1895, pp. 501 *sqq*.

[1] To realise this it is enough to compare what has hitherto been done by the most active societies, such as the Society of the *Monumenta Germaniæ historica* and the *Istituto storico italiano*, with what still remains for them to do. The greater part of the most ancient documents and the hardest to restore, which have long taxed the ingenuity of scholars, have now been placed in a relatively satisfactory condition. But an immense amount of mechanical work has still to be done.

CHAPTER III

CRITICAL INVESTIGATION OF AUTHORSHIP

It would be absurd to look for information about a fact in the papers of some one who knew nothing, and could know nothing, about it. The first questions, then, which we ask when we are confronted with a document is: Where does it come from? who is the author of it? what is its date? A document in respect of which we necessarily are in total ignorance of the author, the place, and the date is good for nothing.

This truth, which seems elementary, has only been adequately recognised in our own day. Such is the natural *ἀκρισία* of man, that those who were the first to make a habit of inquiring into the authorship of documents prided themselves, and justly, on the advance they had made.

Most modern documents contain a precise indication of their authorship: in our days, books, newspaper articles, official papers, and even private writings, are, in general, dated and signed. Many ancient documents, on the other hand, are anonymous, without date, and have no sufficient indication of their place of origin.

The spontaneous tendency of the human mind is to place confidence in the indications of authorship, when there are any. On the cover and in the preface of the *Châtiments,* Victor Hugo is named as the author; therefore Victor Hugo is the author of the *Châtiments.* In such and such a picture gallery we see an unsigned picture whose frame has been furnished by the management with a tablet bearing the name of Leonardo da Vinci; therefore Leonardo da Vinci painted this picture. A poem with the title *Philomena* is found under the name of Saint Bonaventura in M. Clément's *Extraits des poètes chrétiens,* in most editions of Saint Bonaventura's "works," and in a great number of mediæval manuscripts; therefore *Philomena* was written by Saint Bonaventura, and "we may gather thence much precious knowledge of the very soul" of this holy man.[1] Vrain-Lucas offered to M. Chasles autographs of Vercingetorix, Cleopatra, and Saint Mary Magdalene, duly signed, and with the flourishes complete:[2] here, thought M. Chasles, are autographs of Vercingetorix, Cleopatra, and Saint Mary Magdalene. This is one of the most universal, and at the same time indestructible, forms of public credulity.

Experience and reflection have shown the necessity of methodically checking these instinctive impulses of confiding trust. The autographs of Vercingetorix, Cleopatra, and Mary Magdalene had been manufactured by Vrain-Lucas. The *Philomena,* attributed by mediæval scribes now to Saint Bonaventura, now to Louis of Granada, now to John Hoveden, now to John Peckham, is perhaps by none

[1] R. de Gourmont, *Le Latin mystique* (Paris, 1891, 8vo), p. 258.

[2] See these alleged autographs in the *Bibliothèque nationale,* nouv. acq. fr., No. 709.

of these authors, and certainly not by the first-named. Paintings in which there is not the least gleam of talent have, in the most celebrated galleries of Italy, been tricked out, without the least shadow of proof, with the glorious name of Leonardo. On the other hand, it is perfectly true that Victor Hugo is the author of the *Châtiments.* The conclusion is, that the most precise indications of authorship are never sufficient *by themselves.* They only afford a presumption, strong or weak—very strong, in general, where modern documents are concerned, often very weak in the case of ancient documents. False indications of authorship exist, some foisted upon insignificant works in order to enhance their value, some appended to works of merit in order to serve the reputation of a particular person, or to mystify posterity; and there are a hundred other motives which may easily be imagined, and of which a list has been drawn up:[1] the "pseudepigraphic" literature of antiquity and the middle ages is enormous. There are, in addition, documents which are forged from beginning to end; the forgers have naturally furnished them with very precise indications of their alleged authorship. Verification is therefore necessary. But how is it to be had? When the apparent authorship of a document is suspected, we use for its verification the same method which serves to fix, as far as possible, the origin of documents which are furnished with no indications at all on this head. As the procedure

[1] F. Blass has enumerated the chief of these motives with reference to the pseudepigraphic literature of antiquity (pp. 269 *sqq.* in the work already quoted).

is the same in both cases, it is not necessary to distinguish further between them.

I. The chief instrument used in the investigation of authorship is the *internal analysis* of the document under consideration, performed with a view to bring out any indications it may contain of a nature to supply information about the author, and the time and place in which he lived.

First of all we examine the handwriting of the document. Saint Bonaventura was born in 1221; if poems attributed to him are contained in manuscripts executed in the eleventh century, we have in this circumstance an excellent proof that the attribution is ill-founded: no document of which there exists a copy in eleventh-century handwriting can be posterior in date to the eleventh century. Then we examine the language. It is known that certain forms have only been used in certain places and at certain dates. Most forgers have betrayed themselves by ignorance of facts of this kind; they let slip modern words or phrases. It has been possible to establish the fact that certain Phœnician inscriptions, found in South America, were earlier than a certain German dissertation on a point of Phœnician syntax. In the case of official instruments we examine the formulæ. If a document which purports to be a Merovingian charter does not exhibit the ordinary formulæ of genuine Merovingian charters it must be spurious. Lastly, we note all the positive data which occur in the document—the facts which are mentioned or alluded to. When these facts are otherwise known, from sources which a forger could not have had at his disposal, the *bona fides* of the document is established, and the date fixed approximately between the most recent event of which the author shows knowledge, and the next following event which he does not mention but would have done if he had known of it. Arguments may also be founded on the circumstance that particular facts are mentioned with approval, or particular opinions expressed, and help us to make a conjectural estimate of the status, the environment, and the character of the author.

When the internal analysis of a document is carefully performed, it generally gives us a tolerably accurate notion of its authorship. By means of a methodical comparison, instituted between the various elements of the documents analysed and the corresponding elements of similar documents whose authorship was known with certainty, the detection of many a forgery[1] has been rendered possible, and additional information acquired about the circumstances under which most genuine documents have been produced.

The results obtained by internal analysis are supplemented and verified by collecting all the external evidence relative to the document under criticism which can be found scattered over the documents of the same or later epochs—quotations, biographical details about the author, and so on. Sometimes

[1] E. Bernheim (*Lehrbuch*, pp. 243 *sqq.*) gives a somewhat lengthy list of spurious documents, now recognised as such. Here it will be enough to recall a few famous hoaxes: Sanchoniathon, Clotilde de Surville, Ossian. Since the publication of Bernheim's book several celebrated documents, hitherto exempt from suspicion, have been struck off the list of authorities. See especially A. Piaget, *La Chronique des chanoines de Neuchâtel* (Neuchâtel, 1896, 8vo).

there is a significant absence of any such information: the fact that an alleged Merovingian charter has not been quoted by anybody before the seventeenth century, and has only been seen by a seventeenth-century scholar who has been convicted of fraud, suggests the thought that it is modern.

II. Hitherto we have considered only the simplest case, in which the document under examination is the work of a single author. But many documents have, at different times, received additions which it is important to distinguish from the original text, in order that we may not attribute to X, the author of the text, what really belongs to Y or Z, his unforeseen collaborators.[1] There are two kinds of additions—interpolations and continuations. To interpolate is to insert into the text words or sentences which were not in the author's manuscript.[2] Usually interpolations are accidental, due to the negligence of the copyist, and explicable as the introduction into the text of interlinear glosses or marginal notes; but there are cases where some one has deliberately added to (or substituted for) the author's text words or sentences out of his own head, for the sake of completeness, ornament, or emphasis. If we had before us the manuscript in which the deliberate interpolation was made, the appearance of the added matter and the traces of erasure would make the case clear at once. But the first interpolated copy has nearly always been

[1] When the modifications of the primitive text are the work of the author himself, they are "alterations." Internal analysis, and the comparison of different editions, bring them to light.

[2] See F. Blass, ibid., pp. 254 *sqq*.

lost, and in the copies derived from it every trace of addition or substitution has disappeared. There is no need to define "continuations." It is well known that many chronicles of the middle ages have been "continued" by various writers, none of whom took the trouble to indicate where his own work began or ended.

Sometimes interpolations and continuations can be very readily distinguished in the course of the operations for restoring a text of which there are several copies, when it so happens that some of these copies reproduce the primitive text as it was before any addition was made to it. But if all the copies are founded on previous copies which already contained the interpolations or continuations, recourse must be had to internal analysis. Is the style uniform throughout the document? Does the book breathe one and the same spirit from cover to cover? Are there no contradictions, no gaps in the sequence of ideas? In practice, when the continuators or interpolators have been men of well-marked personality and decided views, analysis will separate the original from the additions as cleanly as a pair of scissors. When the whole is written in a level, colourless style, the lines of division are not so easy to see; it is then better to confess the fact than to multiply hypotheses.

III. The critical investigation of authorship is not finished as soon as a document has been accurately or approximately localised in space and time, and as much information as possible obtained about the author or authors.[1] Here is a book: we

[1] As a rule it matters little whether the *name* of the author has or has not been discovered. We read, however, in the *Histoire*

wish to ascertain the origin of the information contained in it, that is, to be in a position to appreciate its value; is it enough to know that it was written in 1890, at Paris, by So-and-so? Perhaps So-and-so copied slavishly, without mentioning the fact, an earlier work, written in 1850. The responsible guarantor of the borrowed parts is not So-and-so, but the author of 1850. Plagiarism, it is true, is now rare, forbidden by the law, and considered dishonourable; formerly it was common, tolerated, and unpunished. Many historical documents, with every appearance of originality, are nothing but unavowed repetitions of earlier documents, and historians occasionally experience, in this connection, remarkable disillusions. Certain passages in Eginhard, a ninth-century chronicler, are borrowed from Suetonius: they have nothing to do with the history of the ninth century; how if the fact had not been discovered? An event is attested three times, by three chroniclers; but these three attestations, which agree so admirably, are really only one if it is ascertained that two of the three chroniclers copied the third, or that the three parallel accounts have been drawn from one and the same source. Pontifical letters and Imperial charters of the middle ages contain eloquent passages which must not be taken seriously; they are part of the official style, and were copied word for word from chancery formularies.

It belongs to the investigation of authorship to

littéraire de la France (xxvi. p. 388): "We have ignored anonymous sermons: writings of this facile character are of no importance for literary history when their authors are unknown." Are they of any more importance when we know the authors' names?

discover, as far as possible, the *sources* utilised by the authors of documents.

The problem thus presented to us has some resemblance to that of the restoration of texts of which we have already spoken. In both cases we proceed on the assumption that identical readings have a common source: a number of different scribes, in transcribing a text, will not make exactly the same mistakes in exactly the same places; a number of different writers, relating the same facts, will not have viewed them from exactly the same standpoint, nor will they say the same things in exactly the same language. The great complexity of historical events makes it extremely improbable that two independent observers should narrate them in the same manner. We endeavour to group the documents into families in the same way as we make families of manuscripts. Similarly, we are enabled in the result to draw up genealogical tables. The examiners who correct the compositions of candidates for the bachelor's degree sometimes notice that the papers of two candidates who sat next each other bear a family likeness. If they have a mind to find out which is derived from the other, they have no difficulty in doing so, in spite of the petty artifices (slight modifications, expansions, abstracts, additions, suppressions, transpositions) which the plagiarist multiplies in order to throw suspicion off the scent. The two guilty ones are sufficiently betrayed by their common errors; the more culpable of the two is detected by the slips he will have made, and especially by the errors in his own papers which are due to peculiarities in those of his accommodating friend. Similarly when two ancient documents are in question: when the author of one has copied directly from the other, the filiation is generally easy to establish; the plagiarist, whether he abridges or expands, nearly always betrays himself sooner or later.[1]

When there are three documents in a family their mutual relationships are sometimes harder to specify. Let A, B, and C be the documents. Suppose A is the common source: perhaps B and C copied it independently; perhaps C only knew A through the medium of B, or B knew it only through C. If B and C have abridged the common source in different ways, they are evidently independent. When B depends on C, or *vice versâ*, we have the simplest case, treated in the preceding paragraph. But suppose the author of C combined A and B, while B had already used A: the genealogy begins to get complicated. It is more complicated still when there are four, five, or more documents in a family, for the number of possible combinations increases with great rapidity. However, if too many intermediate links have not been lost, criticism succeeds in disentangling the relationships by persistent and ingenious applications of the method of repeated comparisons. Modern scholars (Krusch, for example, who has made a speciality of Merovingian hagiography) have recently constructed, by

[1] In very favourable cases the examination of the plagiarist's mistakes has made it possible to determine even this style of handwriting, the size, and the manner of arrangement of the manuscript source. The deductions of the investigation of sources, like those of textual criticism, are sometimes supported by obvious palæographical considerations.

the use of this method, precise genealogies of the utmost solidity.[1] The results of the critical investigation of authorship, as applied to the filiation of documents, are of two kinds. Firstly, lost documents are reconstructed. Suppose two chroniclers, B and C, have used, each in his own way, a common source X, which has now disappeared. We may form an idea of X by piecing together the fragments of it which occur imbedded in B and C, just as we form an idea of a lost manuscript by comparing the partial copies of it which have been preserved. On the other hand, criticism destroys the authority of a host of "authentic" documents—that is, documents which no one suspects of having been falsified—by showing that they are derivative, that they are worth whatever their sources may be worth, and that, when they embellish their sources with imaginary details and rhetorical flourishes, they are worth just nothing at all. In Germany and England editors of documents have introduced the excellent system of printing borrowed passages in small characters, and original passages whose source is unknown in larger characters. Thanks to this system it is possible to see at a glance that celebrated chronicles, which are often (very wrongly) quoted, are mere compilations, of no value in themselves: thus the *Flores historiarum* of the self-styled Matthew of Westminster, perhaps the most popular of the English mediæval chronicles,

[1] The investigations of Julien Havet (*Questions mérovingiennes*, Paris, 1896, 8vo) are regarded as models. Very difficult problems are there solved with faultless elegance. It is also well worth while to read the memoirs in which M. L. Delisle has discussed questions of origin. It is in the treatment of these questions that the most accomplished scholars win their triumphs.

are almost entirely taken from original works by Wendover and Matthew of Paris.[1]

IV. The critical investigation of authorship saves historians from huge blunders. Its results are striking. By eliminating spurious documents, by detecting false ascriptions, by determining the conditions of production of documents which had been defaced by time, and by connecting them with their sources,[2] it has rendered services of such magnitude that to-day it is regarded as having a special right to the name of "criticism." It is usual to say of an historian that he "fails in criticism" when he neglects to distinguish between documents, when he never mistrusts traditional ascriptions, and when he accepts, as if afraid to lose a single one, all the pieces of information, ancient or modern, good or bad, which come to him, from whatever quarter.[3]

This view is perfectly just. We must not, however, be satisfied with this form of criticism, and we must not abuse it.

[1] See the edition of H. R. Luard (vol. i., London, 1890, 8vo) in the *Rerum Britannicarum medii ævi scriptores.* Matthew of Westminster's *Flores historiarum* figure in the Roman "Index," because of the passages borrowed from the *Chronica majora* of Matthew of Paris, while the *Chronica majora* themselves have escaped censure.

[2] It would be instructive to draw up a list of the celebrated historical works, such as Augustin Thierry's *Histoire de la Conquête de l'Angleterre par les Normands*, whose authority has been completely destroyed after the authorship of their sources has been studied. Nothing amuses the gallery more than to see an historian convicted of having built a theory on falsified documents. Nothing is more calculated to cover an historian with confusion than to find that he has fallen into the error of treating seriously documents which are no documents at all.

[3] One of the crudest (and commonest) forms of "uncritical method" is that which consists in employing as if they were documents, and placing on the same footing as documents, the utterances

We must not abuse it. The extreme of distrust, in these matters, is almost as mischievous as the extreme of credulity. Père Hardouin, who attributed the works of Vergil and Horace to mediæval monks, was every whit as ridiculous as the victim of Vrain-Lucas. It is an abuse of the methods of this species of criticism to apply them, as has been done, indiscriminately, for the mere pleasure of it. The bunglers who have used this species of criticism to brand as spurious perfectly genuine documents, such as the writings of Hroswitha, the *Ligurinus*, and the bull *Unam Sanctam*,[1] or to establish imaginary filiations between certain annals, on the strength of superficial indications, would have discredited criticism before now if that had been possible. It is praiseworthy, certainly, to react against those who never raise a doubt about the authorship of a document; but it is carrying the reaction too far to take an exclusive interest in periods of history which depend on documents of uncertain authorship. The only reason why the documents of modern and contemporary history are found less interesting than those of antiquity and the early middle ages, is that the identity which nearly always obtains between their apparent and their real authorship leaves no room for those knotty problems of attribution in which the *virtuosi* of criticism are accustomed to display their skill.[2]

of modern authors on the subject of documents. Novices do not make a sufficient distinction, in the works of modern authors, between what is added to the original source and what is taken from it.

[1] See a list of examples in Bernheim's *Handbuch*, pp. 283, 289.

[2] It is because it is necessary to subject documents of mediæval

Nor must we be content with it. The critical investigation of authorship, like textual criticism, is preparatory, and its results negative. Its final aim and crowning achievement is to get rid of documents which are not documents, and which would have misled us; that is all. "It teaches us not to use bad documents; it does not teach us how to turn good ones to account."[1] It is not the whole of "historical criticism;" it is only one stone in the edifice.[2]

and ancient history to the most searching criticism in respect of authorship that the study of antiquity and the middle ages passes for more "scientific" than that of modern times. The truth is, that it is merely hampered by more preliminary difficulties.

[1] *Revue philosophique*, 1887, ii. p. 170.

[2] The theory of the critical investigation of authorship is now settled, *ne varietur;* it is given in detail in Bernheim's *Lehrbuch*, pp. 242–340. For this reason we have had no scruple in dismissing it with a short sketch. In French, the introduction of M. G. Monod to his *Études critiques sur les sources de l'histoire mérovingienne* (Paris, 1872, 8vo) contains elementary considerations on the subject. Cf. *Revue Critique*, 1873, i. p. 308.

CHAPTER IV

CRITICAL CLASSIFICATION OF SOURCES

By the help of the preceding operations the documents, all the documents, let us suppose, of a given class, or relating to a given subject, have been found. We know where they are; the text of each has been restored, if necessary, and each has been critically examined in respect of authorship. We know where they have come from. It remains to combine and classify the materials thus verified. This is the last of the operations which may be called preparatory to the work of higher (or internal) criticism and construction.

Whoever studies a point of history is obliged, first of all, to classify his sources. To arrange, in a rational and convenient manner, the verified materials before making use of them, is an apparently humble, but really very important, part of the historian's profession. Those who have learnt how to do it possess, on that account alone, a marked advantage: they give themselves less trouble, and they obtain better results; the others waste their time and labour; they are smothered sometimes under the disorderly mass of notes, extracts, copies, scraps, which they themselves have accumulated. Who was it spoke of those busy people who spend their lives lifting building-stones without knowing where to place them, raising as they do so clouds of blinding dust?

I. Here, again, we have to confess that the first, the natural impulse, is not the right one. The first impulse of most men who have to utilise a number of texts is to make notes from them, one after another, in the order in which they study them. Many of the early scholars (whose papers we possess) worked on this system, and so do most beginners who are not warned beforehand; the latter keep, as the former kept, notebooks, which they fill continuously and progressively with notes on the texts they are interested in. This method is utterly wrong. The materials collected must be classified sooner or later; otherwise it would be necessary, when occasion arose, to deal separately with the materials bearing on a given point, to read right through the whole series of notebooks, and this laborious process would have to be repeated every time a new detail was wanted. If this method seems attractive at first, it is because it appears to save time. But this is false economy; the ultimate result is, an enormous addition to the labour of search, and great difficulty in combining the materials.

Others, well understanding the advantages of systematic classification, have proposed to fit their materials, as fast as collected, into their appropriate places in a prearranged scheme. For this purpose they use notebooks of which every page has first been provided with a heading. Thus all the entries of the same kind are close to one another. This system leaves something to be desired; for additions will not always fit without inconvenience into their proper place; and the scheme of classification, once adopted, is rigid, and can only be modified with difficulty. Many librarians used to draw up their catalogues on this plan, which is now universally condemned.

There is a still more barbarous method, which need not receive more than passing mention. This is simply to register documents in the memory without taking written notes. This method has been used. Historians endowed with excellent memories, and lazy to boot, have indulged this whim, with the result that their quotations and references are mostly inexact. The human memory is a delicate piece of registering apparatus, but it is so little an instrument of precision that such presumption is inexcusable.

Every one admits nowadays that it is advisable to collect materials on separate cards or slips of paper. The notes from each document are entered upon a loose leaf furnished with the precisest possible indications of origin. The advantages of this artifice are obvious: the detachability of the slips enables us to group them at will in a host of different combinations; if necessary, to change their places: it is easy to bring texts of the same kind together, and to incorporate additions, as they are acquired, in the interior of the groups to which they belong. As for documents which are interesting from several points of view, and which ought to appear in several groups, it is sufficient to enter them several times over on different slips; or they may be represented, as often as may be required, on reference-slips. Moreover, the method of slips is the only one mechanically possible for the purpose of forming, classifying, and utilising a collection of documents of any great extent. Statisticians, financiers, and men of letters who observe, have now discovered this as well as scholars.

The method of slips is not without its drawbacks. Each slip ought to be furnished with precise references to the source from which its contents have been derived; consequently, if a document has been analysed upon fifty different slips, the same references must be repeated fifty times. Hence a slight increase in the amount of writing to be done. It is certainly on account of this trivial complication that some obstinately cling to the inferior notebook system. Again, in virtue of their very detachability, the slips, or loose leaves, are liable to go astray; and when a slip is lost how is it to be replaced? To begin with, its disappearance is not perceived, and, if it were, the only remedy would be to go right through all the work already done from beginning to end. But the truth is, experience has suggested a variety of very simple precautions, which we need not here explain in detail, by which the drawbacks of the system are reduced to a minimum. It is recommended to use slips of uniform size and tough material, and to arrange them at the earliest opportunity in covers or drawers or otherwise. Every one is free to form his own habits in these matters. But it is well to realise beforehand that these habits, according as they are more or less rational and practical, have a direct influence on the results of scientific work. Renan speaks of "these points of private librarianship which make up the half of scientific work."[1] This is not too strong. One scholar will owe a good part of his well-deserved reputation to his method of collecting, while another will be, so to speak, paralysed by his clumsiness in that particular.[2]

After having collected the documents, whether copied *in extenso* or abridged, on slips or loose leaves, we classify them. On what scheme? In what order? Clearly different cases must be treated differently, and it would not be reasonable to lay down precise formulæ to govern them all. However, we may give a few general considerations.

II. We distinguish between the historian who classifies verified documents for the purposes of historical work, and the scholar who compiles "*Regesta*." By the words "*Regesta*" and "*Corpus*" we understand methodically classified collections of historical documents. In a "*Corpus*" documents are reproduced *in extenso*; in "*Regesta*" they are analysed and described.

The use of these compilations is to assist researchers in collecting documents. Scholars set themselves to perform, once for all, tasks of search and classification from which, thanks to them, the public will henceforth be free.

Documents may be grouped according to their

[1] Renan, *Feuilles détachées*, p. 103.

[2] It would be very interesting to have information on the methods of work of the great scholars, particularly those who undertook long tasks of collection and classification. Some information of this kind is to be found in their papers, and occasionally in their correspondence. On the methods of Du Cange, see L. Feugère, *Étude sur la vie et les ouvrages de Du Cange* (Paris, 1858, 8vo), pp. 62 *sqq.*

date, according to their place of origin, according to their contents, according to their form.[1] Here we have the four categories of time, place, species, and form; by superposing, then, we obtain divisions of smaller extent. We may undertake, for example, to make a group of all the documents having a given form, of a given country, and lying between two given dates (French royal charters of the reign of Philip Augustus); or of all the documents of a given form (Latin inscriptions); or of a given species (Latin hymns); of a given epoch (antiquity, the middle ages). We may recall, by way of illustration, the existence of a *Corpus Inscriptionum Græcarum*, of a *Corpus Inscriptionum Latinarum*, of a *Corpus Scriptorum Ecclesiasticorum Latinorum*, the *Regesta Imperii* of J. F. Böhmer and his continuators, the *Regesta Pontificum Romanorum* of P. Jaffé and A. Potthast.

Whatever the division chosen, there are two

[1] See J. G. Droysen, *Grundriss der Historik*, p. 19: "Critical classification does not exclusively adopt the chronological point of view. . . . The more varied the points of view which criticism uses to group materials, the more solid are the results yielded by converging lines of inquiry."

The system has now been abandoned of grouping documents in a *Corpus* or in *regesta*, as was done formerly, because they have the common characteristic of being unedited, or possibly for the exactly opposite reason. At one time the compilers of *Analecta*, *Reliquiæ manuscriptorum*, "treasuries of *anecdota*," *spicilegia*, and so on, used to publish all the documents of a certain class which had the common feature of being unedited and of appearing interesting to them; on the other hand, Georgisch (*Regesta Chronologico-diplomatica*), Bréquigny (*Table chronologique des diplômes, chartes et actes imprimés concernant l'histoire de France*), Wauters (*Table chronologique des chartes et diplômes imprimés concernant l'histoire de Belgique*), have grouped together all the documents of a certain species which had the common character of having been printed.

alternatives: either the documents to be placed in this division are dated or they are not.

If they are dated, as is the case, for example, with the charters issued from the chancery of a prince, care will have been taken to place at the head of each slip the date (expressed in modern reckoning) of the document entered upon it. Nothing is then easier than to group in chronological order all the slips, that is, all the documents, which have been collected. The rule is to use chronological classification whenever possible. There is only one difficulty, and that is of a practical order. Even in the most favourable circumstances some of the documents will have accidentally lost their dates; these dates the compiler is bound to restore, or at least to attempt to restore; long and patient research is necessary for the purpose.

If the documents are not dated, a choice must be made between the alphabetical, the geographical, and the systematic order. The history of the *Corpus* of Latin inscriptions bears witness to the difficulty of this choice. "The arrangement according to date was impossible, seeing that most of the inscriptions are not dated. From the time of Smetius it was usual to divide them into classes, that is, a distinction was made, resting solely on the contents of the inscription, and having no regard to their place of origin, between religious, sepulchral, military, and poetical inscriptions, those which have a public character, and those which only concern private persons, and so on. Boeckh, although he had preferred the geographical arrangement for his *Corpus Inscriptionum Græcarum*, was of opinion that the arrangement by subjects, which had been hitherto employed, was the only possible one for a Latin *Corpus*. . . ." [Even those who, in France, proposed the geographical arrangement] "wished to make an exception of texts relating to the general history of a country, certainly, at any rate, in the case of the Empire; in 1845 Zumpt defended a very complicated eclectic system of this kind. In 1847 Mommsen still rejected the geographical arrangement except for municipal inscriptions, and in 1852, when he published the Inscriptions of the Kingdom of Naples, he had not entirely changed his opinion. It was only on being charged by the Academy of Berlin with the publication of the *Corpus Inscriptionum Latinarum*, that, grown wise by experience, he rejected even the exceptions proposed by Egger in the case of the general history of a province, and thought it his duty to keep to the geographical arrangement pure and simple."[1] And yet, considering the nature of epigraphic documents, the arrangement according to place was the only rational one. This has been amply demonstrated for more than fifty years; but collectors of inscriptions did not come to an agreement on the subject till after two centuries of tentative efforts in different directions. For two centuries collections of Latin inscriptions have been made without any perception of the fact that "to group inscriptions according to their subjects is much the same thing as to publish an edition of Cicero in which his speeches, treatises, and letters should be cut up and the fragments

[1] J. P. Waltzing, *Recueil général des inscriptions latines* (Louvain, 1892, 8vo), p. 41.

arranged according to their subject-matter;" that "epigraphic monuments belonging to the same territory mutually explain each other when placed side by side;" and, lastly, that "while it is all but impossible to range in order of subject-matter a hundred thousand inscriptions nearly all of which belong to several categories; on the other hand, each monument has but one place, and a very definite place, in the geographical order."[1]

The alphabetical arrangement is very convenient when the chronological and geographical arrangements are unsuitable. There are documents, such as the sermons, the hymns, and the secular songs of the middle ages, which are not precisely dated or localised. They are arranged in the alphabetical order of their *incipit*—that is, the words with which they begin.[2]

The systematic order, or arrangement by subjects, is not to be recommended for the compilation of a *Corpus* or of *regesta*. It is always arbitrary, and

[1] Ibid. When the geographical order is adopted, a difficulty arises from the fact that the origin of certain documents is unknown; many inscriptions preserved in museums have been brought there no one knows whence. The difficulty is analogous to that which results, for chronological *regesta*, from documents without date.

[2] Here the only difficulty arises in the case of documents whose *incipit* has been lost. In the eighteenth century Séguier devoted a great part of his life to the construction of a catalogue, in the alphabetical order of the *incipit*, of the Latin inscriptions, to the number of 50,000, which had at that time been published: he searched through some twelve thousand works. This vast compilation has remained unpublished and useless. Before undertaking work of such magnitude it is well to make sure that it is on a rational plan, and that the labour—the hard and thankless labour—will not be wasted.

leads to inevitable repetition and confusion. Besides, given collections arranged in chronological, geographical, or alphabetical order, nothing more than the addition of a good table of contents is needed to make them available for all the purposes which would be served by a systematic arrangement. One of the chief rules of the art of *Corpus* and *regesta*-making, that great art which has been carried to such perfection in the second half of the nineteenth century,[1] is to provide these collections, whatever the grouping adopted, with a variety of tables and indexes of a kind to facilitate the use of them: *incipit* tables in chronological *regesta* which lend themselves to such treatment, indexes of names and dates in *regesta* arranged by order of *incipit*, and so on.

Corpus and *regesta*-makers collect and classify for the use of others documents in which, at any rate in *all* of which, they have no direct interest, and are absorbed in this labour. Ordinary workers, on the other hand, only collect and classify materials useful for their individual studies. Hence certain differences arise. For example, the arrangement by subjects, on a predetermined system, which is so little to be recommended for great collections, often provides those who are composing monographs on their own account with a scheme of classification preferable to any other. But it will always be well to cultivate the mechanical habits of which professional compilers have learnt the value by experience: to write at the head of every slip its date,

[1] See G. Waitz, *Ueber die Herausgabe und Bearbeitung von Regesten*, in the *Historische Zeitschrift*, xl. (1878), pp. 280–95.

if there is occasion for it, and a heading[1] in any case; to multiply cross-references and indices; to keep a record, on a separate set of slips, of all the sources utilised, in order to avoid the danger of having to work a second time through materials already dealt with. The regular observance of these maxims goes a great way towards making scientific historical work easier and more solid. The possession of a well-arranged, though incomplete, collection of slips has enabled M. B. Hauréau to exhibit to the end of his life an undeniable mastery over the very special class of historical problems which he studied.[2]

[1] In the absence of a predetermined logical order, and when the chronological order is not suitable, it is sometimes an advantage to provisionally group the documents (that is, the slips) in the alphabetical order of the words chosen as headings (*Schlagwörter*). This is what is called the "dictionary system."

[2] See Langlois, *Manuel de bibliographie historique*, i. p. 88.

CHAPTER V

CRITICAL SCHOLARSHIP AND SCHOLARS

THE sum of the operations described in the preceding chapters (restoration of texts, investigation of authorship, collection and classification of verified documents) constitutes the vast domain of external criticism, or critical scholarship.

The public at large, with its vulgar and superficial standards, has nothing but disdain for the whole of critical scholarship. Some of its votaries, on the other hand, are inclined to exalt it unduly. But there is a happy medium between these extremes of over-appreciation and contempt.

The crude opinion of those who pity and despise the minute analysis of external criticism hardly deserves refutation. There is only one argument for the legitimacy and honourable character of the obscure labours of erudition, but it is a decisive argument: it rests on their indispensability. No erudition, no history. "*Non sunt contemnenda quasi parva*," says St. Jerome, "*sine quibus magna constare non possunt.*"[1]

On the other hand, scholars by profession, in their zeal to justify their pride in their work, are not con-

[1] This argument is easy to develop, and often has been, recently by M. J. Bédier, in the *Revue des Deux Mondes*, February 15, 1894, pp. 932 *sqq.*

There are some who willingly admit that the labours of erudition

tent with maintaining its necessity; they allow themselves to be carried away into an exaggeration of its merit and importance. It has been said that the sure methods of external criticism have raised history to the dignity of a science, "of an exact science;" that critical investigations of authorship "enable us, better than any other study, to gain a profound insight into past ages;" that the habit of criticising texts refines or even confers the "historical sense." It has been tacitly assumed that external criticism is the whole of historical criticism, and that beyond the purgation, emendation, and classification of documents there is nothing left to do. This illusion, common enough among specialists, is too crude to need express refutation; the fact is, that it is the psychological criticism which deals with interpretation and examines into the good faith and accuracy of authors that has, better than any other study, enabled us to gain a profound insight into past ages, not external criticism.[1] An historian who should be fortunate enough to find all the documents bearing on his studies already edited correctly, classified, and critically

are useful, but ask impatiently whether "the editing of a text" or "the deciphering of a Gothic parchment" is "the supreme effort of the human mind," and whether the intellectual ability implied by the practice of external criticism does or does not justify "all the fuss made over those who possess it." On this question, obviously devoid of importance, a controversy was held between M. Brunetière, who recommended scholars to be modest, and M. Boucherie, who insisted on their reasons for being proud, in the pages of the *Revue des langues romanes*, 1880, vols. i. and ii.

[1] There have been men who were critics of the first water where external criticism alone was concerned, but who never rose to the conception of higher criticism, or to a true understanding of history.

examined as to authorship, would be in just as good a position to use them for writing history as if he had performed all the preliminary operations himself. It is quite possible, whatever may be said, to have the historical sense in full measure without having ever, both literally and figuratively, wiped away the dust from original documents—that is, without having discovered and restored them for oneself. We need not interpret in the Jewish or etymological sense the dictum of Renan: "I do not think it possible for any one to acquire a clear notion of history, its limits, and the amount of confidence to be placed in the different categories of historical investigation, unless he is in the habit of *handling* original documents."[1] This is to be understood as simply referring to the habit of going direct to the sources, and treating definite problems.[2] Without doubt a day will come when all the documents relating to the history of classical antiquity shall have been edited and treated critically. There will then be no more room, in this department of study, for textual criticism or the investigation of sources; but, for all that, the conditions for the treatment of general ancient history, or special parts of it, will be then eminently favourable. External criticism, as we cannot too often repeat, is entirely preparatory; it is a means, not an end; the ideal state of things would be that it should have been already sufficiently practised

[1] Renan, *Essais de morale et de critique*, p. 36.

[2] "If it were only for the sake of the severe mental discipline, I should not think very highly of the philosopher who had not, at least once in his life, worked at the elucidation of some special point" (*L'Avenir de la science*, p. 136).

that we might dispense with it for the future; it is only a temporary necessity. Theoretically, not only is it unnecessary for those who wish to make historical syntheses to do for themselves the preparatory work on the materials which they use, but we have a right to ask, as has been often asked, whether there is any advantage in their doing it.[1] Would it not be preferable that workers in the field of history should specialise? On the one class—the specialists—would devolve the absorbing tasks of external or erudite criticism; the others, relieved of the weight of these tasks, would have greater liberty to devote themselves to the work of higher criticism, of combination and construction. Such was the opinion of Mark Pattison, who said, *History cannot be written from manuscripts,* which is as much as to say: "It is impossible for a man to write history from documents which he is obliged to put for himself into a condition in which they can be used."

Formerly the professions of "critical scholar" and "historian" were, in fact, clearly distinguished. The "historians" cultivated the empty and pompous species of literature which then was known as "history," without considering themselves bound to keep in touch with the work of the scholars. The latter, for their part, determined by their critical researches the conditions under which history must be written, but were at no pains to write it themselves. Content to collect, emend, and classify historical documents,

[1] On the question whether it is necessary for every one to do "all the preliminary grubbing for himself," cf. J. M. Robertson, "Buckle and His Critics" (London, 1895, 8vo), p. 299.

they took no interest in history, and understood the past no better than did the mass of their contemporaries. The scholars acted as though erudition were an end in itself, and the historians as if they had been able to reconstruct vanished realities by the mere force of reflection and ingenuity applied to the inferior documents, which were common property. So complete a divorce between erudition and history seems to-day almost inexplicable, and it was in truth mischievous enough. We need not say that the present advocates of the division of labour in history have nothing of the kind in view. It is admittedly necessary that close relations should obtain between the world of historians and that of critical scholars, for the work of the latter has no reason for existence beyond its utility to the former. All that is meant is, that certain analytical and all synthetic operations are not necessarily better performed when they are performed by the same person; that though the characters of historian and scholar may be combined, there is nothing illegitimate in their separation; and that perhaps this separation is desirable in theory, as, in practice, it is often a necessity.

In practice, what happens is as follows. Whatever part of history a man undertakes to study, there are only three possible cases. In the first the sources have already been emended and classified; in the second the preliminary work on the sources, which has been only partially done, or not at all, offers no great difficulty; in the third the sources are in a very bad state, and require a great deal of labour to fit them for use. We may observe, in passing, that there is naturally no proportion between the intrinsic importance of the subject and the amount of preliminary work which must be done before it can be treated: there are some subjects of the highest interest, for example the history of the origin and early development of Christianity, which could not be properly attacked till after the completion of investigations which occupied several generations of scholars; but the material criticism of the sources of the history of the French Revolution, another subject of the first rank, gave much less trouble; and there are comparatively unimportant problems in mediæval history which will not be solved till after an immense amount of external criticism shall have been performed.

In the two first cases the expediency of a division of labour does not come in question. But take the third case. A man of ability discovers that the documents which are necessary for the treatment of a point of history are in a very bad condition; they are scattered, corrupt, and untrustworthy. He must take his choice; either he must abandon the subject, having no taste for the mechanical operations which he knows to be necessary, but which, as he foresees, would absorb the whole of his energy; or else he resolves to enter upon the preparatory critical work, without concealing from himself that in all probability he will never have time to utilise the materials he has verified, and that he will therefore be working for those who will come after him. If he adopts the second alternative he becomes a critical scholar by profession, as it were in spite of himself. *A priori*, it is true, there is nothing to prevent those who make great collections of texts and publish critical editions from using their own compilations and editions for the writing of history; and we see, as a matter of fact, that several men have divided themselves between the preparatory tasks of external criticism and the more exalted labours of historical construction: it is enough to mention the names of Waitz, Mommsen, and Hauréau. But this combination is very rare, for several reasons. The first is the shortness of life; there are catalogues, editions, *regesta* on a great scale, the construction of which entails so much mechanical labour as to exhaust the strength of the most zealous worker. The second is the fact that, for many persons, the tasks of critical scholarship are not without their charm; nearly every one finds in them a singular satisfaction in the long run; and some have confined themselves to these tasks who might, strictly speaking, have aspired to higher things.

Is it a good thing in itself that some workers should, voluntarily or not, confine themselves to the researches of critical scholarship? Yes, without a doubt. In the study of history, the results of the division of labour are the same as in the industrial arts, and highly satisfactory—more abundant, more successful, better regulated production. Critics who have been long habituated to the restoration of texts restore them with incomparable dexterity and sureness; those who devote themselves exclusively to investigations of authorship and sources have intuitions which would not occur to others less versed in this difficult and highly specialised branch; those who have spent their lives in the construction of catalogues and the compilation of *regesta* construct and compile them more easily, more quickly, and better than the man in the street. Thus, not only is there no special reason for requiring every "historian" to be at the same time an active worker in the field of critical scholarship, but even those scholars who are engaged in the operations of external criticism come under different categories. Similarly, in a stoneyard there is no point in the architect being at the same time a workman, nor have all the workmen the same functions. Although most critical scholars have not rigorously specialised so far, and although they vary their pleasures by voluntarily executing different kinds of critical work, it would be easy to name some who are specialists in descriptive catalogues and indexes (archivists, librarians, and the like), others who are more particularly "critics" (purifiers, restorers, and editors of texts), and others who are pre-eminently compilers of *regesta*. "The moment it is admitted that erudition is only valuable for the sake of its results, it becomes impossible to carry the division of scientific labour too far;"[1] and the progress of the historical sciences corresponds to the narrower and narrower specialisation of the workers. It was possible, not very long ago, for the same man to devote himself successively to all the operations of historical inquiry, but that was because he appealed to a not very exacting public: nowadays we require of those who criticise documents a minute accuracy and an absolute perfection which presuppose real professional

[1] Renan, *L'Avenir de la science*, p. 230.

skill. The historical sciences have now reached a stage in their evolution at which the main lines have been traced, the great discoveries made, and nothing remains but a more precise treatment of details. We feel instinctively that any further advance must be by dint of investigations of such extent, and analyses of such depth, as none but specialists are capable of.

But the best justification of the division of workers into "scholars" and "historians" (and of the distribution of the former among the various branches of external criticism) is to be found in the fact that different persons have a natural vocation for different tasks. One of the chief justifications of the institution of higher historical teaching is, in our opinion, the opportunity afforded the teachers (presumably men of experience) of discerning in the students, in the course of their university career, either the germ of a vocation for critical scholarship, or fundamental unfitness for critical work, as the case may be.[1] *Criticus non fit, sed nascitur.* For one who is not endowed by nature with certain aptitudes, a career of technical erudition has nothing but disappointments in store: the greatest service that can be rendered to young men hesitating whether to adopt such a career or not is to warn them of the fact. Those who hitherto have devoted themselves to the preparatory tasks of criticism have either chosen them in preference to others because

[1] A university professor is in a very good position for discouraging and encouraging vocations; but "it is by personal effort that the goal (critical skill) must be attained by the students, as Waitz well said in an academic oration; the teacher's part in this work is small . . ." (*Revue Critique*, 1874, ii. p. 232).

they had a taste for them, or else have submitted to them because they knew they were necessary; those who engaged in them by choice have less merit, from the ethical point of view, than those who submitted to them, but, for all that, they have mostly obtained better results, because they have worked, not as a matter of duty, but joyfully and whole-heartedly. It is important that every one should realise the situation, and, in his own as well as the general interest, embrace the special work which suits him best.

We now propose to examine the natural aptitudes which fit, and the truly prohibitory defects which disqualify, for the labours of external criticism. We shall, then, devote a few words to the effects produced on the character by professional habituation to the labours of critical scholarship.

The chief condition of success in these labours is to like them. Those who are exceptionally gifted as poets or thinkers—that is, those who are endowed with creative power—have much difficulty in adapting themselves to the technical drudgery of preparatory criticism: they are far from despising it; on the contrary, they hold it in honour, if they are clear-sighted; but they shrink from devoting themselves to it, for fear of using a razor, as is said, to cut stones. "I have no mind," wrote Leibnitz to Basnage, who had exhorted him to compile an immense *Corpus* of unpublished and printed documents relating to the history of the law of nations; "I have no mind to turn transcriber. . . . Does it not occur to you that the advice you give me resembles that of a man who should wish to marry his friend to a shrew? For to engage a man in a lifelong work is much the same as to find him a wife."[1] And Renan, speaking of those immense preliminary labours "which have rendered possible the researches of the higher criticism" and attempts at historical construction, says: "The man who, with livelier intellectual needs [than those of the men who performed these labours], should now accomplish such an act of abnegation, would be a hero. . . ."[2] Although Renan directed the publication of the *Corpus Inscriptionum Semiticarum*, and Leibnitz was the editor of the *Scriptores rerum Brunsvicensium*, neither Leibnitz, nor Renan, nor their peers have, fortunately, had the heroism to sacrifice their higher faculties to purely critical learning.

Outside the class of superior men (and the infinitely more numerous class of those who wrongly think themselves such), nearly every one, as we have already said, finds in the long run a kind of satisfaction in the minutiæ of preparatory criticism. The reason is, that the practice of this criticism appeals to and develops two very widespread tastes—the taste for collecting and the taste for puzzles. The pleasure of collecting is one which is felt not by children only, but by adults as well, no matter whether the collection be one of various readings or of postage-stamps. The deciphering of rebuses, the solution of small problems of strictly definite scope, are occupations which attract many able minds. Every find brings pleasure, and in the

[1] Quoted by Fr. X. von Wegele, *Geschichte der deutschen Historiographie* (München, 1885, 8vo), p. 653.

[2] Renan, ibid., p. 125.

field of erudition there are innumerable finds—some lying exposed and obvious, some guarded by all but impenetrable barriers—to reward both those who do and those who do not delight in surmounting difficulties. All the scholars of any distinction have possessed in an eminent degree the instincts of the collector and the puzzle-solver, and some of them have been quite conscious of the fact. "The more difficulties we encountered in our chosen path," says M. Hauréau, "the more the enterprise pleased us. This species of labour, which is called bibliography [investigations of authorship, principally from the point of view of pseudepigraphy], could not aspire to the homage of the public, but it has a great attraction for those who devote themselves to it. Yes, it is doubtless a humble study, but how many others are there which so often compensate the trouble they give by affording us opportunity to cry Eureka."[1] Julien Havet, when he was "already known to the learned men of Europe," used to divert himself "by apparently frivolous amusements, such as guessing square words or deciphering cryptograms."[2] Profound instincts, and, for all the childish or ridiculous perversions which they may exhibit in certain individuals, of the highest utility! After all, these are forms, the most rudimentary forms, of the scientific spirit. Those who are devoid of them have no place in the world of

[1] B. Hauréau, *Notices et extraits de quelques manuscrits latins de la Bibliothèque nationale*, i. (Paris, 1890, 8vo), p. v.

[2] *Bibliothèque de l'École des chartes*, 1896, p. 88. Compare analogous traits in the interesting intellectual biography of the Hellenist, palæographer, and bibliographer, Charles Graux, by E. Lavisse (*Questions d'enseignement national*, Paris, 1885, 18mo, pp. 265 *sqq.*).

critical scholarship. But those who aspire to be critical scholars will always be numerous; for the labours of interpretation, construction, and exposition require the rarest gifts: all those whom chance has thrown into the study of history, who desire to do useful work in that department, but are wanting in psychological tact, or find composition irksome, will always allow themselves to be fascinated by the simple and calm pleasures of the preliminary tasks.

But in order to succeed in critical labours it is not enough to like them. It is necessary to possess qualifications "for which zeal is no substitute." What qualifications? Those who have asked this question have answered vaguely: "Qualifications of the moral rather than the intellectual order, patience, intellectual honesty. . . ." Is it not possible to be more precise?

There are young students with no *a priori* repugnance for the labours of external criticism, who perhaps are even disposed to like them, who yet are—experience has shown it—totally incapable of performing them. There would be nothing perplexing in this if these persons were intellectually feeble; this incapacity would then be but one manifestation of their general weakness; nor yet if they had gone through no technical apprenticeship. But we are concerned with men of education and intelligence, sometimes of exceptional ability, who do not labour under the above disadvantages. These are the people of whom we hear: "He works badly, he has the genius of inaccuracy." Their catalogues, their editions, their *regesta*, their monographs swarm with imperfections, and never inspire confidence; try as they may, they never attain, I do not say absolute accuracy, but any decent degree of accuracy. They are subject to "chronic inaccuracy," a disease of which the English historian Froude is a typical and celebrated case. Froude was a gifted writer, but destined never to advance any statement that was not disfigured by error; it has been said of him that he was constitutionally inaccurate. For example, he had visited the city of Adelaide in Australia: "We saw," says he, "below us, in a basin with a river winding through it, a city of 150,000 inhabitants, none of whom has ever known or will ever know one moment's anxiety as to the recurring regularity of his three meals a day." Thus Froude, now for the facts: Adelaide is built on an eminence; no river runs through it; when Froude visited it the population did not exceed 75,000, and it was suffering from a famine at the time. And more of the same kind.[1] Froude was perfectly aware of the utility of criticism, and he was even one of the first in England to base the study of history on that of original documents, as well unpublished as published; but his mental conformation rendered him altogether unfit for the emendation of texts; indeed, he murdered them, unintentionally, whenever he touched them. Just as Daltonism (an affection of the organs of sight which prevents a man from distinguishing correctly between red and green signals) incapacitates for employment on a railway, so chronic inaccuracy, or "Froude's Disease" (a malady not very difficult to diagnose) ought to be regarded as incompatible with the professional practice of critical scholarship.

[1] See H. A. L. Fisher in the *Fortnightly Review*, Dec. 1894, p. 815.

Froude's Disease does not appear to have ever been studied by the psychologists, nor, indeed, is it to be considered as a separate pathological entity. Every one makes mistakes "out of carelessness," "through inadvertence," and in many other ways. What is abnormal is to make many mistakes, to be always making them, in spite of the most persevering efforts to be exact. Probably this phenomenon is connected with weakness of the attention and excessive activity of the involuntary (or subconscious) imagination which the will of the patient, lacking strength and stability, is unable sufficiently to control. The involuntary imagination intrudes upon intellectual operations only to vitiate them; its part is to fill up the gaps of memory by conjecture, to magnify and attenuate realities, and to confuse them with the products of pure invention. Most children distort everything by inexactitude of this kind, and it is only after a hard struggle that they ever attain to a scrupulous accuracy—that is, learn to master their imagination. Many men remain children, in this respect, the whole of their lives.

But, let the psychological causes of Froude's Disease be what they may, another point claims our attention. The man of the sanest and best-balanced mind is liable to bungle the simplest kinds of critical work if he does not allow them the necessary time. In these matters precipitancy is the source of innumerable errors. It is rightly said that patience is the cardinal virtue of the scholar. Do not work too fast, act as if there were always something to be gained by waiting, leave work undone rather than spoil it: these are maxims easy enough to pronounce, but not to be followed in practice by any but persons of calm temperament. There are nervous, excitable persons, who are always in a hurry to get to the end, always seeking variety in their occupations, and always anxious to dazzle and astonish: these may possibly find honourable employment in other careers; but if they embrace erudition, they are doomed to pile up a mass of provisional work, which is likely to do more harm than good, and is sure in the long run to cause them many a vexation. The true scholar is cool, reserved, circumspect. In the midst of the turmoil of life, which flows past him like a torrent, he never hurries. Why should he hurry? The important thing is, that the work he does should be solid, definitive, imperishable. Better "spend weeks polishing a masterpiece of a score of pages" in order to convince two or three among the scholars of Europe that a particular charter is spurious, or take ten years to construct the best possible text of a corrupt document, than give to the press in the same interval volumes of moderately accurate *anecdota* which future scholars will some day have to put through the mill again from beginning to end.

Whatever special branch of critical scholarship a man may choose, he ought to be gifted with prudence, an exceptionally powerful attention and will, and, moreover, to combine a speculative turn of mind with complete disinterestedness and little taste for action; for he must make up his mind to work for distant and uncertain results, and, in nearly every case, for the benefit of others. For textual criticism and the investigation of sources, it is, moreover, very useful to have the puzzle-solving instinct—that is, a nimble, ingenious mind, fertile in hypotheses, prompt to seize and even to guess the relations of things. For tasks of description and compilation (the preparation of inventories and catalogues, *corpus* and *regesta*-making) it is absolutely necessary to possess the collector's instinct, together with an exceptional appetite for work, and the qualities of order, industry, and perseverance.[1] These are the aptitudes required. The labours of external criticism are so distasteful to those who lack these aptitudes, and the results obtained are, in their case, so small in comparison with the time expended, that it is impossible for a man to make too sure of his vocation before entering upon a career of critical scholarship. It is pitiful to see those who, for want of a wise word spoken in due season, lose their way and vainly exhaust themselves in such a career, especially when they have good reason for believing that they might have employed their talents to better advantage in other directions.[2]

II. As critical and preparatory tasks are remarkably well suited to the temperament of a very large

[1] Most of those who have a vocation for critical scholarship possess both the power of solving problems and the taste for collecting. It is, however, easy to divide them into two categories according as they show a marked preference for textual criticism and investigation of authorship on the one hand, or for the more absorbing and less intellectual labours of collection on the other. J. Havet, a past-master in the study of erudite problems, always declined to undertake a general collection of Merovingian royal charters, a work which his admirers expected from him. In this connection he readily admitted his "want of taste for feats of endurance" (*Bibliothèque de l'École des chartes*, 1896, p. 222).

[2] It is common to hear the opposite of this maintained, namely, that the labours of critical scholarship (external criticism) have this

number of Germans, and as the activity of German erudition during the present century has been enormous, it is to Germany that we must go for the best cases of those mental deformations which are produced, in the long run, by the habitual practice of external criticism. Hardly a year passes but complaints are heard, in and about the German universities, of the ill effects produced on scholars by the tasks of criticism.

In 1890, Herr Philippi, as Rector of the University of Giessen, forcibly deplored the chasm which, as he said, is opening between preparatory criticism and general culture: textual criticism loses itself in insignificant minutiæ; scholars collate for the mere pleasure of collating; infinite precautions are employed in the restoration of worthless documents; it is thus evident that "more importance is attached to the materials of study than to its intellectual results." The Rector of Giessen sees in the diffuse style of German scholars and in the bitterness of their polemical writings an effect of the habit they have contracted of "excessive preoccupation with little things."[1] In the same year the same note

advantage over other labours in the field of history that they are within the range of average ability, and that the most moderate intellects, after a suitable preliminary drilling, may be usefully employed in them. It is quite true that men with no elevation of soul or power of thought can make themselves useful in the field of criticism, but then they must have special qualities. The mistake is to think that with good will and a special drilling every one without exception can be fitted for the operations of external criticism. Among those who are incapable of these operations, as well as among those who are fitted for them, there are both men of sense and blockheads.

[1] A. Philippi, *Einige Bemerkungen über den philologischen Unterricht*, Giessen, 1890, 4to. Cf. *Revue Critique*, 1892, i. p. 25.

was sounded, at the University of Bâle, by Herr J. v. Pflugk-Harttung. "The highest branches of historical science are despised," says this author in his *Geschichtsbetrachtungen*[1]: "all that is valued is microscopic observations and absolute accuracy in unimportant details. The criticism of texts and sources has become a branch of sport: the least breach of the rules of the game is considered unpardonable, while conformity to them is enough to assure the approval of connoisseurs, irrespectively of the intrinsic value of the results obtained. Scholars are mostly malevolent and discourteous towards each other; they make molehills and call them mountains; their vanity is as comic as that of the citizen of Frankfort who used complacently to observe, 'All that you can see through yonder archway is Frankfort territory.'"[2] We, for our part, are inclined to draw a distinction between three professional risks to which scholars are subject: dilettantism, hypercriticism, and loss of the power to work.

To take the last first: the habit of critical analysis has a relaxing and paralysing action on certain intelligences. Men, of naturally timid dispositions, discover that whatever pains they take with their critical work, their editing or classifying of documents, they are very apt to make slight mistakes, and these slight mistakes, as a result of their critical education, fill them with horror and dread. To discover blunders in their signed work when the time for correction is past, causes them acute suffering. They reach at length a state of morbid anxiety

[1] J. von Pflugk-Harttung, *Geschichtsbetrachtungen*, Gotha, 1890, 8vo
[2] Ibid., p. 21.

and scrupulosity which prevents them from doing anything at all, for fear of possible imperfections. The *examen rigorosum* to which they are continually subjecting themselves brings them to a standstill. They give the same measure to the productions of others, and in the end they see in historical works nothing but the authorities and the notes, the *apparatus criticus*, and in the *apparatus criticus* they see nothing but the faults in it which require correction.

Hypercriticism.—The excess of criticism, just as much as the crudest ignorance, leads to error. It consists in the application of critical canons to cases outside their jurisdiction. It is related to criticism as logic-chopping is to logic. There are persons who scent enigmas everywhere, even where there are none. They take perfectly clear texts and subtilise on them till they make them doubtful, under the pretext of freeing them from imaginary corruptions. They discover traces of forgery in authentic documents. A strange state of mind! By constantly guarding against the instinct of credulity they come to suspect everything.[1] It is to be observed that in proportion as the criticism of texts and sources makes positive progress, the danger of hypercriticism increases. When all the sources of history have been properly criticised (for certain parts of ancient history this is no distant prospect), good sense will call a halt. But scholars will refuse to halt; they will refine, as they do already on the best established texts, and those who refine will inevitably fall into hypercriticism. "The peculiarity of the study of history and its auxiliary philological sciences," says

[1] Cf. *supra*, p. 99.

Renan, "is that as soon as they have attained their relative perfection they begin to destroy themselves."[1] Hypercriticism is the cause of this.

Dilettantism.—Scholars by profession and vocation have a tendency to treat the external criticism of documents as a game of skill, difficult, but deriving an interest, much as chess does, from the very complication of its rules. Some of them are indifferent to the larger questions—to history itself, in fact. They criticise for the sake of criticism, and, in their view, the elegance of the method of investigation is much more important than the results, whatever they may be. These *virtuosi* are not concerned to connect their labours with some general idea—to criticise systematically, for example, all the documents relating to a question, in order to understand it; they criticise indiscriminately texts relating to all manner of subjects, on the one condition of being sufficiently corrupt. Armed with their critical skill, they range over the whole of the domain of history, and stop wherever a knotty problem invites their services; this problem solved, or at least discussed, they go elsewhere to look for others. They leave behind them no coherent work, but a heterogeneous collection of memoirs on every conceivable subject, which resembles, as Carlyle says, a curiosity shop or an archipelago of small islands.

Dilettanti defend their dilettantism by sufficiently plausible arguments. To begin with, say they, everything is important; in history there is no document which has not its value: "No scientific

[1] Renan, *L'Avenir de la science*, p. xiv.

work is barren, no truth is without its use for science . . .; in history there is no such thing as a trivial subject;" consequently, "it is not the nature of the subject which makes work valuable, but the method employed."[1] The important thing in history is not "the ideas one accumulates; it is the mental gymnastics, the intellectual training—in short, the scientific spirit." Even supposing that there are degrees of importance among the data of history, no one has a right to maintain *a priori* that a document is "useless." What, pray, is the criterion of utility in these matters? How many documents are there not which, after being long despised, have been suddenly placed in the foreground by a change of standpoint or by new discoveries? "All exclusion is rash; there is no research which it is possible to brand beforehand as necessarily sterile. That which has no value in itself may become valuable as a necessary means." Perhaps a day may come when, science being in a sense complete, indifferent documents and facts may be safely thrown overboard; but we are not at present in a position to distinguish the superfluous from the necessary, and in all probability the line of demarcation will never be easy to trace. This justifies the most special researches and the most futile in all appearance. And, if it come to the worst, what does it matter if there is a certain amount of work wasted? "It is a law in science, as in all human effort," and indeed in all the operations of nature, "to work in broad outlines, with a wide margin of what is superfluous."

[1] *Revue historique*, lxiii. (1897), p. 320.

We shall not undertake to refute these arguments to the full extent in which this is possible. Besides, Renan, who has put the case for both sides of the question with equal vigour, definitively closed the debate in the following words: "It may be said that some researches are useless in the sense of taking up time which would have been better spent on more serious questions. . . . Although it is not necessary for an artisan to have a complete knowledge of the work he is employed to execute, it is still to be desired that those who devote themselves to special labours should have some notion of the more general considerations which alone give value to their researches. If all the industrious workers to whom modern science owes its progress had had a philosophical comprehension of what they were doing, how much precious time would have been saved! . . . It is deeply to be regretted that there should be such an immense waste of human effort, merely for want of guidance, and a clear consciousness of the end to be pursued."[1]

Dilettantism is incompatible with a certain elevation of mind, and with a certain degree of "moral perfection," but not with technical proficiency. Some of the most accomplished critics merely make a trade of their skill, and have never reflected on the ends to which their art is a means. It would, however, be wrong to infer that science itself has nothing to fear from dilettantism. The dilettanti

[1] Renan, ibid., pp. 122, 243. The same thought has been more than once expressed, in different language, by E. Lavisse, in his addresses to the students of Paris (*Questions d'enseignement national*, pp. 14, 86, &c.).

of criticism who work as fancy or curiosity bids them, who are attracted to problems not by their intrinsic importance, but by their difficulty, do not supply historians (those whose work it is to combine materials and use them for the main purposes of history) with the materials of which the latter have the most pressing need, but with others which might have waited. If the activity of specialists in external criticism were exclusively directed to questions whose solution is important, and if it were regulated and guided from above, it would be more fruitful.

The idea of providing against the dangers of dilettantism by a rational "organisation of labour" is already ancient. Fifty years ago it was common to hear people talking of "supervision," of "concentrating scattered forces;" dreams were rife of "vast workshops" organised on the model of those of modern industry, in which the preparatory labours of critical scholarship were to be performed on a great scale, in the interests of science. In nearly all countries, in fact, governments (through the medium of historical committees and commissions), academies, and learned societies have endeavoured in our day, much as monastic congregations did of old, to group professed scholars for the purposes of vast collective enterprises, and to co-ordinate their efforts. But this banding of specialists in external criticism for the service and under the supervision of competent men presents great mechanical difficulties. The problem of the "organisation of scientific labour" is still the order of the day.[1]

[1] One of us (M. Langlois) proposes to give elsewhere a detailed account of all that has been done in the last three hundred years,

III. Scholars are often censured for pride and excessive harshness in the judgments which they pass on the labours of their colleagues; and these faults, as we have seen, are often attributed to their excessive "preoccupation with little things," especially by persons whose attempts have been severely judged. In reality there do exist modest and kindly scholars: it is a question of character; professional "preoccupation with little things" is not enough to change natural disposition in this respect. "Ce bon monsieur Du Cange," as the Benedictines said, was modest to excess. "Nothing more is required," says he, in speaking of his labours, "but eyes and fingers in order to do as much and more;" he never blamed any one, on principle. "If I study it is for the pleasure of studying, and not to give pain to any one else, any more than to myself."[1] It is, however, true that most scholars have no compunction in exposing each other's mistakes, and that their austere zeal sometimes finds expression in harsh and overbearing language. Barring the harshness they are quite right. Like physicians, chemists, and other members of learned and scientific professions, they have a keen appreciation of the value of scientific truth, and it is for this reason that they make a point of calling offenders

but especially in the nineteenth century, for the organisation of historical work in the principal countries of the world. Some information has already been collected on this subject by J. Franklin Jameson, "The Expenditures of Foreign Governments in behalf of History," in the "Annual Report of the American Historical Association for 1891," pp. 38-61.

[1] L. Feugère, *Étude sur la vie et les ouvrages de Du Cange*, pp. 55, 58.

to account. They are thus enabled to bar the door against the tribe of incapables and charlatans who once infested their profession.

Among the youths who propose to devote themselves to the study of history there are some in whom the commercial spirit and vulgar ambition are stronger than the love of science. These are apt to say to themselves: "Historical work, if it is to be done according to the rules of method, requires an infinite amount of labour and caution. But do we not see historical writings whose authors have more or less seriously violated the rules? Are these authors thought any the less of on this account? Is it always the most conscientious writer who enjoys the highest consideration? Cannot tact supply the place of knowledge?" If tact really could supply the place of knowledge, then, as it is easier to do bad work than good, and as the important thing with these people is success, they might be tempted to conclude that it does not matter how badly they work as long as they succeed. Why should not things go in these matters as they do in life, where it is not necessarily the best men that get on best? Well, it is due to the pitiless severity of the critics that calculations of this kind would be as disastrous as they are despicable.

Towards the end of the Second Empire there was in France no enlightened public opinion on the subject of historical work. Bad books of historical erudition were published with impunity, and sometimes even procured undeserved rewards for their authors. It was then that the founders of the *Revue Critique d'histoire et de littérature* undertook to combat a state of things which they rightly deemed demoralising. With this object they administered public chastisement to those scholars who showed lack of conscience or method, in a manner calculated to disgust them with erudition for ever. They performed sundry notable executions, not for the pleasure of it, but with the firm resolve to establish a censorship and a wholesome dread of justice, in the domain of historical study. Bad workers henceforth received no quarter, and though the *Revue* did not exert any great influence on the public at large, its police-operations covered a wide enough radius to impress most of those concerned with the necessity of sincerity and respect for method. During the last twenty-five years the impulse thus given has spread beyond all expectation.

It is now a matter of great difficulty to impose on the world of scholars, in matters connected with their studies, or at least to keep up the deception for any length of time. In the case of the historical sciences, as well as the sciences proper, it is now too late to found a new error or to discredit an old truth. It may be a few months, possibly a few years, before a bungled experiment in chemistry or a scamped edition is recognised as such; but inexact results, though temporarily accepted under reserve, are always sooner or later, and generally very soon, discovered, denounced, and eliminated. The theory of the operations of external criticism is now so well established, the number of specialists thoroughly versed in them is now so great in every country, that, with rare exceptions, descriptive catalogues of documents, editions, *regesta*, monographs, are scrutinised, dissected, and judged as soon as they appear. It is well to be warned. It will for the future be the height of imprudence to risk publishing a work of erudition without having first done everything possible to make it unassailable; otherwise it will immediately, or after brief delay, be attacked and demolished. Not knowing this, certain well-meaning persons still show themselves, from time to time, simple enough to enter the lists of critical scholarship insufficiently prepared; they are filled with a desire to be useful, and are apparently convinced that here, as in politics and elsewhere, it is possible to work by extemporised and approximate methods without any "special knowledge." They are sorry afterwards. The knowing ones do not take the risk; the tasks of critical scholarship have no seductions for them, for they are aware that the labour is great and the glory moderate, and that the field is engrossed by clever specialists not too well disposed towards intruders. They see plainly there is no room for them here. The blunt uncompromising honesty of the scholars thus delivers them from undesirable company of a kind which the "historians" proper have still occasionally to put up with.

Bad workers, in fact, on the hunt for a public less closely critical than the scholars, are very ready to take refuge in historical exposition. The rules of method are here less obvious, or, rather, not so well known. While the criticism of texts and sources has been placed on a scientific basis, historical synthesis is still performed haphazard. Mental confusion, ignorance, negligence — faults which stand out so clearly in works of critical scholarship—may in historical works be disguised up to a certain point by literary artifices, and the public at large, which is not well educated in this respect, is not shocked.[1] In short, there is still, in this department, a certain chance of impunity. This chance, however, is diminishing, and a day will come, before so very long, when the superficial writers who make incorrect syntheses will be treated with as little consideration as is now received by those who show themselves unscrupulous or unskilful in the technique of preparatory criticism. The works of the most celebrated historians of the nineteenth century, those who died but yesterday, Augustin Thierry, Ranke, Fustel de Coulanges, Taine, and others, are already battered and riddled with criticism. The faults of their methods have already been seen, defined, and condemned.

Those who are insensible to other considerations ought to be moved to honesty in historical work by the reflection that the time is now past, or nearly so, when it was possible to do bad work without having to suffer for it.

[1] Even the specialists in external criticism themselves, when they do not take the line of despising all synthesis *a priori*, are almost as easily dazzled as anybody else by incorrect syntheses, by a show of "general ideas," or by literary artifices, in spite of their clear-sightedness where works of critical scholarship are concerned.

SECTION II.—INTERNAL CRITICISM

CHAPTER VI

INTERPRETATIVE CRITICISM (HERMENEUTIC)

I. When a zoologist describes the form and situation of a muscle, when a physiologist gives the curve of a movement, we are able to accept their results without reserve, because we know by what method, by what instruments, by what system of notation they have obtained them.[1] But when Tacitus says of the Germans, *Arva per annos mutant*, we do not know beforehand whether he took the right method to inform himself, nor even in what sense he used the words *arva* and *mutant*; to ascertain this a preliminary operation is required.[2] This operation is internal criticism.

The object of criticism is to discover what in a document may be accepted as true. Now the document is only the final result of a long series of operations, on the details of which the author gives

[1] The sciences of observation do, however, need a species of criticism. We do not accept without verification results obtained by anybody, but only results obtained by those who know how to work. But this criticism is made once for all, and applies to the author, not to his works; historical criticism, on the contrary, is obliged to deal separately with every part of a document.

[2] Cf. *supra*, book ii. chap. i. p. 67.

us no information. He had to observe or collect facts, to frame sentences, to write down words; and these operations, which are perfectly distinct one from another, may not all have been performed with the same accuracy. It is therefore necessary to *analyse* the product of the author's labour in order to distinguish which operations have been incorrectly performed, and reject their *results*. *Analysis* is thus necessary to criticism; all criticism begins with analysis.

In order to be logically complete, the analysis ought to reconstruct *all* the operations which the author must have performed, and to examine them *one by one*, to see whether each has been performed correctly. It would be necessary to pass in review all the successive acts by which the document was produced, from the moment when the author observed the fact which is its subject up to the movements of his hand by which he traced the letters of the document; or, rather, it would be necessary to proceed in the opposite direction, step by step, from the movements of the hand back to the observation. This method would be so long and so tedious that no one would ever have the time or the patience to apply it.

Internal criticism is not, like external criticism, an instrument used for the mere pleasure of using it;[1] it yields no immediate satisfaction, because it does not definitively solve any problem. It is only applied because it is necessary, and its use is restricted to a bare minimum. The most exacting historian is satisfied with an abridged method which

[1] Cf. *supra*, p. 122.

concentrates all the operations into two groups: (1) the analysis of the contents of the document, and the positive interpretative criticism which is necessary for ascertaining what the author meant; (2) the analysis of the conditions under which the document was produced, and its negative criticism, necessary for the verification of the author's statements. This twofold division of the labour of criticism is, moreover, only employed by a select few. The natural tendency, even of historians who work methodically, is to read the text with the object of extracting information directly from it, without any thought of first ascertaining what exactly was in the author's mind.[1] This procedure is excusable at most in the case of nineteenth-century documents, written by men whose language and mode of thought are familiar to us, and then only when there is not more than one possible interpretation. It becomes dangerous as soon as the author's habits of language or thought begin to differ from those of the historian who reads him, or when the meaning of the text is not obvious and indisputable. Whoever, in reading a text, is not exclusively occupied with the effort to understand it, is sure to read impressions of his own into it; he is struck by phrases or words in the document which correspond to his own ideas, or agree with his own *a priori* notion of the facts; unconsciously he detaches these phrases or words,

[1] Taine appears to have proceeded thus in vol. ii., *La Révolution*, of his *Origines de la France contemporaine*. He had made extracts from unpublished documents and inserted a great number of them in his work, but it would seem that he did not first methodically analyse them in order to determine their meaning.

and forms out of them an imaginary text which he puts in the place of the real text of the author.[1]

[1] Fustel de Coulanges explains very clearly the danger of this *method:* "Some students begin by forming an opinion . . . and it is not till afterwards that they begin to read the texts. They run a great risk of not understanding them at all, or of understanding them wrongly. What happens is that a kind of tacit contest goes on between the text and the preconceived opinions of the reader; the mind refuses to grasp what is contrary to its idea, and the issue of the contest commonly is, not that the mind surrenders to the evidence of the text, but that the text yields, bends, and accommodates itself to the preconceived opinion. . . . To bring one's personal ideas into the study of texts is the subjective method. A man thinks he is contemplating an object, and it is his own idea that he is contemplating. He thinks he is observing a fact, and the fact at once assumes the colour and the significance his mind wishes it to have. He thinks he is reading a text, and the words of the text take a particular meaning to suit a ready-made opinion. It is this subjective method which has done most harm to the history of the Merovingian epoch. . . . To read the texts was not enough; what was required was to read them before forming any convictions . . ." (*Monarchie franque*, p. 31). For the same reason Fustel de Coulanges deprecated the reading of one document in the light of another; he protested against the custom of explaining the *Germania* of Tacitus by the barbaric laws. In the *Revue des questions historiques*, 1897, vol. i., a lesson on method, *De l'analyse des textes historiques*, is given apropos of a commentary by M. Monod on Gregory of Tours: "The historian ought to begin his work with an exact analysis of each document. . . . The analysis of a text . . . consists in determining the sense of each word, and eliciting the true meaning of the writer. . . Instead of searching for the sense of each of the historian's words, and for the thought he has expressed in them, he [M. Monod] comments on each sentence in the light of what is found in Tacitus or the Salic law. . . . We should understand what analysis really is. Many talk about it, few use it. . . . The use of analysis is, by an attentive study of every detail, to elicit from a text all that is in it; not to introduce into the text what is not there."

After reading this excellent advice it will be instructive to read M. Monod's reply (in the *Revue historique*); it will be seen that Fustel de Coulanges himself did not always practise the method he recommended.

II. Here, as always in history, method consists in repressing the first impulse. It is necessary to be penetrated by the principle, sufficiently obvious but often forgotten, that a document only contains the ideas of the man who wrote it, and to make it a rule to begin by understanding the text by itself, *before* asking what can be extracted from it for the purposes of history. We thus arrive at this general rule of method: the study of every document should begin with an analysis of its contents, made with the sole aim of determining the real meaning of the author.

This analysis is a preliminary operation, distinct and independent. Experience here, as in the tasks of critical scholarship,[1] has decided in favour of the system of slips. Each slip will contain the analysis of a document, of a separate part of a document, or of an episode in a narrative; the analysis ought to indicate not only the general sense of the text, but also, as far as possible, the object and views of the author. It will be well to reproduce verbally any expressions which may seem characteristic of the author's thought. Sometimes it will be enough to have analysed the text mentally: it is not always necessary to put down in black and white the whole contents of a document; in such cases we simply enter the points of which we intend to make use. But against the ever-present danger of substituting one's personal impressions for the text there is only one real safeguard; it should be made an invariable rule never on any account to make an extract from a document, or a partial analysis of it, without

[1] Cf. *supra*, p. 103.

having *first* made a comprehensive analysis[1] of it mentally, if not on paper.

To analyse a document is to discern and isolate all the ideas expressed by the author. Analysis thus reduces to *interpretative criticism.*

Interpretation passes through two stages; the first is concerned with the literal, the second with the real meaning.

III. The determination of the literal meaning of a document is a linguistic operation; accordingly, Philology (in the narrow sense) has been reckoned among the auxiliary sciences of history. To understand a text it is first necessary to know the language. But a *general* knowledge of the language is not enough. In order to interpret Gregory of Tours, it is not enough to know Latin in a general way; it is necessary to add a special study of the particular kind of Latin written by Gregory of Tours.

The natural tendency is to attribute the same meaning to the same word wherever it occurs. We instinctively treat a language as if it were a fixed system of signs. Fixity, indeed, is a characteristic of the signs which have been expressly invented for scientific use, such as algebraical notation or the nomenclature of chemistry. Here every expression has a single precise meaning, which is absolute and invariable; it expresses an accurately analysed and defined idea, only one such idea, and that always the same in whatever context the expression may occur,

[1] The work of analysis may be entrusted to a second person; this is what happens in the case of *regesta* and catalogues of records; if the analysis has been correctly performed by the compiler of *regesta*, there is no need to do it over again.

and by whatever author it may be used. But ordinary language, in which documents are written, fluctuates: each word expresses a complex and ill-defined idea; its meanings are manifold, relative, and variable; the same word may stand for several different things, and is used in different senses by the same author according to the context; lastly, the meaning of a word varies from author to author, and is modified in the course of time. *Vel*, which in classical Latin only has the meanings *or* and *even*, means *and* in certain epochs of the middle ages; *suffragium*, which is classical Latin for *suffrage*, takes in mediæval Latin the sense of *help*. We have, then, to learn to resist the instinct which leads us to explain all the expressions of a text by their classical or ordinary meanings. The grammatical interpretation, based on the general rules of the language, must be supplemented by an historical interpretation founded on an examination of the particular case.

The method consists in determining the special meaning of the words in the document; it rests on a few very simple principles.

(1) Language changes by continuous evolution. Each epoch has a language of its own, which must be treated as a separate system of signs. In order to understand a document we must know the *language of the time*—that is, the meanings of words and forms of expression in use at the time when the text was written. The meaning of a word is to be determined by bringing together the passages where it is employed: it will generally be found that in one or other of these the remainder of the sentence leaves

no doubt as to the meaning of the word in question.[1] Information of this kind is given in historical dictionaries, such as the *Thesaurus Linguæ Latinæ;* or the glossaries of Du Cange. In these compilations the article devoted to each word is a collection of the passages in which the word occurs, accompanied by indications of authorship which fix the epoch.

When the author wrote in a dead language which he had learnt out of books—this is the case with the Latin texts of the earlier middle ages—we must be on our guard against words used in an arbitrary sense, or selected for the sake of elegance: for example, *consul* (count, earl), *capite census* (censitary), *agellus* (grand domain).

(2) Linguistic usage may vary from one region to another; we have, then, to know the *language of the country* where the document was written—that is, the peculiar meanings current in the country.

(3) Each author has his own manner of writing; we have, then, to study the *language of the author,* the peculiar senses in which he used words.[2] This purpose is served by lexicons to a single author, as Meusel's *Lexicon Cæsarianum,* in which are brought

[1] Practical examples of this procedure will be found in Deloche, *La Trustis et l'antrustion royal* (Paris, 1873, 8vo), and, above all, in Fustel de Coulanges. See especially the study of the words *marca* (*Recherches sur quelques problèmes d'histoire*, pp. 322–56), *mallus* (ibid., 372–402), *alleu* (*L'Alleu et le domaine rural*, pp. 149–70), *portio* (ibid., pp. 239–52).

[2] The theory and an example of this procedure will be found in Fustel de Coulanges, *Recherches sur quelques problèmes d'histoire* (pp. 189–289), with reference to the statements of Tacitus about the Germans. See especially pp. 263–89, the discussion of the celebrated passage on the German mode of culture.

together all the passages in which the author used each word.

(4) An expression changes its meaning according to the passage in which it occurs; we must therefore interpret each word and sentence not as if it stood isolated, but with an eye to the general sense of the context. This is the *rule of context*,[1] a fundamental rule of interpretation. Its meaning is that, before making use of a phrase taken from a text, we must have read the text in its entirety; it prohibits the stuffing of a modern work with *quotations*—that is, shreds of phrases torn from passages without regard to the special sense given to them by the context.[2]

These rules, if rigorously applied, would constitute an exact method of interpretation which would hardly leave any chance of error, but would require an enormous expenditure of time. What an immense amount of labour would be necessary if, in the case of *each* word, we had to determine by a special operation its meaning in the language of

[1] Fustel de Coulanges formulates it thus: "It is never safe to separate two words from their context; this is just the way to mistake their meaning" (*Monarchie franque*, p. 228, note 1).

[2] This is how Fustel de Coulanges condemns this practice: "I am not speaking of pretenders to learning who quote second-hand, and at most take the trouble to verify whether the phrase they have seen quoted really occurs in the passage indicated. To verify quotations is one thing and to read texts quite another, and the two often lead to opposite results" (*Revue des questions historiques*, 1887, vol. i.). See also (*L'Alleu et le domaine rural*, pp. 171–98) the lesson given to M. Glasson on the theory of the community of land: forty-five quotations are studied in the light of their context, with the object of proving that none of them bears the meaning M. Glasson attributed to it. We may also compare the reply: Glasson, *Les Communaux et le domaine rural à l'époque franque*, Paris, 1890.

the time, of the country, of the author, and in the context! Yet this is the labour demanded by a well-made translation: in the case of some ancient works of great literary value it has been submitted to; for the mass of historical documents we content ourselves, in practice, with an abridged method.

All words are not equally subject to variations of meaning; most of them keep a fairly uniform meaning in all authors and in all periods. We may therefore be satisfied to study specially those expressions which, from their nature, are liable to take different meanings: first, ready-made expressions which, being fixed, do not follow the evolution of the words of which they are composed; secondly, and chiefly, words denoting things which are in their nature subject to evolution; classes of men (*miles, colonus, servus*); institutions (*conventus, justitia, judex*); usages (*alleu, bénéfice, élection*); feelings, common objects. In the case of all words of such classes it would be imprudent to assume a fixed meaning; it is an absolutely necessary precaution to ascertain what is the sense in which they are used in the text to be interpreted. "These studies of words," said Fustel de Coulanges, "have a great importance in historical science. A badly interpreted term may be the source of serious error."[1] And, in fact, simply by a methodical application of interpretative criticism to a hundred words or so, he succeeded in revolutionising the study of the Merovingian epoch.

[1] All that is original in Fustel de Coulanges rests on his interpretative criticism; he never did personally any work in external criticism, and his critical examination of authors' good faith and accuracy was hampered by a respect for the statements of ancient authors which amounted to credulity.

IV. When we have analysed the document and determined the literal meaning of its phrases, we cannot even yet be sure that we have reached the real thoughts of the author. It is possible that he may have used some expressions in an oblique sense; there are several kinds of cases where this occurs: allegory and symbolism, jests and hoaxes, allusion and implication, even the ordinary figures of speech, metaphor, hyperbole, litotes.[1] In all these cases it is necessary to pierce through the literal meaning to the real meaning, which the author has purposely disguised under an inexact form.

Logically the problem is very embarrassing: there is no fixed external criterion by which we can make sure of detecting an oblique sense; in the case of the hoax, which in the present century has become a branch of literature, it is an essential part of the author's plan to leave no indication which would betray the jest. In practice we may be morally certain that an author is not using an oblique sense wherever his prime object is to be understood; we are therefore not likely to meet with difficulties of this kind in official documents, in charters, and in historical narratives. In all these cases the general form of the document permits us to assume that it is written in the literal sense of the words.

On the other hand, we must be prepared for

[1] A parallel difficulty occurs in the interpretation of illustrative monuments; the representations are not always to be taken literally. In the Behistun monument Darius tramples the vanquished chiefs under foot: this is a metaphor. Mediæval miniatures show us persons lying in bed with crowns on their heads: this is to symbolise their royal rank; the painter did not mean that they wore their crowns to sleep in.

oblique senses when the author had other interests than that of being understood, or when he wrote for a public which could understand his allusions and read between the lines, or when his readers, in virtue of a religious or literary initiation, might be expected to understand his symbolisms and figures of speech. This is the case with religious texts, private letters, and all those literary works which form so large a part of the documents on antiquity. Thus the art of recognising and determining hidden meanings in texts has always occupied a large space in the theory of *hermeneutic*[1] (which is Greek for interpretative criticism), and in the *exegesis* of the sacred texts and of classical authors.

The different modes of introducing an oblique sense behind the literal sense are too varied, and depend too much on special circumstances, for it to be possible to reduce the art of detecting them to definite rules. Only one general principle can be laid down, and that is, that when the literal sense is absurd, incoherent, or obscure, or in contradiction with the ideas of the author or the facts known to him, then we ought to presume an oblique sense.

In order to determine this sense, the procedure is the same as for studying the language of an author: we compare the passages in which the expressions occur in which we suspect an oblique sense, and look to see whether there is not one

[1] A. Boeckh, in the *Encyclopædie und Methodologie der philologischen Wissenschaften*, second edition (1886), has given a theory of *hermeneutic* to which Bernheim has been content to refer.

where the meaning may be guessed from the context. A celebrated instance of this procedure is the discovery of the allegorical meaning of the Beast in the Apocalypse. But as there is no certain method of solving these problems, we never have a right to say we have discovered all the hidden meanings or seized all the allusions contained in a text; and even when we think we have found the sense, we shall do well to draw no inferences from a necessarily conjectural interpretation.

On the other hand, it is necessary to guard against the temptation to look for allegorical meanings everywhere, as the neo-Platonists did in Plato's works and the Swedenborgians in the Bible. This attack of *hyper-hermeneutic* is now over, but we are not yet safe from the analogous tendency to look for allusions everywhere. Investigations of this kind are always conjectural, and are better calculated to flatter the vanity of the interpreter than to furnish results of which history can make use.

V. When we have at length reached the real sense of the text, the operation of positive analysis is concluded. Its result is to make us acquainted with the author's conceptions, the images he had in his mind, the general notions in terms of which he represented the world to himself. This information belongs to a very important branch of knowledge, out of which is constituted a whole group of historical sciences:[1] the history of the illustrative arts and of literature, the history of science, the

[1] The method of extracting information on external facts from a writer's conceptions forms part of the theory of constructive reasoning. *See* book iii.

history of philosophical and moral doctrine, mythology and the history of dogmas (wrongly called religious beliefs, because here we are studying official doctrines without inquiring whether they are believed), the history of law, the history of official institutions (so far as we do not inquire how they were applied in practice), the assemblage of popular legends, traditions, opinions, conceptions (inexactly called beliefs) which are comprised under the name of folk-lore.

All these studies need only the external criticism which investigates authorship and origin and interpretative criticism; they require one degree less elaboration than the history of objective facts, and accordingly they have been earlier established on a methodical basis.

CHAPTER VII

THE NEGATIVE INTERNAL CRITICISM OF THE GOOD FAITH AND ACCURACY OF AUTHORS

I. ANALYSIS and positive interpretative criticism only penetrate as far as the inward workings of the mind of the author of a document, and only help us to know his ideas. They give no direct information about external facts. Even when the author was able to observe them, his text only indicates how he wished to represent them, not how he really saw them, still less how they really happened. What an author expresses is not always what he believed, for he may have lied; what he believed is not necessarily what happened, for he may have been mistaken. These propositions are obvious. And yet a first and natural impulse leads us to accept as true every statement contained in a document, which is equivalent to assuming that no author ever lied or was deceived; and this spontaneous credulity seems to possess a high degree of vitality, for it persists in spite of the innumerable instances of error and mendacity which daily experience brings before us.

Reflection has been forced on historians in the course of their work by the circumstance of their finding documents which contradicted each other; in such cases they have been obliged to doubt, and, after examination, to admit the existence of error or mendacity; thus negative criticism has appeared as a practical necessity for the purpose of eliminating statements which are obviously false or erroneous. But the instinct of confidence is so indestructible that it has hitherto prevented even those professionally concerned from systematising the internal criticism of statements in the same way as the external criticism which deals with the origin of documents has been systematised. Historians, in their works, and even theoretical writers on historical method,[1] have been satisfied with common notions and vague formulæ in striking contrast with the precise terminology of the critical investigation of sources. They are content to examine whether the author was roughly *contemporary* with the events, whether he was an ocular *witness*, whether he was *sincere* and *well-informed*, whether he knew the truth and desired to tell it, or even—summing up the whole question in a single formula—whether he was *trustworthy*.

This superficial criticism is certainly better than no criticism at all, and has sufficed to give those who have applied it the consciousness of incontestable superiority. But it is only a halfway-house between common credulity and scientific method. Here, as in every science, the starting-point must be methodical doubt.[2] All that has not been proved must be temporarily regarded as doubtful: no pro-

[1] For example, Père de Smedt, Tardif, Droysen, and even Bernheim.

[2] Descartes, who came at a time when history still consisted in the reproduction of pre-existing narratives, did not see how to apply methodical doubt to the subject; he therefore refused to allow it a place among the sciences.

position is to be affirmed unless reasons can be adduced in favour of its truth. Applied to the statements contained in documents, methodical doubt becomes *methodical distrust.*

The historian ought to distrust *a priori* every statement of an author, for he cannot be sure that it is not mendacious or mistaken. At the best it affords a presumption. For the historian to adopt it and affirm it afresh on his own account implies that he regards it as a scientific truth. To take this decisive step is what he has no right to do without good reasons. But the human mind is so constituted that this step is often taken unconsciously (cf. book ii. chap. i.). Against this dangerous tendency criticism has only one means of defence. We must not postpone doubt till it is forced upon us by conflicting statements in documents; we must *begin* by doubting. We must never forget the interval which separates a statement made by any author whatsoever from a scientifically established truth, so that we may continually keep in mind the responsibility which we assume when we reproduce a statement.

Even after we have accepted the principle and resolved to apply this unnatural distrust in practice, we tend instinctively to free ourselves from it as soon as possible. The natural impulse is to perform the criticism of the whole of an author, or at least of the whole of a document, in the lump; to divide authorities into two categories, the sheep on the right, the goats on the left; on the one side trustworthy authors and good documents, on the other suspected authors and bad documents. Having thus exhausted our powers of distrust, we proceed to reproduce without discussion all the statements contained in the "good document." We consent to distrust suspected authors such as Suidas or Aimo, but we affirm as established truth everything that has been said by Thucydides or Gregory of Tours.[1] We apply to authors that judicial procedure which divides witnesses into admissible and inadmissible: having once accepted a witness, we feel ourselves bound to admit all his testimony; we dare not doubt any of his statements without a special reason. Instinctively we take sides with the author on whom we have bestowed our approval, and we go so far as to say, as in the law courts, that the burden of proof rests with those who reject valid testimony.[2]

[1] Fustel de Coulanges himself did not rise above this kind of timidity. With reference to a speech attributed to Clovis by Gregory of Tours, he says: "Doubtless we are unable to affirm that these words were ever pronounced. But, all the same, we ought not to affirm, in contradiction to Gregory of Tours, that they were not. . . . The wisest course is to accept Gregory's text" (*Monarchic franque*, p. 66). The wisest, or rather the only scientific course, is to admit that we know nothing about the words of Clovis, for Gregory himself had no knowledge of them.

[2] Quite recently, E. Meyer, one of the most critically expert historians of antiquity, has in his work, *Die Entstehung des Judenthums* (Halle, 1896, 8vo), revived this strange juridical argument in favour of the narrative of Nehemiah. M. Bouché-Leclercq, in a remarkable study on "The Reign of Seleucus II. (Callinicus) and Historical Criticism" (*Revue des Universités du Midi*, April-June 1897), seems, by way of reaction against the hypercriticism of Niebuhr and Droysen, to incline towards an analogous theory: "Historical criticism, if it is not to degenerate into agnosticism—which would be suicidal—or into individual caprice, must place a certain amount of trust in testimony which it cannot verify, as long as it is not flatly contradicted by other testimony of equal value." M. Bouché-Leclercq is right as against the historian who, "after having discredited all his witnesses, claims to put himself in their place, and sees with their

The confusion is still further increased by the use of the word *authentic*, borrowed from judicial language. It has reference to the origin only, not to the contents; to say that a document is authentic is merely to say that its origin is certain, not that its contents are free from error. But authenticity inspires a degree of respect which disposes us to accept the contents without discussion. To doubt the statements of an authentic document would seem presumptuous, or at least we think ourselves bound to wait for overwhelming proof before we impeach the testimony of the author.

II. These natural instincts must be methodically resisted. A document (still more a literary work) is not all of a piece; it is composed of a great number of independent statements, any one of which may be intentionally or unintentionally false, while the others are *bonâ fide* and accurate, or conversely, since each statement is the outcome of a mental operation which may have been incorrectly performed, while others were performed correctly. It is not, therefore, enough to examine a document as a whole; each of the statements in it must be examined separately; *criticism* is impossible without *analysis*.

Thus internal criticism conducts us to two general rules.

(1) A scientific truth is not established by *testimony*. In order to affirm a proposition we must

eyes something quite different from what they themselves saw." But when the "testimony" is insufficient to give us the scientific knowledge of a fact, the only correct attitude is "agnosticism," that is, a confession of ignorance; we have no right to shirk this confession because chance has permitted the destruction of the documents which might have contradicted the testimony.

have special reasons for believing it true. It may happen in certain cases that an author's statement is a sufficient reason for belief; but we cannot know that beforehand. The rule, then, will be to examine each separate statement in order to make sure whether it is of a nature to constitute a sufficient reason for belief.

(2) The criticism of a document is not to be performed *en bloc*. The rule will be to *analyse* the document into its elements, in order to isolate the different statements of which it is composed and to examine each of them separately. Sometimes a single sentence contains several statements; they must be separated and criticised one by one. In a sale, for example, we distinguish the date, the place, the vendor, the purchaser, the object, the price, and each one of the conditions.

In practice, criticism and analysis are performed simultaneously, and, except in the case of texts in a difficult language, may proceed *pari passu* with interpretative analysis and criticism. As soon as we understand a phrase we analyse it and criticise each of its elements.

It thus appears that *logically* criticism comprises an enormous number of operations. In describing them, with all the details necessary for the understanding of their mechanism and the reasons for their employment, we are likely to give the impression of a procedure too slow to be practicable. Such an impression is inevitably produced by every verbal description of a complicated process. Compare the time occupied in describing a movement in fencing with that required to execute it; compare the tedium of the grammar and dictionary with the rapidity of reading. Like every practical art, criticism consists in the habit of performing certain acts. In the period of apprenticeship, before the habit is acquired, we are obliged to think of each act separately before performing it, and to analyse the movements; accordingly we perform them all slowly and with difficulty; but the habit once acquired, the acts, which have now become instinctive and unconscious, are performed with ease and rapidity. The reader must therefore not be uneasy about the slowness of the critical processes; he will see later on how they are abridged in practice.

III. The problem of criticism may be stated as follows. Given a statement made by a man of whose mental operations we have no experience, and the value of the statement depending exclusively on the manner in which these operations were performed; to ascertain whether these operations were performed correctly. The mere statement of the problem shows that we cannot hope for any direct or definitive solution of it; we lack the essential datum, namely, the manner in which the author performed the mental operations concerned. Criticism therefore does not advance beyond indirect and provisional solutions, and does no more than furnish data which require a final elaboration.

A natural instinct leads us to judge of the value of statements by their form. We think we can tell at a glance whether an author is sincere or a narrative accurate. We seek for what is called "the accent of sincerity," or "an impression of truth." This impression is almost irresistible, but it is none the less an illusion. There is no external criterion either of good faith or of accuracy. "The accent of sincerity" is the appearance of conviction; an orator, an actor, an habitual liar will put more of it into his lies than an undecided man into his statement of what he believes to be the truth. Energy of affirmation does not always mean strength of conviction, but sometimes only cleverness or effrontery.[1] Similarly, abundance and precision of detail, though they produce a vivid impression on unexperienced readers, do not guarantee the accuracy of the facts;[2] they give us no information about anything but the imagination of the author when he is sincere, or his impudence when he is the reverse. We are apt to say of a circumstantial narrative: "Things of this kind are not invented." They are not invented, but they are very easy to transfer from one person, country, or time to another. There is thus no external characteristic of a document which can relieve us of the obligation to criticise it.

The value of an author's statement depends solely on the conditions under which he performed certain mental operations. Criticism has no other resource

[1] The "Memoirs of Cardinal de Retz" furnish a conclusive instance: the anecdote of the ghosts met by Retz and Turenne. A. Feillet, who edited Retz in the *Collection des Grands Écrivains de la France*, has shown (vol. i. p. 192) that this story, so vividly narrated, is false from beginning to end.

[2] A good example of the fascination exerted by a circumstantial narrative is the legend respecting the origin of the League of the three primitive Swiss cantons (Gessler and the Grütli conspirators), which was *fabricated* by Tschudi in the sixteenth century, became classical on the production of Schiller's "William Tell," and has only been extirpated with the greatest difficulty. (See Rilliet, *Origines de la Confédération suisse*, Geneva, 1869, 8vo.)

than the examination of these conditions. But it is not a case of reconstructing all of them; it is enough to answer a single question: did the author perform these operations correctly or not? The question may be approached on two sides.

(1) The critical investigation of authorship has often taught us the *general* conditions under which the author operated. It is probable that some of these influenced each one of the operations. We ought therefore to begin by studying the information we possess about the author and the composition of the document, taking particular pains to look in the habits, sentiments, and personal situation of the author, or in the circumstances in which he composed, for all the reasons which could have existed for incorrectness on the one hand, or exceptional accuracy on the other. In order to perceive these reasons it is necessary to be on the lookout for them beforehand. The only method, therefore, is to draw up a general set of questions having reference to the possible causes of inaccuracy. We shall then apply it to the general conditions under which the document was composed, in order to discover those causes which may have rendered the author's mental operations incorrect and vitiated the results. But all that we shall thus obtain—even in the exceptionally favourable cases in which the conditions of origin are well known—will be *general* indications, which will be insufficient for the purposes of criticism, for criticism must always deal with each separate statement.

(2) The criticism of particular statements is confined to the use of a single method, which, by a

curious paradox, is the study of the *universal* conditions under which documents are composed. The information which is not furnished by the general study of the author may be sought for by a consideration of the necessary processes of the human mind; for, since these are universal, they must appear in each particular case. We know what are the cases in which men in general are inclined to alter or distort facts. What we have to do in the case of each statement is to examine whether it was made under such circumstances as to lead us to suspect, from our knowledge of the habits of normal humanity, that the operations implied in the making of it were incorrectly performed. The practical procedure will be to draw up a set of questions relating to the habitual causes of inaccuracy.

The whole of criticism thus reduces to the drawing up and answering of two sets of questions: one for the purpose of bringing before our minds those general conditions affecting the composition of the document, from which we may deduce general motives for distrust or confidence; the other for the purpose of realising the special conditions of each statement, from which special motives may be drawn for distrust or confidence. These two sets of questions ought to be drawn up beforehand in such a form as may enable us to examine methodically both the document in general and each statement in particular; and as they are the same for all documents, it is useful to formulate them once for all.

IV. The critical process comprises two series of

questions, which correspond to the two series of operations by which the document was produced. All that interpretative criticism tells us is what the author meant; it remains to determine (1) what he really believed, for he may not have been sincere; (2) what he really knew, for he may have been mistaken. We may therefore distinguish a *critical examination of the author's good faith*, by which we seek to determine whether the author of the document lied or not, and a *critical examination* of his *accuracy*, by which we seek to determine whether he was or was not mistaken.

In practice we rarely need to know what an author believed, unless we are making a special study of his character. We have no direct interest in the author; he is merely the medium through which we reach the external facts he reports. The aim of criticism is to determine whether the author has reported the facts correctly. If he has given inexact information, it is indifferent whether he did so intentionally or not; to draw a distinction would complicate matters unnecessarily. There is thus little occasion to make a separate examination of an author's good faith, and we may shorten our labours by including in a single set of questions all the causes which lead to misstatement. But for the sake of clearness it will be well to discuss the questions to be asked in two separate series.

The questions in the first series will help us to inquire whether we have any reason to distrust the sincerity of a statement. We ask whether the author was in any of those situations which normally incline a man to be insincere. We must ask what these situations are, both as affecting the general composition of a document, and as affecting each particular statement. Experience supplies the answer. Every violation of truth, small or great, is due to a wish on the part of the author to produce a particular impression upon the reader. Our set of questions thus reduces to a list of the motives which may, in the general case, lead an author to violate truth. The following are the most important cases:—

(1) The author seeks to gain a practical advantage for himself; he wishes to deceive the reader of the document, in order to persuade him to an action, or to dissuade him from it; he knowingly gives false information: we then say the author has an interest in deceiving. This is the case with most official documents. Even in documents which have not been composed for a practical purpose, every interested statement has a chance of being mendacious. In order to determine which statements are to be suspected, we are to ask what *can* have been the general aim of the author in writing the document as a whole; and again, what can have been his particular purpose in making each of the separate statements which compose the document. But there are two natural tendencies to be resisted. The first is, to ask what interest the author could have *had* in lying, meaning what interest should *we* have had in his place; we must ask instead what interest can he have *thought* he had in lying, and we must look for the answer in his tastes and ideals. The other tendency is to take sole account of the *individual* interest of the author; we ought, however, to remember that the author may have given

false information in order to serve a *collective* interest. This is one of the difficulties of criticism. An author is a member at one and the same time of several different groups, a family, a province, a country, a religious denomination, a political party, a class in society, whose interests often conflict; we have to discover the group in which he took most interest, and for which he worked.

(2) The author was placed in a situation which compelled him to violate truth. This happens whenever he has to draw up a document in conformity with rule or custom, while the actual circumstances are in some point or other in conflict with rule or custom; he is then obliged to state that the conditions were normal, and thus make a false declaration in respect of all the irregularities. In nearly every report of proceedings there is some slight deviation from truth as to the day, the hour, the place, the number or the names of those present. Most of us have observed, if not taken part in, some of these petty fictions. But we are too apt to forget them when we come to criticise documents relating to the past. The *authentic* character of the documents contributes to the illusion; we instinctively make *authentic* a synonym of *sincere*. The rigid rules which govern the composition of every authentic document seem to guarantee sincerity; they are, on the contrary, an incentive to falsify, not the main facts, but the accessory circumstances. From the fact of a person having signed a report we may infer that he agreed to it, but not that he was actually present at the time when the report mentions him as having been present.

(3) The author viewed with sympathy or antipathy a group of men (nation, party, denomination, province, city, family), or an assemblage of doctrines or institutions (religion, school of philosophy, political theory), and was led to distort facts in such a manner as to represent his friends in a favourable and his opponents in an unfavourable light. These are instances of a general bias which affects all the statements of an author, and they are so obvious that the ancients perceived them and gave them names (*studium* and *odium*); from ancient times it has been a literary commonplace for historians to protest that they have steered clear of both.

(4) The author was induced by private or collective vanity to violate truth for the purpose of exalting himself or his group. He made such statements as he thought likely to give the reader the impression that he and his possessed qualities deserving of esteem. We have therefore to inquire whether a given statement may not be influenced by vanity. But we must take care not to represent the author's vanity to ourselves as being exactly like our own vanity or that of our contemporaries. Different people are vain for different reasons; we must inquire what was our author's particular vanity; he may have lied in order to attribute to himself or his friends actions which we should consider dishonourable. Charles IX. falsely boasted of having organised the Massacre of St. Bartholomew. There is, however, a kind of vanity which is universal, and that is, the desire to appear to be a person of exalted rank playing an important part in affairs. We must, therefore, always distrust a statement

which attributes to the author or his group a high place in the world.[1]

(5) The author desired to please the public, or at least to avoid shocking it. He has expressed sentiments and ideas in harmony with the morality or the fashion of his public; he has distorted facts in order to adapt them to the passions and prejudices of his time, even those which he did not share. The purest types of this kind of falsehood are found in ceremonial forms, official formulæ, declarations prescribed by etiquette, set speeches, polite phrases. The statements which come under this head are so open to suspicion that we are unable to derive from them any information about the facts stated. We are all aware of this so far as relates to the contemporary formulæ of which we see instances every day, but we often forget it in the criticism of documents, especially those belonging to an age from which few documents have come down to us. No one would think of looking for the real sentiments of a man in the assurances of respect with which he ends his letters. But people believed for a long time in the humility of certain ecclesiastical dignitaries of the middle ages, because, on the day of their election, they began by refusing an office of which they declared themselves unworthy, till at last comparison showed that this refusal was a mere conventional form. And there are still scholars who, like the Benedictines of the eighteenth century, look in the chancery-formulæ

[1] Striking examples of falsehoods due to vanity are to be found in abundance in the *Économies royales* of Sully and the *Mémoires* of Retz.

of a prince for information as to his piety or his liberality.[1]

In order to recognise these conventional declarations there are two lines of general study to be pursued: the one is directed to the author, and seeks to discover what was the public he addressed, for in one and the same country there are usually several different publics, each of which has its own code of morals or propriety; the other is directed towards the public, and seeks to determine its morals or its manners.

(6) The author endeavoured to please the public by literary artifices. He distorted facts in order to embellish them according to his own æsthetic notions. We have therefore to look for the ideal of the author or of his time, in order to be on our guard against passages distorted to suit that ideal. But without special study we may calculate on the common kinds of literary distortion. Rhetorical distortion consists in attributing to persons noble attitudes, acts, sentiments, and, above all, words: this is a natural tendency in young boys who are beginning to practise the art of composition, and in writers still in a semi-barbarous stage; it is the common defect of the mediæval chroniclers.[2] Epic

[1] Fustel de Coulanges himself went to the formulæ of the inscriptions in honour of the emperors for a proof that the peoples liked the imperial *régime*. "If we read the inscriptions, the sentiment which they exhibit is always one of satisfaction and gratitude. . . . See the collection of Orelli, the most frequent expressions are . . ." And the enumeration of the titles of respect given to the emperors ends with this strange aphorism: "It would show ignorance of human nature to see nothing but flattery in all this." There is not even flattery here; there is nothing but formulæ.

[2] Suger, in his life of Louis VI., is a model of this type.

distortion embellishes the narrative by adding picturesque details, speeches delivered by the persons concerned, numbers, sometimes names of persons; it is dangerous, because the precision of the details produces an illusive appearance of truth.[1] Dramatic distortion consists in grouping the facts in such a way as to enhance the dramatic effect by concentrating facts, which in reality were separate, upon a single moment, a single person, or a single group. Writing of this kind is what we call "truer than the truth." It is the most dangerous form of distortion, the form employed by artistic historians, by Herodotus, Tacitus, the Italians of the Renaissance. Lyrical distortion exaggerates the intensity of the sentiments and the emotions of the author and his friends: we should remember this when we attempt to reconstruct "the psychology" of a person.

Literary distortion does not much affect archives (though instances of it are found in most charters of the eleventh century); but it profoundly modifies all literary texts, including the narratives of historians. Now, the natural tendency is to trust writers more readily when they have talent, and to admit statements with less difficulty when they are presented in good literary form. Criticism must counteract this tendency by the application of the paradoxical rule, that the more interesting a statement is from the artistic point of view,[2] the more it ought to be suspected. We must distrust every narrative which

[1] The *Chronicon Helveticum* of Tschudi is a striking instance.

[2] Aristophanes and Demosthenes are two striking examples of the power great writers have of paralysing critics and obscuring facts. Not till the close of the nineteenth century has any one ventured to recognise frankly their lack of good faith.

is very picturesque or very dramatic, in which the personages assume noble attitudes or manifest great intensity of feeling.

This first series of questions will yield the *provisional* result of enabling us to note the statements which have a *chance* of being mendacious.

V. The second series of questions will be of use in determining whether there is any reason to distrust the accuracy of a statement. Was the author in one of those situations which cause a man to make mistakes? As in dealing with good faith, we must look for these conditions both as affecting the document as a whole, and as affecting each of the particular statements in it.

The practice of the established sciences teaches us the conditions of an exact knowledge of facts. There is only one scientific procedure for gaining knowledge of a fact, namely, *observation*; every statement, therefore, must rest, directly or indirectly, upon an observation, and this observation must have been made correctly.

The set of questions by the aid of which we investigate the probabilities of error may be drawn up in the light of experience, which brings before us the most common cases of error.

(1) The author was in a situation to observe the fact, and supposed he really had observed it; he was, however, prevented from doing so by some interior force of which he was unconscious, an hallucination, an illusion, or a mere prejudice. It would be useless, as well as impossible, to determine which of these agencies was at work; it is enough to ascertain whether the author had a tendency to

observe badly. It is scarcely possible in the case of a particular statement to recognise that it was the result of an hallucination or an illusion. At the most we may learn, either from information derived from other sources or by comparison, that an author had a *general* propensity to this kind of error.

There is a better chance of recognising whether a statement was due to prejudice. In the life or the works of an author we may find the traces of his dominant prejudices. With reference to each of his particular statements, we ought to ask whether it is not the result of a preconceived idea of the author on a class of men or a kind of facts. This inquiry partly coincides with the search for motives of falsehood: interest, vanity, sympathy, and antipathy give rise to prejudices which alter the truth in the same manner as wilful falsehood. We therefore employ the questions already formulated for the purpose of testing good faith. But there is one to be added. In putting forward a statement has the author been led to distort it unconsciously by the circumstance that he was answering a question? This is the case of all statements obtained by interrogating witnesses. Even apart from the cases where the person interrogated seeks to please the proposer of the question by giving an answer which he thinks will be agreeable to him, every question suggests its own answer, or at least its form, and this form is dictated beforehand by some one unacquainted with the facts. It is therefore necessary to apply a special criticism to every statement obtained by interrogation; we must ask what was the question put, and what were the preconceptions to which it may have given rise in the mind of the person interrogated.

(2) The author was badly situated for observing. The practice of the sciences teaches us what are the conditions for correct observation. The observer ought to be placed where he can see correctly, and should have no practical interest, no desire to obtain a particular result, no preconceived idea about the result. He ought to record the observation immediately, in a precise system of notation; he ought to give a precise indication of his method. These conditions, which are insisted on in the sciences of observation, are never completely fulfilled by the authors of documents.

It would be useless, therefore, to ask whether there have been chances of inaccuracy; *there always have been,* and it is just this that distinguishes a *document* from an *observation.* It only remains to look for the obvious causes of error in the conditions of observation: to inquire whether the observer was in a place where he could not see or hear well, as would be the case, for example, with a subordinate who should presume to narrate the secret deliberations of a council of dignitaries; whether his attention was greatly distracted by the necessity for action, as it would be on the field of battle, for example; whether he was inattentive because the facts had little interest for him; whether he lacked the special experience or general intelligence necessary for understanding the facts; whether he analysed his impressions badly, or confused different events. Above all, we must ask when he *wrote down* what he saw or heard. This is the most important point:

the only exact observation is the one which is recorded immediately it is made; such is the constant procedure in the established sciences; an impression committed to writing later on is only a recollection, liable to be confused in the memory with other recollections. *Memoirs* written several years after the facts, often at the very end of the author's career, have introduced innumerable errors into history. It must be made a rule to treat *memoirs* with special distrust, as second-hand documents, in spite of their appearance of being contemporary testimony.

(3) The author states facts which he could have observed, but to which he did not take the trouble to attend. From idleness or negligence he reported details which he has merely inferred, or even imagined at random, and which turn out to be false. This is a common source of error, though it does not readily occur to one, and is to be suspected wherever the author was obliged to procure information in which he took little interest, in order to fill up a blank form. Of this kind are answers to questions put by an authority (it is enough to observe how most official inquiries are conducted in our own day), and detailed accounts of ceremonies or public functions. There is too strong a temptation to write the account from the programme, or in agreement with the usual order of the proceedings. How many accounts of meetings of all kinds have been published by reporters who were not present at them! Similar efforts of imagination are suspected—sometimes, it is thought, clearly recognised—in the writings of mediæval chroniclers.[1]

[1] For example, the account of the election of Otto I. in the *Gesta Ottonis* of Wittekind.

The rule, then, will be to distrust all narratives conforming too closely to a set formula.

(4) The fact stated is of such a nature that it could not have been learnt by observation alone. It may be a hidden fact—a private secret, for example. It may be a fact relating to a collectivity, and applying to an extensive area or a long period of time; for example, the common act of a whole army, a custom common to a whole people or a whole age, a statistical total obtained by the addition of numerous items. It may be a comprehensive judgment on the character of a man, a group, a custom, an event. Here we have to do with propositions derived from observations by synthesis or inference: the author can only have arrived at them indirectly; he began with data furnished by observation, and elaborated them by the logical processes of abstraction, generalisation, reasoning, calculation. Two questions arise. Does it appear that the author had sufficient data to work upon? Was he accurate, or the reverse, in his use of the data he had?

On the probable inaccuracies of an author, general indications may be obtained from an examination of his writings. This examination will show us how he worked: whether he was capable of abstraction, reasoning, generalisation, and what were the mistakes he was in the habit of making. In order to determine the value of the data, we must criticise each statement separately; we must imagine the conditions under which the author observed, and ask ourselves whether he was able to procure the necessary data for his statement. This is an indispensable precaution in dealing with large totals in statistics and descriptions of popular usages; for it is possible that the author may have obtained the total he gives by a process of conjectural valuation (this is the ordinary practice in stating the number of combatants or killed in a battle), or by combining subsidiary totals, all of which were not accurate; it is possible that he may have extended to a whole people, a whole country, a whole period, that which was true only of a small group known to him.[1]

VI. These two first series of questions bearing on the good faith and the accuracy of the statements in the document are based on the supposition that the author has observed the fact himself. This is a feature common to all reports of observations in the established sciences. But in history there is so great a dearth of direct *observations*, of even moderate value, that we are obliged to turn to account documents which every other science would reject.[2] Take any narrative at random, even if it be the work of a contemporary, it will be found that the facts observed by the author are never more than a part of the whole number. In nearly every document the majority of the statements do not come from the author at first hand, but are reproductions of the statements of others. Even where a general relates a battle in which he commanded, he does not communicate his own observations, but those of

[1] For example, the statistics on the population, the commerce, and the wealth of European countries given by the Venetian ambassadors of the sixteenth century, and the descriptions of the usages of the Germans in the *Germania* of Tacitus.

[2] It would be interesting to examine how much of Roman or Merovingian history would be left if we rejected all documents but those which represent direct observation.

his officers; his narrative is in a large measure a "second-hand document."[1]

In order to criticise a second-hand statement it is no longer enough to examine the conditions under which the author of the document worked: this author is, in such a case, a mere agent of transmission; the true author is the person who supplied him the information. The critic, therefore, must change his ground, and ask whether the informant observed and reported correctly; and if he too had the information from some one else (the commonest case), the chase must be pursued from one intermediary to another, till the person is found who first launched the statement on its career, and with regard to him the question must be asked: Was he an accurate observer?

Logically such a search is not inconceivable; ancient collections of Arab traditions give lists of their successive guarantors. But, in practice, lack of documents nearly always prevents us from getting as far as the observer of a fact; the observation remains anonymous. A general question then presents itself: How are we to criticise an anonymous statement? It is not only "anonymous documents"

[1] It will be seen why we have not separately defined and studied "first-hand documents." The question has not been raised in the proper manner in historical practice. The distinction ought to apply to *statements*, not to documents. It is not the document which comes to us at first, second, or third hand; it is the statement. What is called a "first-hand document" is nearly always composed in part of second-hand statements about facts of which the author had no personal knowledge. The name "second-hand document" is given to those which, like the work of Livy, contain nothing first-hand; but the distinction is too crude to serve as a guide in the critical examination of statements.

with which we are concerned, where the composition as a whole is the work of an unknown author; even when the author is known, this question arises with respect to each statement of his drawn from an unknown source.

Criticism works by reproducing the conditions under which an author wrote, and has hardly anything to take hold of where a statement is anonymous. The only method left is to examine the general conditions of the document. We may inquire whether there is any feature common to all the statements of a document indicating that they all proceed from persons having the same prejudices or passions: in this case the tradition followed by the author is biassed; the tradition followed by Herodotus has both an Athenian bias and a Delphic bias. In respect of each fact derived from such a tradition we must ask whether it has not been distorted by the interest, the vanity, or the prejudices of the group concerned. We may even ignore the author, and ask whether there was anything likely to make for or against correct observation, common to all the men of the time and country in which the observation must have been made: for example, what means of information, and what prejudices, had the Greeks of Herodotus' time with respect to the Scythians.

The most useful of all these general inquiries has reference to that mode of transmitting anonymous statements which is called *tradition*. No second-hand statement has any value except in so far as it reproduces its source; every addition is an alteration, and ought to be eliminated. Similarly, all the intermediary sources are valueless except as copies of the original statement founded directly on observation. The critic needs to know whether this transmission from hand to hand has preserved or distorted the original statement; above all, whether the tradition embodied in the document was *written* or *oral*. Writing fixes a statement, and ensures its being transmitted faithfully; when a statement is communicated orally, the impression in the mind of the hearer is apt to be modified by confusion with other impressions; in passing from one intermediary to another the statement is modified at every step,[1] and as these modifications arise from different causes, there is no possibility of measuring or correcting them.

Oral tradition is by its nature a process of continual alteration; hence in the established sciences only written transmission is accepted. Historians have no avowable motive for proceeding differently, at any rate when it is a case of establishing a particular fact. We must therefore search documents for statements derived from oral tradition in order that we may suspect them. We rarely have direct information as to statements being thus derived; authors who borrow from oral tradition are not anxious to proclaim the fact.[2] There is thus only

[1] There is much less modification where the oral tradition assumes a regular or striking form, as is the case with verses, maxims, proverbs.

[2] Sometimes the *form* of the phrase tells its own tale, when, in the midst of a detailed narrative, obviously of legendary origin, we come across a curt, dry entry in annalistic style, obviously copied from a written document. That is what we find in Livy (see Nitzsch, *Die römische Annalistik*, Leipzig, 1873, 8vo), and in Gregory of Tours (see Loebell, *Gregor von Tours*, Leipzig, 1868, 8vo).

an indirect method, and that is to ascertain that written transmission was impossible; we may then be sure that the fact reached the author only by oral tradition. We have therefore to ask the question: In this period and in this group of men was it customary to commit to writing facts of this kind? If the answer is negative, the fact considered rests on oral tradition alone.

The most striking form of oral tradition is *legend*. It arises among groups of men with whom the spoken word is the only means of transmission, in barbarous societies, or in classes of little culture, such as peasants or soldiers. In this case it is the whole group of facts which is transmitted orally and assumes the legendary form. There is a legendary period in the early history of every people: in Greece, at Rome, among the Germanic and Slavonic races, the most ancient memories of the people form a stratum of legend. In periods of civilisation popular legends continue to exist in reference to events which strike the imagination of the people.[1] Legend is exclusively oral tradition.

When a people has emerged from the legendary period and begun to commit its history to writing, oral tradition does not come to an end, but only applies to a narrower sphere; it is now restricted to

[1] The events which strike the popular imagination and are transmitted by legend are not generally those which seem to us the most important. The heroes of the *chansons de gestes* are hardly known historically. The Breton epic songs relate, not to the great historical events, as Villemarqué's collection led people to believe, but to obscure local episodes. The same holds of the Scandinavian sagas; for the most part they relate to quarrels among the villagers of Iceland or the Orkneys.

facts which are not registered, whether because they are by their nature secret, or because no one takes the trouble to record them, such as private actions, words, the details of events. Thus arise *anecdotes*, which have been named "the legends of civilised society." Like legends they have their origin in confused recollections, allusions, mistaken interpretations, imaginings of all kinds which fasten upon particular persons and events.

Legends and anecdotes are at bottom mere popular beliefs, arbitrarily attached to historical personages; they belong to folk-lore, not to history.[1] We must therefore guard against the temptation to treat legend as an alloy of accurate facts and errors out of which it is possible by analysis to extract grains of historical truth. A legend is a conglomerate in which there may be some grains of truth, and which may even be capable of being analysed into its elements; but there is no means of distinguishing the elements taken from reality from those which are the work of imagination. To use Niebuhr's expression, a legend is "a mirage produced by an invisible object according to an unknown law of refraction."

The crudest analytical procedure consists in rejecting those details in the legendary narrative which appear impossible, miraculous, contradictory, or absurd, and retaining the rational residue as historical. This is how the Protestant rationalists of the eighteenth century treated biblical narratives.

[1] The theory of legend is one of the most advanced parts of criticism. Bernheim (in his *Lehrbuch*, pp. 380-90) gives a good summary and a bibliography of it.

One might as well amputate the marvellous part of a fairy tale, suppress Puss in Boots, and keep the Marquis of Carabas as an historical character. A more refined but no less dangerous method is to compare different legends in order to deduce their common historical basis. Grote[1] has shown, with reference to Greek tradition, that it is impossible to extract any trustworthy information from legend by any process whatever.[2] We must make up our minds to treat legend as a product of imagination; we may look in it for a people's conceptions, not for the external facts in that people's history. The rule will be to reject every statement of legendary origin; nor does this apply only to narratives in legendary form: a narrative which has an historical appearance, but is founded on the data of legend, the opening chapters of Thucydides for example, ought equally to be discarded.

In the case of written transmission it remains to inquire whether the author reproduced his source without altering it. This inquiry forms part of the critical investigation of the sources,[3] so far as it can be pursued by a comparison of texts. But when the source has disappeared we are reduced to internal criticism. We ask, first of all, whether the author can have had exact information, otherwise his state-

[1] "History of Greece," vols. i. and ii. Compare Renan, *Histoire du peuple d'Israël*, vol. i. (Paris, 1887, 8vo), Introduction.

[2] And yet Niebuhr made use of the Roman legends to construct a theory, which it was afterwards necessary to demolish, of the struggle between the patricians and the plebeians; and Curtius, twenty years after Grote, looked for historical facts in the Greek legends.

[3] See *supra*, pp. 93 *sqq*.

ment is valueless. We next put to ourselves the general question: Was the author in the habit of altering his sources, and in what manner? And in regard to each separate second-hand statement we ask whether it has the appearance of being an exact reproduction or an arrangement. We judge by the form: when we meet with a passage whose style is out of harmony with the main body of the composition, we have before us a fragment of an earlier document; the more servile the reproduction the more valuable is the passage, for it can contain no exact information beyond what was already in the source.

VII. In spite of all these investigations, criticism never succeeds in determining the parentage of all the statements to the extent of finding out who it was that observed, or even recorded, each fact. In most cases the inquiry ends in leaving the statement anonymous.

We are thus confronted with a fact, observed we know not by whom nor how, recorded we know not when nor how. No other science accepts facts which come in such a condition, without possibility of verification, subject to incalculable chances of error. But history can turn them to account, because it does not, like the other sciences, need a supply of facts which are difficult to ascertain.

The notion of a *fact*, when we come to examine it precisely, reduces to an affirmative judgment having reference to external reality. The operations by which we arrive at such a judgment are more or less difficult, and the risk of error is greater or smaller according to the nature of the realities investigated and the degree of precision with which we wish to formulate them. Chemistry and biology need to discern facts of a delicate order, rapid movements, transient states, and to measure them in exact figures. History can work with facts of a much coarser kind, spread over a large extent of space or time, such as the existence of a custom, of a man, of a group, even of a people; and these facts may be roughly expressed in vague words conveying no idea of accurate measurement. With such easily observed facts as these to deal with, history can afford to be much less exacting with regard to the conditions of observation. The imperfection of the means of information is compensated by a natural faculty of being satisfied with information which can easily be obtained.

Documents supply little else besides ill-verified facts, subject to many risks of falsehood or error. But there are some facts in respect of which it is very difficult to lie or be mistaken. The last series of questions which the critic should ask is intended to distinguish, in the mass of alleged facts, those which by their nature are little subject to the risk of alteration, and which are therefore very probably correct. We know what, in general, are the classes of facts which enjoy this privilege; we are thus enabled to draw up a list of questions for general use, and in applying them to any particular case we ask whether the fact in question comes under any of the heads specified in advance.

(1) The fact is of a nature to render falsehood improbable. A man lies in order to produce an impression, and has no motive to lie in a case

where he believes that the false impression would be of no use, or that the falsehood would be ineffectual. In order to determine whether the author was in such a situation there are several questions to be asked.

(*a*) Is the fact stated manifestly prejudicial to the effect which the author wished to produce? Does it run counter to the interest, the vanity, the sentiments, the literary tastes of the author and his group; or to the opinions which he made a point of not offending? In such a case there is a probability of good faith. But in the application of this criterion there is danger; it has often been wrongly used, and in two ways. One of these is to take for a confession what was meant for a boast, as the declaration of Charles IX. that he was responsible for the Massacre of St. Bartholomew. Or again, we trust without examination an Athenian who speaks ill of the Athenians, or a Protestant who accuses other Protestants. But it is quite possible the author's notions of his interest or honour were very different from ours;[1] or he may have wished to calumniate fellow-citizens who did not belong to his own party, or co-religionists who did not belong to his own sect. This criterion must therefore be restricted to cases where we know exactly what *effect* he wished to produce, and in what *group* he was mainly interested.

(*b*) Was the fact stated so obviously known to the public that the author, even if tempted to falsehood, would have been restrained by the certainty of being detected? This is the case with facts which are

[1] Cf. *supra*, p. 166.

easy to verify, which are not remote in point of time or space, which apply to a wide area or a long period, especially if the public had any interest in verifying them. But the fear of detection is only an intermittent check, opposed by interest whenever the author has any motive for deceiving. It acts unequally on different minds—strongly on men of culture and self-control who understand their public, feebly in barbarous ages and on passionate men.[1] This criterion, therefore, is to be restricted to cases where we know what idea the author had of his readers, and whether he was dispassionate enough to keep them in mind.

(*c*) Was the fact stated *indifferent* to the author, so that he had no temptation to misrepresent it? This is the case with facts of a general kind, usages, institutions, objects, persons, which the author mentions incidentally. A narrative, even a false one, cannot be composed exclusively of falsehoods; the author must localise his facts, and needs to surround them with a framework of truth. The facts which form this framework had no interest for him; at that time every one knew them. But for us they are instructive, and we can depend on them, for the author had no intention of deceiving us.

(2) The fact was of a kind to render error improbable. Numerous as the chances of error are, still there are facts so "big" it is hard to be mistaken about them. We have, then, to ask

[1] It is often said, "The author would not have dared to write this if it had not been true." This argument does not apply to societies in a low state of civilisation. Louis VIII. dared to write that John Lackland had been condemned by the verdict of his peers.

whether the alleged fact was easy to ascertain: (*a*) Did it cover a long period of time, so that it must have been frequently observed? Take, for example, the case of a monument, a man, a custom, an event which was in progress for a considerable time. (*b*) Did it cover a wide area, so that many people observed it?—as, for example, a battle, a war, a custom common to a whole people. (*c*) Is it expressed in such general terms that superficial observation was enough to discover it?—as the mere existence of a man, a city, a people, a custom. Facts of this large and general kind make up the bulk of historical knowledge.

(3) The fact was of such a nature that it would not have been stated unless it was true. A man does not declare that he has seen something contrary to his expectations and habits of mind unless observation has compelled him to admit it. A fact which seems very improbable to the man who relates it has a good chance of being true. We have, then, to ask whether the fact stated was in contradiction with the author's opinions, whether it is a phenomenon of a kind unknown to him, an action or a custom which seems unintelligible to him; whether it is a saying whose import transcends his intelligence, such as the sayings of Christ reported in the Gospels, or the answers made by Joan of Arc to questions put to her in the course of her trial. But we must guard against judging of the author's ideas by our own standards: when men who are accustomed to believe in the marvellous speak of monsters, of miracles, of wizards, there is nothing in these to contradict their expectations, and the criterion does not apply.

VIII. We have at last reached the end of this description of the critical operations; its length is due to the necessity of describing successively operations which are performed simultaneously. We will now consider how these methods are applied in practice.

If the text be one whose interpretation is debatable, the examination is divided into two stages: the first comprises the reading of the text with a view to the determination of the meaning, without attempting to draw any information from it; the second comprises the critical study of the facts contained in the document. In the case of documents whose meaning is clear, we may begin the critical examination on the first reading, reserving for separate study any individual passages of doubtful meaning.

We begin by collecting the *general* information we possess about the document and the author, with the special purpose of discovering the conditions which may have influenced the production of the document—the epoch, the place, the purpose, the circumstances of its composition; the author's social status, country, party, sect, family, interests, passions, prejudices, linguistic habits, methods of work, means of information, culture, abilities, and mental defects; the nature of the facts and the mode of their transmission. Information on all these points is supplied by the preparatory critical investigation of authorship and sources. We now combine the different heads, mentally applying the set of general critical questions; this should be done at the outset, and the results impressed on the memory, for they will need to be present to the mind during the remainder of the operations.

Thus prepared, we attack the document. As we read we mentally analyse it, destroying all the author's combinations, discarding all his literary devices, in order to arrive at the facts, which we formulate in simple and precise language. We thus free ourselves from the deference imposed by artistic form, and from all submission to the author's ideas —an emancipation without which criticism is impossible.

The document thus analysed resolves into a long series of the author's conceptions and statements as to facts.

With regard to each statement, we ask ourselves whether there is a probability of their being false or erroneous, or whether, on the other hand, there are exceptional chances in favour of good faith and accuracy, working through the list of critical questions prepared for particular cases. This list of questions must be always present to the mind. At first it may seem cumbersome, perhaps pedantic; but as it will be applied more than a hundred times in each page of the document, it will in the end be used unconsciously. As we read a text, all the reasons for distrust or confidence will occur to the mind simultaneously, combined into a single impression.

Analysis and critical questioning will then have become a matter of instinct, and we shall have acquired for ever that methodically analytical, distrustful, not too respectful turn of mind which is often mystically called "the critical sense," but which is nothing else than an unconscious *habit* of criticism.

CHAPTER VIII

THE DETERMINATION OF PARTICULAR FACTS

CRITICAL analysis yields in the result a number of conceptions and statements, accompanied by comments on the probability of the facts stated being accurate. It remains to examine how we can deduce from these materials those particular historical facts which are to form the basis of scientific knowledge. Conceptions and statements are two different kinds of results, and must be treated by different methods.

I. Every conception which is expressed in writing or by any illustrative representation is in itself a definite, unimpeachable fact. That which is expressed must have first been present in the mind of some one—if not in that of the author, who may have reproduced a formula he did not understand, then in the mind of the man who originated the formula. The existence of a conception may be learnt from a single instance and proved from a single document. Analysis and interpretation are thus sufficient for the purpose of drawing up the complete list of those facts which form the basis of the history of the arts, the sciences, or of doctrines.[1]

[1] See above, p. 153. Similarly, the particular facts which compose the history of forms (palæography, linguistic science) are directly established by the analysis of the document.

It is the task of external criticism to localise these facts by determining the epoch, the country, the author of each conception. The duration, geographical distribution, origin, and filiation of conceptions belong to historical synthesis. Internal criticism has nothing to do here; the fact is taken directly from the document.

We may advance a step farther. In themselves conceptions are nothing but facts in psychology; but imagination does not create its objects, it takes the elements of them from reality. Descriptions of imaginary facts are constructed out of the real facts which the author has observed in his experience. These elements of knowledge, the raw material of the imaginary description, may be sought for and isolated. In dealing with periods and with classes of facts for which documents are rare—antiquity, for example, and the usages of private life—the attempt has been made to lay under contribution works of literature, epic poems, novels, plays.[1] The method is legitimate, but only within the limits of certain restrictions which one is very apt to forget.

(1) It does not apply to social facts of a psychological order, the moral or artistic standards of a society; the moral and æsthetic conceptions in a document give at most the individual standards of the author; we have no right to conclude from these to the morals or the æsthetic tastes of the age. We must at least wait till we have

[1] Primitive Greece has been studied in the Homeric poems. Mediæval private life has been reconstructed principally from the *chansons de gestes*. (See C. V. Langlois, *Les Traditions sur l'histoire de la société française au moyen âge d'après les sources littéraires*, in the *Revue historique*, March-April, 1897.)

compared several different authors of the same period.

(2) Descriptions even of physical facts and objects may be products of the author's imagination. It is only the *elements* of them which we know to be certainly real; all that we can assert is the separate existence of the irreducible elements, form, material, colour, number. When the poet speaks of golden gates or silver bucklers, we cannot infer that golden gates and silver bucklers ever existed in reality; nothing is certain beyond the separate existence of gates, bucklers, gold, and silver. The analysis must therefore be carried to the point of distinguishing those elements which the author must necessarily have taken from experience: objects, their purpose, ordinary actions.

(3) The conception of an object or an action proves that it existed, but not that it was common; the object or action may have been unique, or restricted to a very small circle; poets and novelists are fond of taking their models from an exceptional world.

(4) The facts yielded by this method are not localised in space or time; the author may have taken them from a time or country not his own.

All these restrictions may be summarised as follows: before drawing any inference from a work of literature as to the state of the society in which the author lived, we should ask ourselves what would be the worth of a similar inference as to contemporary manners drawn from a modern novel.

With the facts yielded by conceptions we may join those indifferent facts of an obvious and elementary character which the author has stated almost without thinking. Logically we have no right to call them certain, for we do sometimes meet with men who make mistakes about obvious and elementary facts, and others who lie even on indifferent matters. But such cases are so rare that there is not much danger in admitting as certain facts of this kind which are supported by a single document, and this is how we deal, in practice, with periods of which little is known. The institutions of the Gauls and Germans are described from the unique texts of Cæsar and Tacitus. Facts so easy to discover are forced upon the authors of descriptions much as realities are forced upon poets.

II. On the other hand, a statement in a document as to an objective fact is never enough to establish that fact. The chances of falsehood or error are so many, the conditions which gave rise to the statement are so little known, that we cannot be sure that none of these chances has taken effect. The critical examination provides no definitive solution; it is indispensable if we are to avoid error, but it is insufficient to conduct us to truth.

Criticism can *prove* no fact; it only yields probabilities. Its end and result is to decompose documents into statements, each labelled with an estimate of its value—worthless statement, statement open to suspicion (strong or weak), statement probably (or, very probably) true, statement of unknown value.

Of all these different kinds of results one only is definitive—*the statement of an author who can have had no information on the fact he states is null and void;*

it is to be rejected as we reject an apocryphal document.[1] But criticism here merely destroys illusory sources of information; it supplies nothing certain to take their place. The only sure results of criticism are *negative.* All the positive results are subject to doubt; they reduce to propositions of the form: "There are chances for or against the truth of such and such a statement." Chances only. A statement open to suspicion may turn out to be true; a statement whose truth is probable may, after all, be false. Instances occur continually, and we are never sufficiently well acquainted with the conditions under which the observation was made to *know* whether it was made ill or well.

In order to obtain a definitive result we require a final operation. After passing through the ordeal of criticism, statements present themselves as probable or improbable. But even the most probable of them, taken by themselves, remain mere probabilities: to pass from them to categorical propositions in scientific form is a step we have no right to take; a proposition in a science is an assertion not open to debate, and that is what the statements we have before us are not. It is a principle common to all sciences of observation not to base a scientific conclusion on a single observation; the fact must have been corroborated by several independent observations before it is affirmed categorically. History,

[1] Most historians refrain from rejecting a legend till its falsity has been proved, and if by chance no document has been preserved to contradict it, they adopt it provisionally. This is how the first five centuries of Rome are still dealt with. This method, unfortunately still too general, helps to prevent history from being established as a science.

with its imperfect modes of acquiring information, has less right than any other science to claim exemption from this principle. An historical statement is, in the most favourable case, but an indifferently made observation, and needs other observations to corroborate it.

It is by combining observations that every science is built up: a scientific fact is a centre on which several different observations converge.[1] Each observation is subject to chances of error which cannot be entirely eliminated; but if several observations agree, this can hardly be in virtue of a common error: the more probable explanation of the agreement is that the observers have all seen the same reality and have all described it correctly. Errors are personal and tend to diverge; it is the correct observations that agree.

Applied to history, this principle leads to a last series of operations, intermediate between purely analytical criticism and the synthetic operations—the comparison of statements.

We begin by classifying the results yielded by critical analysis in such a way as to bring together those statements which relate to the same fact. The operation is facilitated mechanically by the method of slips. Either each statement has been entered on a separate slip, or else a single slip has been assigned for each fact, and the different statements relating to it entered upon the slip as met with in

[1] For the logical justification of this principle in history see C. Seignobos, *Revue Philosophique*, July–August 1887. Complete scientific certitude is only produced by an agreement between observations made on different *methods*; it is to be found at the junction of two different paths of research.

the course of reading. By bringing the statements together we learn the extent of our information on the fact; the definitive conclusion depends on the relation between the statements. We have, then, to study separately the different cases which may occur.

I. Most frequently, except in contemporary history, the documents only supply a single statement on a given fact. In such a case all the other sciences follow an invariable rule: an isolated observation is not admitted into science; it is quoted (with the observer's name), but no conclusions are drawn from it. Historians have no avowable motive for proceeding otherwise. When a fact is supported by no more than the statement of a single man, however honest he may be, historians ought not to assert it, but to do as men of science do—give the reference (Thucydides states, Cæsar says that . . .); this is all they have a right to affirm. In reality they all retain the habit of stating facts, as was done in the middle ages, on the *authority* of Thucydides or of Cæsar; many are simple enough to do so in express terms. Thus, allowing themselves to be guided by natural credulity, unchecked by science, historians end by admitting, on the insufficient presumption afforded by a unique document, any statement which does not happen to be contradicted by another document. Hence the absurd consequence that history is more positive, and seems better established in regard to those little known periods which are represented by a single writer than in regard to facts known from thousands of documents which contradict each other. The wars of the Medes known to Herodotus alone, the adventures of Fredegonda related by none but Gregory of Tours, are less subject to discussion than the events of the French Revolution, which have been described by hundreds of contemporaries. This is a discreditable state of things which cannot be ended except by a revolution in the minds of historians.

IV. When we have several statements relating to the same fact, they may contradict each other or they may agree. In order to be certain that they really do contradict each other, we have to make sure that they do actually relate to the same fact. Two apparently contradictory statements may be merely parallel; they may not relate exactly to the same moment, the same place, the same persons, the same episodes of an event, and they may be both correct.[1] We must not, however, infer that they confirm each other; each comes under the category of unique statements.

If the contradiction is real, at least one of the statements is false. In such cases it is a natural tendency to seek to reconcile them by a compromise—to split the difference. This peace-making spirit is the reverse of scientific. A says two and two make four; B says they make five. We are not to conclude that two and two make four and a half; we must examine and see which is right. This examination is the work of criticism. Of two contradictory statements, it nearly always happens that one is open to suspicion; this should be rejected if the competing statement has been judged very probably true. If both are open to suspicion,

[1] This case is studied and a good example given by Bernheim, *Lehrbuch*, p. 421.

we abstain from drawing any conclusion. We do the same if several statements open to suspicion agree together as against a single statement which is not suspected.[1]

V. When several statements agree, it is still necessary to resist the natural tendency to believe that the fact has been demonstrated. The first impulse is to count each document as one source of information. We are well aware in matters of everyday life that men are apt to copy each other, that a single narrative often serves the turn of several narrators, that several newspapers sometimes happen to publish the same correspondence, that several reporters sometimes agree to let one of their number do the work for all. We have, in such a case, several documents, several statements—have we the same number of observations? Obviously not. When one statement reproduces another, it does not constitute a new observation, and even if an observation were to be reproduced by a hundred different authors, these hundred copies would amount to no more than one observation. To count them as a hundred would be the same thing as to count a hundred printed copies of the same book as a hundred different documents. But the respect paid to "historical documents" is sometimes stronger than obvious truth. The same statement occurring in several different documents by different authors has an illu-

[1] It is hardly necessary to enter a caution against the childish method of counting the documents on each side of a question and deciding by the majority. The statement of a single author who was acquainted with a fact is evidently worth more than a hundred statements made by persons who knew nothing about it. The rule has been formulated long ago: *Ne numerentur, sed ponderentur.*

sory appearance of multiplicity; an identical fact related in ten different documents at once gives the impression of being established by ten agreeing observations. This impression is to be distrusted. An agreement is only conclusive when the agreeing statements represent *observations* which are independent of each other. Before we draw any conclusion from an agreement we must examine whether it is an agreement between *independent* observations. Two operations are thus required.

(1) We begin by inquiring whether the statements are independent, or are reproductions of one and the same observation. This inquiry is partly the work of that part of external criticism which deals with the investigation of sources;[1] but that investigation only touches the relations between written documents, and stops short when it has determined which passages of an author are borrowed from other authors. Borrowed passages are to be rejected without discussion. But the same work remains to be done in reference to statements which were not committed to writing. We have to compare the statements which relate to the same fact, in order to find out whether they proceeded originally from different observers, or at least from different observations.

The principle is analogous to that employed in the investigation of sources. The details of a social fact are so manifold, and there are so many different ways of looking at the same fact, that two independent observers cannot possibly give completely coincident accounts; if two statements present the

[1] Cf. *supra*, p. 94.

same details in the same order, they must be derived from a common observation; different observations are bound to diverge somewhere. We may often apply an *a priori* principle: if the fact was of such a nature that it could only be observed or reported by a single observer, then all the accounts of it must be derived from a single observation. These principles[1] enable us to recognise many cases of different observations, and still more numerous cases of observations being reproduced.

There remains a great number of doubtful cases. The natural tendency is to treat them as if they were cases of independent observation. But the scientific procedure would be the exact reverse of this: as long as the statements are not proved to be independent we have no right to assume that their agreement is conclusive.

It is only after we have determined the relations between the different statements that we can begin to count them and examine into their agreement. Here again we have to distrust the first impulse; the kind of agreement which is really conclusive is not, as one would naturally imagine, a perfect similarity between two narratives, but an occasional coincidence between two narratives which only partially resemble each other. The natural tendency is to think that the closer the agreement is, the greater is its demonstrative power; we ought, on the contrary, to adopt as a rule the paradox that

[1] It is hardly possible to study here the special difficulties which arise in the application of these principles, as when the author, wishing to conceal his indebtedness, has introduced deviations in order to put his readers off the scent, or when the author has combined statements taken from different documents.

an agreement proves more when it is confined to a small number of circumstances. It is at such points of coincidence between diverging statements that we are to look for scientifically established historical facts.

(2) Before drawing any conclusions it remains to make sure whether the *different* observations of the same fact are entirely *independent;* for it is possible that one may have influenced another to such a degree that their agreement is inconclusive. We have to guard against the following cases:—

(*a*) The different observations have been made by the same author, who has recorded them either in the same or in different documents; special reasons must then be had before it can be assumed that the author really made the observation afresh, and did not content himself with merely repeating a single observation.

(*b*) There were several observers, but they commissioned one of their number to write a single document. We have to ascertain whether the document merely gives the statements of the writer, or whether the other observers checked his work.

(*c*) Several observers recorded their observations in different documents, but under similar conditions. We must apply the list of critical questions in order to ascertain whether they were not all subject to the same influences, predisposing to falsehood or error; whether, for example, they had a common interest, a common vanity, or common prejudices.

The only observations which are certainly independent are those which are contained in different documents, written by different authors, who belonged to different groups, and worked under different conditions. Cases of perfectly conclusive agreement are thus rare, except in reference to modern periods.

The possibility of proving an historical fact depends on the number of independent documents relating to it which have been preserved, and the preservation of the documents is a matter of chance; this explains the share which chance has in the formation of historical science.

The facts which it is possible to establish are chiefly those which cover a large extent of space or time (sometimes called *general* facts), customs, doctrines, institutions, great events; they were easier to observe than the others, and are now easier to prove. Historical method is not, however, essentially powerless to establish facts of short duration and limited extent (those which are called *particular facts*), such as a saying, a momentary act. It is enough that several persons should have been present when the fact occurred, that they should have recorded it, and that their writings should have come down to us. We know what were the words which Luther uttered at the Diet of Worms; we know that he did not say what tradition puts in his mouth. This concurrence of favourable conditions becomes more and more frequent with the organisation of newspapers, of shorthand writers, and of depositories of documents.

In the case of antiquity and the middle ages historical knowledge is limited to general facts by the scarcity of documents. In dealing with contemporary history it is possible to include more and more particular facts. The general public supposes the opposite of this; it is suspicious about contemporary facts, with reference to which it sees contradictory narratives circulating, and believes without hesitation ancient facts, which it does not see contradicted anywhere. Its confidence is at its greatest in respect of that history which we have not the means of knowing, and its scepticism increases with the means of knowledge.

VI. *Agreement between documents* leads to conclusions which are not all of them definitive. In order to complete and rectify our conclusions we have still to study *the harmony of the facts.*

Several facts which, taken in isolation, are only imperfectly proved, may confirm each other in such a manner as to produce a collective certainty. The facts which the documents present in isolation have sometimes been in reality sufficiently near each other to be connected. Of this kind are the successive actions of the same man or of the same group of men, the habits of the same group at different epochs separated by short intervals, or of similar groups at the same epoch. It is no doubt possible that one of several analogous facts may be true and another false; the certainty of the first does not justify the categorical assertion of the second. But yet the harmony of several such facts, each proved imperfectly, yields a kind of certainty; the facts do not, in the strict sense of the word, prove, but they *confirm* [1] each other. The doubt which attached to each one of them disappears; we obtain that species

[1] Here we merely indicate the principle of the method of confirmation; its applications would require a very lengthy study.

of certainty which is produced by the interconnection of facts. Thus the comparison of conclusions which are separately doubtful yields a whole which is morally certain. In an itinerary of a sovereign, the days and the places confirm each other when they harmonise so as to form a coherent whole. An institution or a popular usage is established by the harmony of accounts, each of which is no more than probable, relating to different times and places.

This method is a difficult one to apply. The notion of harmony is a much vaguer one than that of agreement. We cannot assign any precise general rules for distinguishing facts which are sufficiently connected to form a whole, the harmony of whose parts would be conclusive; nor can we determine beforehand the duration and extent of that which may be taken to form a whole. Facts separated by half a century of time and a hundred leagues of space may confirm each other in such a way as to establish a popular usage (for example, among the ancient Germans); but they would prove nothing if they were taken from a heterogeneous society subject to rapid evolution (take, for example, French society in 1750, and again in 1800, in Alsace and in Provence). Here we have to study the relation between the facts. This brings us to the beginnings of historical construction; here is the transition from analytical to synthetic operations.

VII. But it remains to consider cases of discordance between facts established by documents and other facts established by other methods. It happens sometimes that a fact obtained as an historical conclusion is in contradiction with a body of known historical facts, or with the sum of our knowledge of humanity founded on direct observation, or with a scientific law established by the regular method of an established science. In the first two cases the fact is only in conflict with history, psychology, or sociology, all imperfectly established sciences; we then simply call the fact *improbable.* If it is in conflict with a true science it becomes a *miracle.* What are we to do with an improbable or miraculous fact? Are we to admit it after examination of the documents, or are we to pass on and shelve the question?

Improbability is not a scientific notion; it varies with the individual. Each person finds improbable what he is not accustomed to see: a peasant would think the telephone much more improbable than a ghost; a king of Siam refused to believe in the existence of ice. It is important to know who precisely it is to whom the fact appears to be improbable. Is it to the mass who have no scientific culture? For these, science is more improbable than miracle, physiology than spiritualism; their notions of improbability are worthless. Is it to the man who possesses scientific culture? If so, we have to deal with that which seems improbable to a scientific mind, and it would be more accurate to say that the fact is contrary to the results of science—that there is disagreement between the direct observations of men of science and the indirect testimony of the documents.

How is this conflict to be decided? The question has no great practical interest; nearly all the documents which relate miraculous facts are already open to suspicion on other grounds, and would be discarded by a sound criticism. But the question of miracles has raised such passions that it may be well to indicate how it affects the historian.[1]

The general tendency to believe in the marvellous has filled with miraculous facts the documents of nearly every people. Historically the existence of the devil is much better proved than that of Pisistratus: there has not been preserved a single word of a contemporary of Pisistratus saying that he has seen him; thousands of "ocular witnesses" declare they have seen the devil; few historical facts have been established by so great a number of independent testimonies. However, we do not hesitate to reject the devil and to accept Pisistratus. For the existence of the devil would be irreconcilable with the laws of all the established sciences.

For the historian the solution of the problem is obvious.[2] The observations whose results are contained in historical documents are never of equal value with those of contemporary scientists; we have already shown why. The indirect method of history is always inferior to the direct methods of the sciences of observation. If its results do not harmonise with

[1] Père de Smedt has devoted to this question a part of his *Principes de la critique histoire* (Paris, 1887, 12mo).

[2] The solution of the question is different in the case of the sciences of direct observation, especially the biological sciences. Science knows nothing of the possible and the impossible; it only recognises facts which have been correctly or incorrectly observed: facts which had been declared impossible, as the existence of aerolites, have been discovered to be genuine. The very notion of a miracle is metaphysical; it implies a conception of the universe as a whole which transcends the limits of observation. (See Wallace, "Miracles and Modern Spiritualism.")

theirs, it is history which must give way; historical science, with its imperfect means of information, cannot claim to check, contradict, or correct the results of other sciences, but must rather use their results to correct its own. The progress of the direct sciences sometimes modifies the results of historical interpretation; a fact established by direct observation aids in the comprehension and criticism of documents. Cases of stigmata and nervous anæsthesia which have been scientifically observed have led to the admission as true of historical narratives of analogous facts, as in the case of the stigmata of certain saints and the possessed nuns of Loudun. But history cannot aid the progress of the direct sciences. It is kept at a distance from reality by its indirect means of information, and must accept the laws that are established by those sciences which come into immediate contact with reality. In order to reject one of these laws new direct observations are necessary. Such revolutions are possible, but they must be brought about from within. History has no power to take the initiative in them.

The solution is not so clear in the case of facts which do not harmonise with a body of historical knowledge or with the sciences, still in the embryonic stage, which deal with man. It depends on the opinion we form as to the value of such knowledge. We can at least lay down the practical rule that in order to contradict history, psychology, or sociology, we must have very strong documents, and this is a case which hardly ever occurs.

BOOK III

SYNTHETIC OPERATIONS

BOOK III

SYNTHETIC OPERATIONS

CHAPTER I

GENERAL CONDITIONS OF HISTORICAL CONSTRUCTION

THE criticism of documents only yields isolated facts. In order to organise them into a body of science it is necessary to perform a series of synthetic operations. The study of these processes of historical construction forms the second half of Methodology.

The mode of construction cannot be regulated by the ideal plan of the science we desire to construct; it depends on the materials we have at our disposal. It would be chimerical to formulate a scheme which the materials would not allow us to carry out; it would be like proposing to construct an Eiffel tower with building-stones. The fundamental defect of philosophies of history is that they forget this practical necessity.

I. Let us begin by considering the materials of history. What is their form and their nature? How do they differ from the materials of other sciences?

Historical facts are derived from the critical analysis of documents. They issue from this process in the form to which analysis has reduced them, chopped small into individual statements; for a single sentence contains several statements: we have often accepted some and rejected others; each of these statements represents a fact.

Historical facts have the common characteristic of having been taken from documents; but they differ greatly among themselves.

(1) They represent phenomena of very different nature. From the same document we derive facts bearing on handwriting, language, style, doctrines, customs, events. The Mesha inscription furnishes facts bearing on Moabite handwriting and language, the belief in the god Chemosh, the practices belonging to his cult, the war between the Moabites and Israel. Thus the facts reach us pell-mell, without distinction of nature. This mixture of heterogeneous facts is one of the characteristics which differentiate history from the other sciences. The sciences of direct observation choose the facts to be studied, and systematically limit themselves to the observation of facts of a single species. The documentary sciences receive the facts, already observed, at the hands of authors of documents, who supply them in disorder. For the purpose of remedying this disorder it is necessary to sort the facts and group them by species. But, for the purpose of sorting them, it is necessary to know precisely what it is that constitutes a *species* of historical facts; in order to group them we need a principle of classification applicable to them. But on these two questions of capital importance historians have not as yet succeeded in formulating precise rules.

(2) Historical facts present themselves in very

different degrees of generality, from the highly general facts which apply to a whole people and which lasted for centuries (institutions, customs, beliefs), down to the most transient actions of a single man (a word, a movement). Here again history differs from the sciences of direct observation, which regularly start from particular facts and labour methodically to condense them into general facts. In order to form groups the facts must be reduced to a common degree of generality, which makes it necessary to inquire to what degree of generality we can and ought to reduce the different species of facts. And this is what historians do not agree about among themselves.

(3) Historical facts are localised; each belongs to a given time and a given country. If we suppress the time and place to which they belong, they lose their historical character; they now contribute only to the knowledge of universal humanity, as is the case with facts of folk-lore whose origin is unknown. This necessity of localisation is also foreign to the general sciences; it is confined to the descriptive sciences, which deal with the geographical distribution and with the evolution of phenomena. It obliges the historian to study separately the facts belonging to different countries and different epochs.

(4) The facts which have been extracted from documents by critical analysis present themselves accompanied by a critical estimate of their probability.[1] In every case where we have not reached complete certainty, whenever the fact is merely probable—still more when it is open to suspicion—

[1] See above, p. 194.

criticism supplies the fact to the historian accompanied by a label which he has no right to remove, and which prevents the fact from being definitively admitted into the science. Even those facts which, after comparison with others, end by being established, are subject to temporary exclusion, like the clinical cases which accumulate in the medical reviews before they are considered sufficiently proved to be received as scientific facts.

Historical construction has thus to be performed with an incoherent mass of minute facts, with detail-knowledge reduced as it were to a powder. It must utilise a heterogeneous medley of materials, relating to different subjects and places, differing in their degree of generality and certainty. No method of classifying them is provided by the practice of historians; history, which began by being a form of literature, has remained the least methodical of the sciences.

II. In every science the next step after observing the facts is to formulate a series of questions according to some methodical system;[1] every science is composed of the answers to such a series of questions. In all the sciences of direct observation, even if the questions to be answered have not been put down in advance, the facts which are observed suggest questions, and require them to be formulated precisely. But historians have no discipline of this kind; many of them are accustomed to imitate artists, and do not even think of asking themselves what they are looking for. They take from their

[1] In the experimental sciences an hypothesis is a form of question accompanied by a provisional answer.

documents those parts which strike them, often for purely personal reasons, and reproduce them, changing the language and adding any miscellaneous reflections which come into their minds.

If history is not to be lost in the confusion of its materials, it must be made a rule to proceed here, as in the other sciences, by way of question and answer.[1] But how are the questions to be chosen in a science so different from the others? This is the fundamental problem of method. The only way to solve it is to begin by determining the essential characteristic of historical facts by which they are differentiated from the facts of the other sciences.

The sciences of direct observation deal with *realities*, taken in their entirety. The science which borders most closely on history in respect of its subject-matter, descriptive zoology, proceeds by the examination of a real and complete animal. This animal is first observed, as a whole, by actual vision; it is then dissected into its parts; this dissection is *analysis* in the original sense of the word (*ἀναλύειν*, to break up into parts). It is then possible to put the parts together again in such a way as to exhibit the structure of the whole; this is *real* synthesis. It is possible to watch the *real* movements which are the functions of the organs in such a way as to observe the mutual actions and reactions of the different parts of the organism. It is possible to

[1] Fustel de Coulanges saw the necessity of this. In the preface to his *Recherches sur quelques problèmes d'histoire* (Paris, 1885, 8vo) he announces his intention of presenting his researches "in the form which all my works have, that is, in the form of questions which I ask myself, and on which I endeavour to throw light."

compare *real* wholes and see what are the parts in which they resemble each other, so as to be able to classify them according to real points of resemblance. The science is a body of objective knowledge founded on *real* analysis, synthesis, and comparison; actual sight of the things studied guides the scientific researcher and dictates the questions he is to ask himself.

In history there is nothing like this. One is apt to say that history is the "vision" of past events, and that it proceeds by "analysis": these are two metaphors, dangerous if we suffer ourselves to be misled by them.[1] In history we see nothing real except paper with writing on it—and sometimes monuments or the products of art or industry. The historian has nothing before him which he can analyse physically, nothing which he can destroy and reconstruct. "Historical analysis" is no more real than is the vision of historical facts; it is an abstract process, a purely intellectual operation. The analysis of a document consists in a *mental* search for the items of information it contains, with the object of criticising them one by one. The analysis of a fact consists in the process of distinguishing *mentally* between its different details (the various episodes of an event, the characteristics of

[1] Fustel de Coulanges himself seems to have been misled by them: "History is a science; it does not imagine, it only sees" (*Monarchie franque*, p. 1). "History, like every science, consists in a process of discerning facts, analysing them, comparing them, and noting their connections. . . . The historian . . . seeks facts and attains them by the minute observation of texts, as the chemist finds his in the course of experiments conducted with minute precision" (Ibid., p. 39).

an institution), with the object of paying special attention to each detail in turn; that is what is called examining the different "aspects" of a fact,—another metaphor. The human mind is vague by nature, and spontaneously revives only vague collective impressions; to impart clearness to these it is necessary to ask what individual impressions go to form a given collective impression, in order that precision may be attained by a successive consideration of them. This is an indispensable operation, but we must not exaggerate its scope. It is not an objective method which yields a knowledge of real objects; it is only a subjective method which aims at detecting those abstract elements which compose our impressions.[1] From the very nature of its materials history is necessarily a subjective science. It would be illegitimate to extend to this intellectual analysis of subjective impressions the rules which govern the real analysis of real objects.

History, then, must guard against the temptation to imitate the method of the biological sciences. Historical facts are so different from the facts of the other sciences that their study requires a different method.

III. Documents, the sole source of historical knowledge, give information on three categories of facts:

(1) Living beings and material objects. Documents make us acquainted with the existence of human beings, physical conditions, products of art and industry. In all these cases physical facts

[1] The subjective character of history has been brought out into strong relief by the philosopher G. Simmel, *Die Probleme der Geschichtsphilosophie* (Leipzig, 1892, 8vo).

have been brought before the author by physical perception. But we have before us nothing but intellectual phenomena, facts seen "through the author's imagination," or, to speak accurately, mental images representative of the author's impressions—images which we form on the *analogy* of the images which were in his mind. The Temple at Jerusalem was a material object which men saw, but we cannot see it now; all we can now do is to form a mental image of it, analogous to that which existed in the minds of those who saw and described it.

(2) Actions of men. Documents relate the actions (and words) of men of former times. Here, too, are physical facts which were known to the authors by sight and hearing, but which are now for us no more than the author's recollections, subjective images which are reproduced in our minds. When Cæsar was stabbed the dagger-thrusts were seen, the words of the murderers were heard; we have nothing but mental images. Actions and words all have this characteristic, that each was the action or the word of an individual; the imagination can only represent to itself *individual* acts, copied from those which are brought before us by direct physical observation. As these are the actions of men living in a society, most of them are performed simultaneously by several individuals, or are directed to some common end. These are collective acts; but, in the imagination as in direct observation, they always reduce to a sum of individual actions. The "social fact," as recognised by certain sociologists, is a philosophical construction, not an historical fact.

(3) Motives and conceptions. Human actions do not contain their own cause within themselves; they have *motives.* This vague word denotes both the stimulus which occasions the performance of an action, and the *representation* of the action which is in the mind of a man at the moment when he performs it. We can imagine motives only as existing in a man's mind, and in the form of vague interior representations, analogous to those which we have of our own inward states; we can express them only by words, generally metaphorical. Here we have *psychic* facts, generally called feelings and ideas. Documents exhibit three kinds of such facts: (*a*) motives and conceptions in the authors' minds and expressed by them; (*b*) motives and ideas attributed by the authors to contemporaries of theirs whose actions they have seen; (*c*) motives which we ourselves may suppose to have influenced the actions related in the documents, and which we represent to ourselves on the model of our own motives.

Physical facts, human actions (both individual and collective), psychic facts—these form the objects of historical knowledge; they are none of them observed directly, they are all *imagined.* Historians—nearly all of them unconsciously and under the impression that they are observing realities—are occupied solely with images.

IV. How, then, is it possible to imagine facts without their being wholly imaginary? The facts, as they exist in the historian's mind, are necessarily subjective; that is one of the reasons given for refusing to recognise history as a science. But subjective is not a synonym of unreal. A recollection is only an image; but it is not therefore a chimera, it is the representation of a vanished reality. It is true that the historian who works with documents has no personal recollections of which he can make direct use; but he forms mental images on the model of his own recollections. He assumes that realities (objects, actions, motives), which have now disappeared, but were formerly observed by the authors of the documents, resembled the realities of his own day which he has himself seen and which he retains in his memory. This is the postulate of all the documentary sciences. If former humanity did not resemble the humanity of to-day, documents would be unintelligible. Starting from this assumed resemblance, the historian forms a mental representation of the bygone facts of history similar to his own recollection of the facts he has witnessed.

This operation, which is performed unconsciously, is one of the principal sources of error in history. The things of the past which are to be pictured in imagination were not wholly similar to the things of the present which we have seen; we have never seen a man like Cæsar or Clovis, and we have never experienced the same mental states as they. In the established sciences it is equally true that one man will work on facts which another has observed, and which he must therefore represent to himself by analogy; but these facts are defined by precise terms which indicate what invariable elements ought to appear in the image. Even in physiology the notions which occur are sufficiently clear and fixed for the same word to evoke in the minds of all naturalists similar images of an organ or a movement. The reason is that each notion which has a name has been formed by a method of observation and abstraction in the course of which all the characteristics which belong to the notion have been precisely determined and described.

But in proportion as a body of knowledge is more nearly concerned with the invisible facts of the mind, its notions become more confused and its language less precise. Even the most ordinary facts of human life, social conditions, actions, motives, feelings, can only be expressed by vague terms (*king*, *warrior*, *to fight*, *to elect*). In the case of more complex phenomena, language is so indefinite that there is no agreement even as to the essential elements of the phenomena. What are we to understand by a tribe, an army, an industry, a market, a revolution? Here history shares the vagueness common to all the sciences of humanity, psychological or social. But its indirect method of representation by mental images renders this vagueness still more dangerous. The historical images in our minds ought, then, to reproduce at least the essential features of the images which were in the minds of the direct observers of past facts; but the terms in which they expressed their mental images never tell us exactly what these essential elements were.

Facts which we did not see, described in language which does not permit us to represent them in our minds with exactness, form the data of history. The historian, however, is obliged to picture the facts in his imagination, and he should make it his constant endeavour to construct his mental images out of none but correct elements, so that he may imagine the facts as he would have seen them if he had been able to observe them personally.[1] But the formation of a mental image requires more elements than the documents supply. Let any one endeavour to form a mental representation of a battle or a ceremony out of the data of a narrative, however detailed; he will see how many features he is compelled to add. This necessity becomes physically perceptible in attempts to restore monuments in accordance with descriptions (for example, the Temple at Jerusalem), in pictures which claim to be representations of historical scenes, in the drawings of illustrated newspapers.

Every historical image contains a large part of fancy. The historian cannot get rid of it, but he can take stock of the real elements which enter into his images and confine his constructions to these; they are the elements which he has derived from the documents. If, in order to understand the battle between Cæsar and Ariovistus, he finds it necessary to make a mental picture of the two opposing armies, he will be careful to draw no conclusions from the general aspect under which he imagines them; he will base his reasonings exclusively on the real details furnished by the documents.

V. The problem of historical method may be finally stated as follows. Out of the different elements we find in documents we form mental images. Some of these, relating entirely to physical

[1] This has been eloquently put by Carlyle and Michelet. It is also the substance of the famous expression of Ranke: "I wish to state how that really was" (*wie es eigentlich gewesen*).

objects, are furnished to us by illustrative monuments, and they directly represent some of the physical aspects of the things of the past. Most of them, however, including all the images we form of psychic facts, are constructed on the model either of ancient representations, or, more frequently, of the facts we have observed in our own experience. Now, the things of the past were only partially similar to the things of the present, and it is precisely the points of difference which make history interesting. How are we to represent to ourselves these elements of difference for which we have no model? We have never seen a company of men resembling the Frankish warriors, and we have never personally experienced the feelings which Clovis had when setting out to fight against the Visigoths. How are we to make our imagination of facts of this kind harmonise with the reality?

Practically, what happens is as follows. Immediately on the reading of a sentence in a document an image is formed in our minds by a spontaneous operation beyond our control. This image is based on a superficial analogy, and is, as a rule, grossly inaccurate. Any one who searches his memory may recall the absurd manner in which he first represented to himself the persons and scenes of the past. It is the task of history to rectify these images gradually, by eliminating the false elements one by one, and replacing them by true ones. We have seen red-haired people, bucklers, and Frankish battle-axes (or at least drawings of these objects); we bring these elements together, in order to correct our first mental image of the Frankish warriors. The historical image thus ends by becoming a combination of features borrowed from different experiences.

It is not enough to represent to oneself isolated persons, objects, and actions. Men and their actions form part of a whole, of a society and of a process of evolution. It is, therefore, further necessary to represent to oneself the relations between different men and different actions (nations, governments, laws, wars).

But in order to imagine relations it is necessary to have a conception of collectivities or wholes, and the documents only give isolated elements. Here again the historian is obliged to use a subjective method. He imagines a society or a process of evolution, and in this imaginary framework he disposes the elements furnished by the documents. Thus, whereas biological classification is guided by the objective observation of physical units, historical classification can only be effected upon subjective units existing in the imagination.

The realities of the past are things which we do not observe, and which we can only know in virtue of their resemblance to the realities of the present. In order to realise the conditions under which past events happened, we must observe the humanity of to-day, and look for the conditions under which analogous events happen now. History thus becomes an application of the descriptive sciences which deal with humanity, descriptive psychology, sociology or social science; but all these sciences are still but imperfectly established, and their defects retard the establishment of a science of history.

Some of the conditions of human life are, however, so necessary and so obvious that the most superficial observation is enough to establish them. These are the conditions common to all humanity; they have their origin either in the physiological organisation which determines the material needs of men, or in the psychological organisation which determines their habits in matters of conduct. These conditions can therefore be provided for by the use of a set of general questions applicable to all the cases that may occur. It is with historical construction as with historical criticism—the impossibility of direct observation compels the use of prearranged sets of questions.

The human actions which form the subject-matter of history differ from age to age and from country to country, just as men and societies have differed from each other; and, indeed, it is the special aim of history to study these differences. If men had always had the same form of government or spoken the same language, there would be no occasion to write the history of forms of government or the history of languages. But these differences are comprised within limits imposed by the general conditions of human life; they are but varieties of certain modes of being and doing which are common to the whole of humanity, or at least to the great majority of men. We cannot know *a priori* what was the mode of government or the language of an historical people; it is the business of history to tell us. But that a given people had a language and had a form of government is something which we are entitled to assume, before examination, in every possible case.

By drawing up the list of the fundamental phenomena which we may expect to find in the life of every individual and every people, we shall have suggested to us a set of general questions which will be summary, but still sufficient to enable us to arrange the bulk of historical facts in a certain number of natural groups, each of which will form a special branch of history. This scheme of general classification will supply the scaffolding of historical construction.

The set of general questions will only apply to phenomena of constant occurrence: it cannot anticipate the thousands of local or accidental events which enter into the life of an individual or a nation; it will, therefore, not contain all the questions which the historian must answer before he can give a complete picture of the past. The detailed study of the facts will require the use of lists of questions entering more into detail, and differing according to the nature of the events, the men, or the societies studied. In order to frame these lists, we begin by setting down those questions or matters of detail which are suggested by the mere reading of the documents; but for the purpose of arranging these questions, often indeed for the purpose of making the list complete, recourse must be had to the systematic *a priori* method. Among the classes of facts, the persons, and the societies with which we are well acquainted (either from direct observation or from history), we look for those which resemble the facts, the persons, or the societies which we wish to study. By analysing the scheme of arrangement used in the scientific treatment of these familiar cases we shall learn what questions ought to be asked in reference to the analogous cases which we propose to investigate. Of course the model must be chosen intelligently; we must not apply to a barbarous society a list of questions framed on the study of a civilised nation, and ask with regard to a feudal domain what agents corresponded to each of our ministers of state—as Boutaric did in his study of the administration of Alphonse of Poitiers.

This method of drawing up lists of questions which bases all historical construction on an *a priori* procedure, would be objectionable if history really were a science of observation; and perhaps some will think it compares very unfavourably with the *a posteriori* methods of the natural sciences. But its justification is simple: it is the only method which it is possible to employ, and the only method which, as a matter of fact, ever has been employed. The moment an historian attempts to put in order the facts contained in documents, he constructs out of the knowledge he has (or thinks he has) of human affairs a scheme of arrangement which is the equivalent of a list of questions—unless, perhaps, he adopts a scheme which one of his predecessors has constructed in a similar manner. But when this work has been performed unconsciously, the scheme of arrangement remains incomplete and confused. Thus it is not a case of deciding whether to work with or without an *a priori* set of questions—we must work with such a set in any case—the choice merely lies between the unconscious use of an incomplete and confused set of questions and the conscious use of a precise and complete set.

VI. We can now sketch the plan of historical construction in a way which will determine the series of synthetic operations necessary to raise the edifice.

The critical analysis of the documents has supplied the materials—historical facts still in a state of dispersion. We begin by *imagining* these facts on the model of what we suppose to be the analogous facts of the present; by combining elements taken from reality at different points, we endeavour to form a mental image which shall resemble as nearly as possible that which would have been produced by direct observation of the past event. This is the first operation, inseparable in practice from the reading of the documents. Considering that it will be enough to have indicated its nature here,[1] we have refrained from devoting a special chapter to it.

The facts having been thus imagined, we *group* them according to schemes of classification devised on the model of a body of facts which we have observed directly, and which we suppose analogous to the body of past facts under consideration. This is the second operation; it is performed by the aid of systematic questions, and its result is to divide the mass of historical facts into homogeneous portions which we afterwards form into groups until the entire history of the past has been systematically arranged according to a general scheme.

When we have arranged in this scheme the facts taken from the documents, there remain gaps whose extent is always considerable, and is enormous for those parts of history in regard to which documents

[1] Cf. pp. 219–23.

are scanty. We endeavour to fill some of these gaps by *reasoning* based on the facts which are known. This is (or should be) the third operation; it increases the sum of historical knowledge by an application of logic.

We still possess nothing but a mass of facts placed side by side in a scheme of classification. We have to condense them into *formulæ,* in order to deduce their general characteristics and their relation to each other. This is the fourth operation; it leads to the final conclusions of history, and crowns the work of historical construction from the scientific point of view.

But as historical knowledge, which is by nature complex and unwieldy, is exceptionally difficult to communicate, we still have to look for the methods of expounding historical results in appropriate form.

VII. This series of operations, easy to conceive in the mind, has never been more than imperfectly performed. It is beset by material difficulties which theories of methodology do not take into account, but which it would be better to face, with the purpose of discovering whether they are after all insurmountable.

The operations of history are so numerous, from the first discovery of the document to the final formula of the conclusion, they require such minute precautions, so great a variety of natural gifts and acquired habits, that there is no man who can perform *by himself* all the work on any one point. History is less able than any other science to dispense with the division of labour; but there is no other science in which labour is so imperfectly divided. We find specialists in critical scholarship writing general histories in which they let their imagination guide them in the work of construction;[1] and, on the other hand, there are constructive historians who use for their work materials whose value they have not tested.[2] The reason is that the division of labour implies a common understanding among the workers, and in history no such understanding exists. Except in the preparatory operations of external criticism, each worker follows the guidance of his own private inspiration; he is at no pains to work on the same lines as the others, nor does he pay any regard to the whole of which his own work is to form a part. Thus no historian can feel perfectly safe in adopting the results of another's work, as may be done in the established sciences, for he does not know whether these results have been obtained by trustworthy methods. The most scrupulous go so far as to admit nothing until they have done the work on the documents over again for themselves. This was the attitude adopted by Fustel de Coulanges. It is barely possible to satisfy this exacting standard in the case of little-known periods, the documents relating to which are confined to a few volumes; and yet some have gone so far as to maintain the dogma that no historian should ever work at second hand.[3] This, indeed, is what an historian is compelled to do when the documents are too numerous for him

[1] Curtius in his "History of Greece," Mommsen in his "History of Rome" (before the Empire), Lamprecht in his "History of Germany."

[2] It will be enough to mention Augustin Thierry, Michelet, and Carlyle.

[3] See P. Guiraud, *Fustel de Coulanges* (Paris, 1896, 12mo), p. 164, for some very judicious observations on this subject.

to be able to read them all; but he does not say so, to avoid scandal.

It would be better to acknowledge the truth frankly. So complex a science as history, where facts must ordinarily be accumulated by the million before it is possible to formulate conclusions, cannot be built up on this principle of continually beginning afresh. Historical construction is not work that can be done with documents, any more than history can be "written from manuscripts," and for the same reason—the shortness of time. In order that science may advance it is necessary to combine the results of thousands of detail-researches.

But how are we to proceed in view of the fact that most researches have been conducted upon methods which, if not defective, are at least open to suspicion? Universal confidence would lead to error as surely as universal distrust would make progress impossible. One useful rule, at any rate, may be stated, as follows: The works of historians should be read with the same critical precautions which are observed in the reading of documents. A natural instinct impels us to look principally for the conclusions, and to accept them as so much established truth; we ought, on the contrary, to be continually applying analysis, we ought to look for the facts, the *proofs,* the fragments of documents—in short, the materials. We shall be doing the author's work over again, but we shall do it very much faster than he did, for that which takes up time is the collection and combination of the materials; and we shall accept no conclusions but those we consider to have been proved.

CHAPTER II

THE GROUPING OF FACTS

I. THE prime necessity for the historian, when confronted with the chaos of historical facts, is to limit the field of his researches. In the ocean of universal history what facts is he to choose for collection? Secondly, in the mass of facts so chosen he will have to distinguish between different groups and make subdivisions. Lastly, within each of these subdivisions he will have to arrange the facts one by one. Thus all historical construction should begin with the search for a principle to guide in the selection, the grouping, and the arrangement of facts. This principle may be sought either in the external conditions of the facts or in their intrinsic nature.

The simplest and easiest mode of classification is that which is founded on external conditions. Every historical fact belongs to a definite time and a definite place, and relates to a definite man or group of men: a convenient basis is thus afforded for the division and arrangement of facts. We have the history of a period, of a country, of a nation, of a man (biography); the ancient historians and those of the Renaissance used no other type. Within this general scheme the subdivisions are formed on the same principle, and facts are arranged in chronological and geographical order, or according to the groups to which they relate. As to the selection of facts to be arranged in this scheme, for a long time it was made on no fixed principle; historians followed their individual fancy, and chose from among the facts relating to a given period, country, or nation all that they deemed interesting or curious. Livy and Tacitus mingle accounts of floods, epidemics, and the birth of monsters with their narratives of wars and revolutions.

Classification of facts by their intrinsic nature was introduced very late, and has made way but slowly and imperfectly. It took its rise outside the domain of history, in certain branches of study dealing with special human phenomena—language, literature, art, law, political economy, religion; studies which began by being dogmatic, but gradually assumed an historical character. The principle of this mode of classification is to select and group together those facts which relate to the same species of actions; each of these groups becomes the subject-matter of a special branch of history. The totality of facts thus comes to be arranged in compartments which may be constructed *a priori* by the study of the totality of human activities; these correspond to the set of general questions of which we have spoken in the preceding chapter.

In the following table we have attempted to provide a general scheme for the classification[1] of

[1] The classification of M. Lacombe (*De l'histoire considérée comme science*, chap. vi.), founded on the motives of actions and the wants they are intended to satisfy, is very judicious from the philosophical point of view, but does not meet the practical needs of historians; it rests on abstract psychological categories (economic, reproductive, sympathetic, ambitious, &c.), and ends by classing

historical facts, founded on the nature of the *conditions* and of the *manifestations* of activity.

I. MATERIAL CONDITIONS. (1) *Study of the body: A.* Anthropology (ethnology), anatomy, and physiology, anomalies and pathological peculiarities. *B.* Demography (number, sex, age, births, deaths, diseases). (2) *Study of the environment: A.* Natural geographical environment (orographic configuration, climate, water, soil, flora, and fauna). *B.* Artificial environment, forestry (cultivation, buildings, roads, implements, &c.).

II. INTELLECTUAL HABITS (not obligatory). (1) *Language* (vocabulary, syntax, phonetics, semasiology). Handwriting. (2) *Arts: A.* Plastic arts (conditions of production, conceptions, methods, works). *B.* Arts of expression, music, dance, literature. (3) *Sciences* (conditions of production, methods, results). (4) *Philosophy and Morals* (conceptions, precepts, actual practice). (5) *Religion* (beliefs, practices).[1]

III. MATERIAL CUSTOMS (not obligatory). (1) *Material life: A.* Food (materials, modes of preparing, stimulants). *B.* Clothes and personal adornment. *C.* Dwellings and furniture. (2) *Private life: A.* Employment of time (toilette, care of the person, meals). *B.* Social ceremonies (funerals and marriages, festivals, etiquette). *C.* Amusements (modes of exercise and hunting, games and spectacles, social meetings, travelling).

IV. ECONOMIC CUSTOMS. (1) *Production: A.* Agriculture and stock-breeding. *B.* Exploitation of minerals. (2) *Transformation, Transport and industries:*[2] technical processes, division of labour, means of communication. (3) *Commerce:*

together very different species of phenomena (military institutions along with economics).

[1] Ecclesiastical institutions form part of the government; in German manuals of antiquities they are found among institutions, while religion is classed with the arts.

[2] Modes of transport, which are often put under commerce, form a species of industry.

exchange and sale, credit. (4) *Distribution:* system of property, transmission, contracts, profit-sharing.

V. SOCIAL INSTITUTIONS. (1) *The family:* *A.* Constitution, authority, condition of women and children. *B.* Economic organisation.[1] Family property, succession. (2) *Education and instruction* (aim, methods, *personnel*). (3) *Social classes* (principle of division, rules regulating intercourse).

VI. PUBLIC INSTITUTIONS (obligatory). (1) *Political institutions:* *A.* Sovereign (*personnel*, procedure). *B.* Administration, services (war, justice, finance, &c.). *C.* Elected authorities, assemblies, electoral bodies (powers, procedure). (2) *Ecclesiastical institutions* (the same divisions). (3) *International institutions:* *A.* Diplomacy. *B.* War (usages of war and military arts). *C.* Private law and commerce.

This grouping of facts according to their nature is combined with the system of grouping by time and place; we thus obtain chronological, geographical, or national sections in each branch. The history of a species of activity (language, painting, government) subdivides into the history of periods, countries, and nations (history of the ancient Greek language, history of the government of France in the nineteenth century).

The same principles aid in determining the order in which the facts are to be arranged. The necessity of presenting facts one after another obliges us to adopt some methodical rule of succession. We may describe successively either all the facts which relate to a given place, or those which relate to a given country, or all the facts of a given species. All historical matter can be distributed in three different kinds of order: *chronological* order, *geogra-*

[1] Property is an institution of mixed character, being at once economic, social, and political.

phical order, that kind of order which is governed by the nature of actions and is generally called *logical* order. It is impossible to use any of these orders exclusively: in every chronological exposition there necessarily occur geographical or logical cross-divisions, transitions from one country to another, or from one species of facts to a different species, and conversely. But it is always necessary to decide which shall be the main order into which the others enter as subdivisions.

It is a delicate matter to choose between these three orders; our choice will be decided by different reasons according to the subject, and according to the public for whom we are working. That is to say, it will depend on the method of exposition; it would take up too much space to give the theory of it.

II. When we come to the selection of historical facts for classification and arrangement, a question is raised which has been disputed with considerable warmth.

Every human action is by its nature an individual transient phenomenon which is confined to a definite time and a definite place. Strictly speaking, every fact is unique. But every action of a man resembles other actions of the same man, or of other members of the same group, and often to so great a degree that the whole group of actions receives a common name, in which their individuality is lost. These groups of similar actions, which the human mind is irresistibly impelled to form, are called habits, usages, institutions. These are merely constructions of the mind, but they are imposed so forcibly on our intellect that many of them must be recognised and constantly employed; habits are collective facts, possessing extension in time and space. Historical facts may therefore be considered under two different aspects: we may regard either the individual, particular, and transient elements in them, or we may look for what is collective, general, and durable. According to the first conception, history is a continuous narrative of the incidents which have happened among men in the past; according to the second, it is the picture of the successive habits of humanity.

On this subject there has been a contest, especially in Germany, between the partisans of the history of civilisation (*Kulturgeschichte*)[1] and the historians who remain faithful to ancient tradition; in France we have had the struggle between the history of institutions, manners, and ideas, and political history, contemptuously nicknamed "battle-history" by its opponents.

This opposition is explained by the difference between the documents which the workers on either side were accustomed to deal with. The historians, principally occupied with political history, read of individual and transient acts of rulers in which it was difficult to detect any common feature. In the special histories, on the contrary (except that of literature), the documents exhibit none but general facts, a linguistic form, a religious rite, a rule of law; an effort of imagination is required to picture the man who pronounced the word, who performed the rite, or who applied the rule in practice.

[1] For the history and biography of this movement see Bernheim, *Lehrbuch*, pp. 45–55.

There is no need to take sides in this controversy. Historical construction in its completeness implies the study of facts under both aspects. The representation of men's habits of thought, life, and action is obviously an important part of history. And yet, supposing we had brought together all the acts of all individuals for the purpose of extracting what is common to them, there would still remain a residue which we should have no right to reject, for it is the distinctively historical element—the circumstance that a particular action was the action of a given man, or group of men, at a given moment. In a scheme of classification which should only recognise the general facts of political life there would be no place for the victory of Pharsalia or the taking of the Bastille—accidental and transient facts, but without which the history of Roman and French institutions would be unintelligible.

History is thus obliged to combine with the study of general facts the study of certain particular facts. It has a mixed character, fluctuating between a science of generalities and a narrative of adventures. The difficulty of classing this hybrid under one of the categories of human thought has often been expressed by the childish question: Is history a science or an art?

III. The general table given above may be used for the determination of all the species of habits (usages or institutions) of which the history may be written. But before applying this general scheme to the study of any particular group of habits, language, religion, private usages, or political institutions, there is always a preliminary question to be answered: Whose were the habits we are about to study? They were common to a great number of individuals; and a collection of individuals with the same habits is what we call a *group.* The first condition, then, for the study of a habit is the determination of the group which has practised it. At this point we must beware of the first impulse; it leads to a negligence which may ruin the whole of our historical construction.

The natural tendency is to conceive the human group on the model of the zoological species—as a body of men who all resemble each other. We take a group united by a very obvious common characteristic, a nation united by a common official government (Romans, English, French), a people speaking the same language (Greeks, ancient Germans), and we proceed as if all the members of this group resembled each other at every point and had the same usages.

As a matter of fact, no real group, not even a centralised society, is a homogeneous whole. For a great part of human activity—language, art, science, religion, economic interests—the group is constantly fluctuating. What are we to understand by the group of those who speak Greek, the Christian group, the group of modern science? And even those groups to which some precision is given by an official organisation, States and Churches, are but superficial unities composed of heterogeneous elements. The English nation comprises Welsh, Scotch, and Irish; the Catholic Church is composed of adherents scattered over the whole world, and differing in everything but religion. There is no group whose members have the same habits in every respect. The same man is at the same time a member of several groups, and in each group he has companions who differ from those he has in the others. A French Canadian belongs to the British Empire, the Catholic Church, the group of French-speaking people. Thus the different groups overlap each other in a way that makes it impossible to divide humanity into sharply distinct societies existing side by side.

In historical documents we find the contemporary names of groups, many of them resting on mere superficial resemblances. It must be made a rule not to adopt popular notions of this kind without criticising them. We must accurately determine the nature and extent of the group, asking: Of what men was it composed? What bond united them? What habits had they in common? In what species of activity did they differ? Not till after such criticism shall we be able to tell what are the habits in respect of which the group in question may be used as a basis of study. In order to study intellectual habits (language, religion, art, science) we shall not take a political unit, the nation, but the group consisting of those who shared the habit in question. In order to study economic facts we shall choose a group united by a common economic interest; we shall reserve the political group for the study of social and political facts, and we shall discard *race* [1] altogether.

[1] It is no longer necessary to demonstrate the nullity of the notion of *race*. It used to be applied to vague groups, formed by a nation or a language; for race as understood by historians (Greek,

Even in those points in which a group is homogeneous it is not entirely so; it is divided into subgroups, the members of which differ in secondary habits; a language is divided into dialects, a religion into sects, a nation into provinces. Conversely, one group resembles other groups in a way that justifies its being regarded as contiguous with them; in a general classification we may recognise "families" of languages, arts, and peoples. We have, then, to ask: How was a given group subdivided? Of what larger group did it form a part?

It then becomes possible to study methodically a given habit, or even the totality of the habits belonging to a given time and place, by following the table given above. The operation presents no difficulties of method in the case of those species of facts which appear as individual and voluntary habits—language, art, sciences, conceptions, private usages; here it is enough to ascertain in what each habit consisted. It is merely necessary to distinguish carefully between those who originated or maintained habits (artists, the learned, philosophers, introducers of fashions) and the mass who accepted them.

But when we come to social or political habits (what we call institutions), we meet with new conditions which produce an inevitable illusion.

Roman, Germanic, Celtic, Slavonic races) has nothing but the name in common with race in the anthropological sense—that is, a group of men possessing the same hereditary characteristics. It has been reduced to an absurdity by the abuse Taine made of it. A very good criticism of it will be found in Lacombe (ibid., chap. xviii.), and in Robertson ("The Saxon and the Celt," London, 1897, 8vo).

The members of the same social or political group do not merely habitually perform *similar* actions; they influence each other by *reciprocal* actions, they command, coerce, pay each other. Habits here take the form of *relations* between the different members; when they are of old standing, formulated in official rules, imposed by a visible authority, maintained by a special set of persons, they occupy so important a place in life, that, to the persons under their influence, they appear as external realities. The men, too, who specialise in an occupation or a function which becomes the dominating habit of their lives, appear as grouped in distinct categories (classes, corporations, churches, governments); and these categories are taken for real existences, or at least for organs of various functions in a real existence, namely, society. We follow the analogy of an animal's body so far as to describe the "structure" and the "functions" of a society, even its "anatomy" and "physiology." These are pure metaphors. By the structure of a society we mean the rules and the customs by which occupations and enjoyments are distributed among its members; by its functions we mean the habitual actions by which each man enters into relations with the others. It may be convenient to use these terms, but it should be remembered that the underlying reality is composed entirely of habits and customs.

The study of institutions, however, obliges us to ask special questions about persons and their functions. In respect of social and economic institutions we have to ask what was the principle of the division of labour and of the division into classes, what were the professions and classes, how were they recruited, what were the relations between the members of the different professions and classes. In respect of political institutions, which are sanctioned by obligatory rules and a visible authority, two new series of questions arise. (1) Who were the persons invested with authority? When authority is divided we have to study the division of functions, to analyse the *personnel* of government into its different groups (supreme and subordinate, central and local), and to distinguish each of the special bodies. In respect of each class of men concerned in the government we shall ask: How were they recruited? What was their official authority? What were their real powers? (2) What were the official rules? What was their form (custom, orders, law, precedent)? What was their content (rules of law)? What was the mode of application (procedure)? And, above all, how did the rules differ from the practice (abuse of power, exploitation, conflicts between executive agents, non-observance of rules)?

After the determination of all the facts which constitute a society, it remains to find the place which this society occupies among the total number of the societies contemporary with it. Here we enter upon the study of international institutions, intellectual, economic, and political (diplomacy and the usages of war); the same questions apply as in the study of political institutions. A study should also be made of the habits common to several societies, and of those relations which do not assume an official form. This is one of the least advanced parts of historical construction

IV. The outcome of all this labour is a tabulated view of human life at a given moment; it gives us the knowledge of a *state* of society (in German, *Zustand*). But history is not limited to the study of simultaneous facts, taken in a state of rest, to what we may call the *statics* of society. It also studies the states of society at different moments, and discovers the differences between these states. The habits of men and the material conditions under which they live change from epoch to epoch; even when they appear to be constant they do not remain unaltered in every respect. There is therefore occasion to investigate these changes; thus arises the study of successive facts.

Of these changes the most interesting for the work of historical construction are those which tend in a common direction,[1] so that in virtue of a series of gradual differentiations a usage or a state of society is transformed into a different usage or state, or, to speak without metaphor, cases where the men of a given period practise a habit very different from that of their predecessors without any abrupt change having taken place. This is *evolution*.

Evolution occurs in all human habits. In order to investigate it, therefore, it is enough to turn once more to the series of questions which we used in constructing a tabulated view of society. In respect of each of the facts, conditions, usages, persons invested with authority, official rules, the question is to be asked: What was the evolution of this fact?

[1] There is no general agreement on the proper place in history of retrograde changes, of those oscillations which bring things back to the point from which they started.

This study will involve several operations: (1) the determination of the fact whose evolution is to be studied; (2) the fixing of the duration of the time during which the evolution took place (the period should be so chosen that while the transformation is obvious, there yet remains a connecting link between the initial and the final condition); (3) the establishing of the different stages of the evolution; (4) the investigation of the means by which it was brought about.

V. A series, even a complete series, of all the states of all societies and of all their evolutions would not be enough to exhaust the subject-matter of history. There remains a number of unique facts which we cannot pass over, because they explain the origin of certain states of society, and form the starting-points of evolutions. How could we study the institutions or the evolution of France if we ignored the conquest of Gaul by Cæsar and the invasion of the Barbarians?

This necessity of studying unique facts has caused it to be said that history cannot be a science, for every science has for its object that which is general. History is here in the same situation as cosmography, geology, the science of animal species: it is not the abstract knowledge of the general relations between facts, it is a study which aims at *explaining* reality. Now, reality exists but once. There has been but a single evolution of the world, of animal life, of humanity. In each of these evolutions the successive facts have not been the product of abstract laws, but of the concurrence, at each moment, of several circumstances of different nature. This concurrence, sometimes called chance, has produced a series of accidents which have determined the particular course taken by evolution.[1] Evolution can only be understood by the study of these accidents; history is here on the same footing as geology or palæontology.

Thus scientific history may go back to the accidents, or events, which traditional history collected for literary reasons, because they struck the imagination, and employ them for the study of evolution. We may thus look for the facts which have influenced the evolution of each one of the habits of humanity. Each event will be arranged under its date in the evolution which it is supposed to have influenced. It will then suffice to bring together the events of every kind, and to arrange them in chronological and geographical order, to have a representation of historical evolution as a whole.

Then, over and above the *special* histories in which the facts are arranged under purely abstract categories (art, religion, private life, political institutions), we shall have constructed a concrete *general* history, which will connect together the various special histories by exhibiting the main stream of evolution which has dominated all the special evolutions. None of the species of facts which we study apart (religion, art, law, constitutions) forms a closed world within which evolution takes place in obedience to a kind of internal impulse, as specialists are prone to imagine. The evolution of

[1] The theory of chance as affecting history has been expounded in a masterly manner by M. Cournot, *Considérations sur la marche des idées et des événements dans les temps modernes* (Paris, 1872, 2 vols. 8vo).

a usage or of an institution (language, religion, church, state) is only a metaphor; a usage is an abstraction, abstractions do not evolve; it is only *existences* that evolve, in the strict sense of the word.[1] When a change takes place in a usage, this means that the men who practise it have changed. Now, men are not built in water-tight compartments (religious, juridical, economic) within which phenomena can occur in isolation; an event which modifies the condition of a man changes his habits in a great variety of respects. The invasion of the Barbarians influenced alike language, private life, and political institutions. We cannot, therefore, understand evolution by confining ourselves to a special branch of history; the specialist, even for the purpose of writing the complete history of his own branch, must look beyond the confines of his own subject into the field of general events. It is the merit of Taine to have asserted, with reference to English literature, that literary evolution depends, not on literary events, but on facts of a general character.

The general history of individual facts was developed before the special histories. It contains the residue of facts which have not found a place in the special histories, and has been reduced in extent by the formation and detachment of special branches. As general facts are principally of a

[1] Lamprecht, in a long article, *Was ist Kulturgeschichte*, published in the *Deutsche Zeitschrift für Geschichtswissenschaft*, New Series, vol. i., 1896, has attempted to base the history of civilisation on the theory of a collective soul of society producing "social-psychic" phenomena common to the whole society, and differing from period to period. This is a metaphysical hypothesis.

political nature, and as it is more difficult to organise these into a special branch, general history has in practice been confounded with political history (*Staatengeschichte*).[1] Thus political historians have been led to make themselves the champions of general history, and to retain in their constructions all the general facts (migrations of peoples, religious reforms, inventions, and discoveries) necessary for the understanding of political evolution.

In order to construct general history it is necessary to look for all the facts which, because they have produced changes, can explain either the state of a society or one of its evolutions. We must search for them among all classes of facts, displacements of population, artistic, scientific, religious, technical innovations, changes in the *personnel* of government, revolutions, wars, discoveries of countries.

That which is important is that the fact should have had a decisive influence. We must therefore resist the natural temptation to divide facts into great and small. It goes against the grain to admit that great effects may have had small causes, that Cleopatra's nose may have made a difference to the Roman Empire. This repugnance is of a metaphysical order; it springs from a preconceived opinion on the government of the world. In all the sciences which deal with an evolution we find individual facts which serve as starting-points for series of vast transformations. A drove of horses brought by the Spanish

[1] The expression *national* history, introduced in the interests of patriotism, denotes the same thing. The history of the nation means practically the history of the State.

has stocked the whole of South America. In a flood a branch of a tree may dam a current and transform the aspect of a valley.

In human evolution we meet with great transformations which have no intelligible cause beyond an individual accident.[1] In the sixteenth century England changed its religion three times on the death of a sovereign (Henry VIII., Edward VI., Mary). Importance is not to be measured by the initial fact, but by the facts which resulted from it. We must not, therefore, deny *a priori* the action of individuals and discard individual facts. We must examine whether a given individual was in a position to make his influence strongly felt. There are two cases in which we may assume that he was: (1) when his action served as an example to a mass of men and created a tradition, a case frequent in art, science, religion, and technical matters; (2) when he had power to issue commands and direct the actions of a mass of men, as is the case with the heads of a state, an army, or a church. The episodes in a man's life may thus become important facts.

Accordingly, in the scheme of historical classification a place should be assigned for persons and events.

VI. In every study of successive facts it is necessary to provide a number of halting-places, to distinguish beginnings and ends, in order that chronological divisions may be made in the enormous mass of facts. These divisions are *periods;* the use of them is as old as history. We need

[1] See Cournot, ibid., i. p. iv.

them, not only in general history, but in the special branches of history as well, whenever we study an extent of time long enough for an evolution to be sensible. It is by means of events that we fix their limits.

In the special branches of history, after having decided what changes of habits are to be considered as reaching deepest, we adopt them as marking *dates* in the evolution; we then inquire what event produced them. The event which led to the formation or the change of a habit becomes the beginning or the end of a period. Sometimes these boundary events are of the same species as the facts whose evolution we are studying—literary facts in the history of literature, political facts in political history. But more often they belong to a different species, and the special historian is obliged to borrow them from general history.

In general history the periods should be divided according to the evolution of several species of phenomena; we look for events which mark an epoch simultaneously in several branches (the Invasion of the Barbarians, the Reformation, the French Revolution). We may thus construct periods which are common to several branches of evolution, whose beginning and whose end are each marked by a single event. It is thus that the traditional division of universal history into periods has been effected. The sub-periods are obtained by the same process, by taking for limits events which have produced consequences of secondary importance.

The periods which are thus constructed according to the events are of unequal duration. We must not be troubled by this want of symmetry; a period ought not to be a fixed number of years, but the time occupied by a distinct phase of evolution. Now, evolution is not a regular movement; sometimes a long series of years passes without notable change, then come moments of rapid transformation. On this difference Saint-Simon has founded a distinction between *organic* periods (of slow change) and *critical* periods (of rapid change).

CHAPTER III

CONSTRUCTIVE REASONING

I. The historical facts supplied by documents are never enough to fill all the blanks in such schemes of classification and arrangement as we have been considering. There are many questions to which no direct answer is given by the documents; many features are lacking without which the complete picture of the various states of society, of evolutions and events, cannot be given. We are irresistibly impelled to endeavour to fill up these gaps.

In the sciences of direct observation, when a fact is missing from a series, it is sought for by a new observation. In history, where we have not this resource, we seek to extend our knowledge by the help of reasoning. Starting from facts known to us from the documents, we endeavour to reach new facts by inference. If the reasoning be correct, this method of acquiring knowledge is legitimate.

But experience shows that of all the methods of acquiring historical knowledge, reasoning is the most difficult to employ correctly, and the one which has introduced the most serious errors. It should not be used without the safeguard of a number of precautions calculated to keep the danger continually before the mind.

(1) Reasoning should never be combined with

the analysis of a document. The reader who allows himself to introduce into a text what the author has not expressly put there ends by making him say what he never intended to say.[1]

(2) Facts obtained by the direct examination of documents should never be confused with the results obtained by reasoning. When we state a fact known to us by reasoning only, we must not allow it to be supposed that we have found it in the documents; we must disclose the method by which we have obtained it.

(3) Unconscious reasoning must never be allowed; there are too many chances of error. It will be enough to make a point of putting every argument into logical form; in the case of bad reasoning the major premiss is generally monstrous to an appalling degree.

(4) If the reasoning leaves the least doubt, no attempt must be made to draw a conclusion; the point treated must be left in the conjectural stage, clearly distinguished from the definitively established results.

(5) It is not permissible to return to a conjecture and endeavour to transform it into a certainty. Here the first impression is most likely to be right. By reflection upon a conjecture we familiarise ourselves with it, and end by thinking it better established; while the truth is, we are merely more accustomed to it. This is a frequent mishap with those who devote themselves to long meditation on a small number of texts.

There are two ways of employing reasoning, one

[1] We have already (p. 143) treated of this fault of method.

negative, the other positive; we shall examine them separately.

II. The negative mode of reasoning, called also the "argument from silence," is based on the absence of indications with regard to a fact.[1] From the circumstance of the fact not being mentioned in any document it is inferred that there was no such fact; the argument is applied to all kinds of subjects, usages of every description, evolutions, events. It rests on a feeling which in ordinary life is expressed by saying: "If it were true, we should have heard of it;" it implies a general proposition which may be formulated thus: "If an alleged event really had occurred, there would be some document in existence in which it would be referred to."

In order that such reasoning should be justified it would be necessary that every fact should have been observed and recorded in writing, and that all the records should have been preserved. Now, the greater part of the documents which have been written have been lost, and the greater part of the events which happen are not recorded in writing. In the majority of cases the argument would be invalid. It must therefore be restricted to the cases where the conditions implied in it have been fulfilled.

(1) It is necessary not only that there should be now no documents in existence which mention the fact in question, but that there should never have been any. If the documents are lost we can conclude

[1] The discussion of this argument, which was formerly much used in religious history, was a favourite subject with the earlier writers who treated of methodology, and still occupies a considerable space in the *Principes de la critique historique* of Père de Smedt.

nothing. The argument from silence ought, therefore, to be employed the more rarely the greater the number of documents that have been lost; it is of much less use in ancient history than in dealing with the nineteenth century. Some, desiring to free themselves from this restriction, are tempted to assume that the lost documents contained nothing interesting; if they were lost, say they, the reason was that they were not worth preserving. But the truth is, every manuscript is at the mercy of the least accident; its preservation or destruction is a matter of pure chance.

(2) The fact must have been of such a kind that it could not fail to be observed and recorded. Because a fact has not been recorded it does not follow that it has not been observed. Any one who is concerned in an organisation for the collection of a particular species of facts knows how much commoner those facts are than people think, and how many cases pass unnoticed or without leaving any written trace. It is so with earthquakes, cases of hydrophobia, whales stranded on the shore. Besides, many facts, even those which are well known to those who are contemporary with them, are not recorded, because the official authorities prevent their publication; this is what happens to the secret acts of governments and the complaints of the lower classes. This silence, which proves nothing, greatly impresses unreflecting historians; it is the origin of the widespread sophism of the "good old times." No document relates any abuse of power by officials or any complaints made by peasants; therefore, everything was regular and nobody was suffering.

Before we argue from silence we should ask: Might not this fact have failed to be recorded in any of the documents we possess? That which is conclusive is not the absence of any document on a given fact, but silence as to the fact in a document in which it would naturally be mentioned.

The negative argument is thus limited to a few clearly defined cases. (1) The author of the document in which the fact is not mentioned had the intention of systematically recording all the facts of the same class, and must have been acquainted with all of them. (Tacitus sought to enumerate the peoples of Germany; the *Notitia dignitatum* mentioned all the provinces of the Empire; the absence from these lists of a people or a province proves that it did not then exist.) (2) The fact, if it was such, must have affected the author's imagination so forcibly as necessarily to enter into his conceptions. (If there had been regular assemblies of the Frankish people, Gregory of Tours could not have conceived and described the life of the Frankish kings without mentioning them.)

III. The positive mode of reasoning begins with a fact established by the documents, and infers some other fact which the documents do not mention. It is an application of the fundamental principle of history, the *analogy* between present and past humanity. In the present we observe that the facts of humanity are connected together. Given one fact, another fact accompanies it, either because the first is the cause of the second, or because the second is the cause of the first, or because both are effects of a common cause. We assume that in the past similar facts were connected in a similar manner, and this assumption is corroborated by the direct study of the past in the documents. From a given fact, therefore, which we find in the past, we may infer the existence of the other facts which were connected with it.

This reasoning applies to facts of all kinds, usages, transformations, individual incidents. We may begin with any known fact and endeavour to infer unknown facts from it. Now the facts of humanity, having a common centre, man, are all connected together, not merely facts of the same class, but facts belonging to the most widely different classes. There are connections, not merely between the different facts relating to art, to religion, to manners, to politics, but between the facts of religion on the one hand and the facts of art, of politics, and of manners on the other; thus from a fact of one species we may infer facts of all the other species.

To examine those connections between facts on which reasonings may be founded would mean tabulating all the known relations between the facts of humanity, that is, giving a full account of all the empirical laws of social life. Such a labour would provide matter for a whole book.[1] Here we shall content ourselves with indicating the general rules governing this kind of reasoning, and the precautions to be taken against the most common errors.

The argument rests on two propositions: one is general, and is derived from experience of human

[1] This is what Montesquieu attempted in his *Esprit des Lois.* In a course of lectures at the Sorbonne, I have endeavoured to give a sketch of such a comprehensive account.—[Ch. S.]

affairs; the other is particular, and is derived from the documents. In practice, we begin with the particular proposition, the historical fact: Salamis bears a Phœnician name. We then look for a general proposition: the language of the name of a city is the language of the people which founded it. And we conclude: Salamis, bearing a Phœnician name, was founded by the Phœnicians.

In order that the conclusion may be certain, two conditions are necessary.

(1) The general proposition must be accurately true; the two facts which it declares to be connected must be connected in such a way that the one is never found without the other. If this condition were completely satisfied we should have a *law*, in the scientific sense of the word; but in dealing with the facts of humanity—apart from those physical conditions whose laws are established by the regular sciences—we can only work with empirical laws obtained by rough determinations of general facts which are not analysed in such a manner as to educe their true causes. These empirical laws are approximately true only when they relate to a numerous body of facts, for we can never quite know how far each is necessary to produce the result. The proposition relating to the language of the name of a city does not go enough into detail to be always true. Petersburg is a German name, Syracuse in America bears a Greek name. Other conditions must be fulfilled before we can be sure that the name is connected with the nationality of the founders. We should, therefore, only employ such propositions as go into detail.

(2) In order to employ a general proposition which goes into detail, we must have a detailed knowledge of the particular fact; for it is not till after this fact has been established that we look for an empirical general law on which to found an argument. We shall begin, then, by studying the particular conditions of the case (the situation of Salamis, the habits of the Greeks and Phœnicians); we shall not work on a single detail, but on an assemblage of details.

Thus, in historical reasoning it is necessary to have (1) an accurate general proposition; (2) a detailed knowledge of a past fact. It is bad workmanship to assume a false general proposition—to suppose, for example, as Augustin Thierry did, that every aristocracy had its origin in a conquest. It is bad workmanship, again, to found an argument on an isolated detail (the name of a city). The nature of these errors indicates the precautions to be taken.

(1) The spontaneous tendency is to take as a basis of reasoning those "common-sense truths" which form nearly the whole of our knowledge of social life. Now, the greater part of these are to some extent false, for the science of social life is still imperfect. And the chief danger in them lies in the circumstance that we use them unconsciously. The safest precaution will be always to formulate the supposed law on which we propose to base an argument. In every instance where such and such a fact occurs, it is certain that such and such another fact occurs also. If this proposition is obviously false, we shall at once see it to be so; if it is too

general, we shall inquire what new conditions may be introduced to make it accurate.

(2) A second spontaneous impulse leads us to draw consequences from isolated facts, even of the slightest kind (or rather, the idea of each fact awakens in us, by association, the idea of other facts). This is the natural procedure in the history of literature. Each circumstance in the life of an author supplies material for reasoning; we construct by conjecture all the influences which could have acted upon him, and we assume that they did act upon him. All the branches of history which study a single species of facts, isolated from every other species (language, arts, private law, religion), are exposed to the same danger, because they deal with fragments of human life, not with comprehensive collections of phenomena. But few conclusions are firmly established except those which rest on a comprehensive body of data. We do not make a diagnosis from a single symptom, but from a number of concurrent symptoms. The precaution to be taken will be to avoid working with an isolated detail or an abstract fact. We must have before our minds actual men, as affected by the principal conditions under which they lived.

We must be prepared to realise but rarely the conditions of a certain inference; we are too little acquainted with the laws of social life, and too seldom know the precise details of an historical fact. Thus most of our reasonings will only afford presumptions, not certainties. But it is with reasonings as with documents.[1] When several presump-

[1] See p. 204.

tions all point in the same direction they confirm each other, and end by producing a legitimate certitude. History fills up some of its gaps by an accumulation of reasonings. Doubts remain as to the Phœnician origin of various Greek cities, but there is no doubt about the presence of the Phœnicians in Greece.

CHAPTER IV

THE CONSTRUCTION OF GENERAL FORMULÆ

I. SUPPOSE we had methodically arranged all the historical facts established by the analysis of documents, or by reasoning; we should possess a systematised inventory of the whole of history, and the work of construction would be complete. Ought history to stop at this point? The question is warmly debated, and we cannot avoid giving an answer, for it is a question with a practical bearing.

Critical scholars, who are accustomed to collect all the facts relating to their speciality, without any personal preference, are inclined to regard a complete, accurate, and objective collection of facts as the prime requisite. All historical facts have an equal right to a place in history; to retain some as being of greater importance, and reject the rest as comparatively unimportant, would be to introduce the subjective element of choice, variable according to individual fancy; history cannot sacrifice a single fact.

Against this very reasonable view there is nothing to be urged except a material difficulty; this, however, is enough, for it is the practical motive of all the sciences: we mean the impossibility of acquiring or communicating complete knowledge. A body of history in which no fact was sacrificed would have to contain all the actions, all the thoughts, all the adventures of all men at all times. It would form a total which no one could possibly make himself master of, not for want of materials, but for want of time. This, indeed, applies, as things are, to certain voluminous collections of documents: the collected reports of parliamentary debates contain the whole history of the various assemblies, but to learn their history from these sources would require more than a lifetime.

Every science must take into consideration the practical conditions of life, at least so far as it claims to be a real science, a science which it is possible to know. Any ideal which ends by making knowledge impossible impedes the establishment of the science.

Science is a saving of time and labour, effected by a process which provides a rapid means of learning and understanding facts; it consists in the slow collection of a quantity of details and their condensation into portable and incontrovertible formulæ. History, which is more encumbered with details than any other science, has the choice between two alternatives: to be complete and unknowable, or to be knowable and incomplete. All the other sciences have chosen the second alternative; they abridge and they condense, preferring to take the risk of mutilating and arbitrarily combining the facts to the certainty of being unable either to understand or communicate them. Scholars have preferred to confine themselves to the periods of ancient history, where chance, which has destroyed nearly all the sources of information, has freed them from the responsibility of choosing between facts by depriving them of nearly all the means of knowing them.

History, in order to constitute itself a science, must elaborate the raw material of facts. It must condense them into manageable form by means of descriptive formulæ, qualitative and quantitative. It must search for those connections between facts which form the ultimate conclusions of every science.

II. The facts of humanity, with their complex and varied character, cannot be reduced like chemical facts to a few simple formulæ. Like the other sciences which deal with life, history needs descriptive formulæ in order to express the nature of the different phenomena.

In order to be manageable, a formula must be short; in order to give an exact idea of the facts, it must be precise. Now, in the knowledge of human affairs, precision can only be obtained by attention to characteristic details, for these alone enable us to understand how one fact differed from others, and what there was in it peculiar to itself. There is thus a conflict between the need of brevity, which leads us to look for concrete formulæ, and the necessity of being precise, which requires us to adopt detailed formulæ. Formulæ which are too short make science vague and illusory, formulæ which are too long encumber it and make it useless. This dilemma can only be evaded by a perpetual compromise, the principle of which is to compress the facts by omitting all that is not necessary for the purpose of representing them to the mind, and to stop at the point where omission would suppress some characteristic feature.

This operation, which is difficult in itself, is still further complicated by the state in which the facts which are to be condensed into formulæ present themselves. According to the nature of the documents from which they are derived, they come to us in all the different degrees of precision: from the detailed narrative which relates the smallest episodes (the battle of Waterloo) down to the barest mention in a couple of words (the victory of the Austrasians at Testry). On different facts of the same kind we possess an amount of details which is infinitely variable according as the documents give us a complete description or a mere mention. How are we to organise into a common whole, items of knowledge which differ so widely in point of precision? When facts are known to us from a vague word of general import, we cannot reduce them to a less degree of generality and a greater degree of precision; we do not know the details. If we add them conjecturally we shall produce an historical novel. This is what Augustin Thierry did in the case of his *Récits mérovingiens.* When facts are known in detail, it is always easy to reduce them to a greater degree of generality by suppressing characteristic details; this is what is done by the authors of abridgements. But the result of this procedure would be to reduce history to a mass of vague generalities, uniform for the whole of time except for the proper names and the dates. It would be a dangerous method of introducing symmetry, to bring all facts to a common degree of generality by levelling them all to the condition of those which are the most imperfectly known. In those cases, therefore, where the documents give details, our descriptive formulæ should always retain the characteristic features of the facts.

In order to construct these formulæ we must return to the set of questions which we employed in grouping the facts, we must answer each question, and compare the answers. We shall then combine them into as condensed and as precise a formula as possible, taking care to keep a fixed sense for every word. This may appear to be a matter of style, but what we have in view here is not merely a principle of exposition, necessary for the sake of being intelligible to the reader, it is a precaution which the author ought to take on his own account. The facts of society are of an elusive nature, and for the purpose of seizing and expressing them, fixed and precise language is an indispensable instrument; no historian is complete without good language.

It will be well to make the greatest possible use of concrete and descriptive terms: their meaning is always clear. It will be prudent to designate collective groups only by collective, not by abstract names (royalty, State, democracy, Reformation, Revolution), and to avoid personifying abstractions. We think we are simply using metaphors, and then we are carried away by the force of the words. Certainly abstract terms have something very seductive about them, they give a scientific appearance to a proposition. But it is only an appearance, behind which scholasticism is apt to be concealed; the word, having no concrete meaning, becomes a purely verbal notion (like the soporific virtue of which Molière speaks). As long as our notions on social phenomena have not been reduced to truly scientific formulæ, the most scientific course will be to express them in terms of every-day experience.

In order to construct a formula, we should know beforehand what elements ought to enter into it. We must here make a distinction between general facts (habits and evolutions) and unique facts (events).

III. General facts consist in actions which are often repeated, and are common to a number of men. We have to determine their *character*, *extent*, and *duration*.

In order to formulate their character, we combine all the features which constitute a fact (habit, institution) and distinguish it from all others. We unite under the same formula all the individual cases which greatly resemble each other, by neglecting the individual differences.

This concentration is performed without effort in the case of habits which have to do with forms (language, handwriting), and in the case of all intellectual habits; those who practised these habits have already given them expression in formulæ, which we have only to collect. The same holds of these institutions which are sanctioned by expressly formulated rules (regulations, laws, private statutes). Accordingly the special branches of history were the first to yield methodical formulæ. On the other hand, these special branches do not go beyond superficial and conventional facts, they do not reach the real actions and thoughts of men:

in language they deal with written words, not the real pronunciation; in religion with official dogmas and rites, not with the real beliefs of the mass of the people; in morals with avowed precepts, not with the effective ideals; in institutions with official rules, not with the real practice. On all these subjects the knowledge of conventional forms must some day be supplemented by a parallel study of the real habits.

It is much more difficult to embrace in a single formula a habit which is composed of real actions, as is the case with economic phenomena, private life, politics; for we have to find in the different actions those common characteristics which constitute the habit; or, if this work has already been done in the documents, and condensed into a formula (the most common case), we must criticise this formula in order to make sure that it really represents a homogeneous habit.

The same difficulty occurs in constructing the formula for a group; we have to describe the characteristic common to all the members of the group and to find a collective name which shall exactly designate it. In documents there is no lack of names of groups; but, as they have their origin in usage, many of them correspond but ill to the real groups; we have to criticise these names to fix their precise meaning, sometimes to correct their application.

This first operation should yield formulæ expressive of the conventional and real characteristics of all the habits of the different groups.

In order to fix the precise *extent* of a habit we

shall seek the most distant points where it appears (this will give the area of distribution), and the region where it is most common (the centre). Sometimes the operation takes the form of a map (for example the map of the *tumuli* and the *dolmens* of France). It will also be necessary to indicate the groups of men who practised each habit, and the sub-groups in which it was most pronounced.

The formula should also indicate the *duration* of the habit. We shall look for the extreme cases, the first and the last appearance of the form, the doctrine, the usage, the institution, the group. But it will not be enough to note the two isolated cases, the earliest and the most recent; we must ascertain the period in which it was really active.

The formula of an evolution ought to indicate the successive variations in the habit, giving in each case precise limits of extent and duration. Then, by comparing all the variations, it will be possible to determine the general course of the evolution. The general formula will indicate when and where the evolution began and ended, and the nature of the change which it effected. All evolutions present common features which enable them to be divided into stages. Every habit (usage or institution) begins by being the spontaneous act of several individuals; when others imitate them it becomes a usage. Similarly social functions are in the first instance performed by persons who undertake them spontaneously, when these persons are recognised by others they acquire an official status. This is the first stage; individual initiative followed by general imitation and recognition. The usage becomes traditional and is transformed into an obligatory custom or rule; the persons acquire a permanent status and are invested with powers of material or moral constraint. This is the stage of tradition and authority; very often it is the last stage, and continues till the society is destroyed. The usage is relaxed, the rules are violated, the persons in authority cease to be obeyed; this is the stage of revolt and decomposition. Finally, in certain civilised societies, the rule is criticised, the persons in authority are censured, by the action of a part of the subjects a rational change is effected in the composition of the governing body, which is subjected to supervision; this is the stage of reform and of checks.

IV. In the case of unique facts we cannot expect to bring several together under a common formula, for the nature of these facts is to occur but once. However, it is imperatively necessary to abridge, we cannot preserve all the acts of all the members of an assembly or of all the officers of a state. Many individuals and many facts must be sacrificed.

How are we to choose? Personal tastes and patriotism give rise to preferences for congenial characters and for local events; but the only principle of selection which can be employed by all historians in common is that which is based on the part played in the evolution of human affairs. We ought to retain those persons and those events which have visibly influenced the course of an evolution. We may recognise them by our inability to describe the evolution without mentioning them. The men are those who have modified the state of a society either by the creation or the introduction of a habit (artists, men of science, inventors, founders, apostles), or as directors of a movement, heads of states, of parties, of armies. The events are those which have brought about changes in the habits or the state of societies.

In order to construct a formula descriptive of an historical person, we must take particulars from his biography and his habits. From his biography we shall take those facts which determined his career, formed his habits, and occasioned the actions by which he influenced society. These comprise physiological conditions (physique, temperament, state of health),[1] the educational influences, the social conditions to which he was subject. The history of literature has accustomed us to researches of this kind.

Among the habits of a man it is necessary to determine his fundamental conceptions relating to the class of facts in which his influence was felt, his conception of life, his knowledge, his predominating tastes, his habitual occupations, his principles of conduct. From these details, in which there is infinite variety, an impression is formed of the man's "character," and the collection of these characteristic features constitutes his "portrait," or, to use a favourite phrase of the day, his "psychology." This exercise, which is still held in great esteem, dates from the time when history was still a branch of literature; it is doubtful whether it can ever be-

[1] Michelet has discredited the study of physiological influences by the abuse which he has made of it in the last part of his "History of France"; it is, however, indispensable for the understanding of a man's career.

come a scientific process. There is perhaps no sure method of summing up the character of a man, even in his lifetime, still less when we can only know him indirectly through the medium of documents. The controversies relative to the interpretation of the conduct of Alexander are a good example of this uncertainty.

If, however, we take the risk of seeking a formula to describe a character, there are two natural temptations against which we must guard: (1) We must not construct the formula out of the person's assertions in regard to himself. (2) The study of imaginary personages (dramas and novels) has accustomed us to seek a logical connection between the various sentiments and the various acts of a man; a character, in literature, is constructed logically. This search for coherency must not be transferred to the study of real men. We are less likely to do so in the case of those whom we observe in their lifetime, because we see too many characteristics in them which could not enter into a coherent formula. But the absence of documents, by suppressing those characteristics which would have checked us, encourages us to arrange the very small number of those which remain in the form of a stage-character. This is why the great men of antiquity seem to us to have been much more logical than our contemporaries are.

How are we to construct a formula for an event? The imperative need of simplification causes us to combine under a single name an enormous mass of minute facts which are perceived in the lump, and between which we vaguely feel that there is a connection (a battle, a war, a reform). The facts which are thus combined are such facts as have conduced to a common result. That is how the common notion of an event arises, and there is no more scientific conception to put in its place. Facts, then, are to be grouped according to their consequences; those which have had no visible consequences disappear, the others are fused into a certain number of aggregates which we call events.

In order to describe an event, it is necessary to give precise indications (1) of its character, (2) of its extent.

(1) By the character of an event we mean the features which distinguish it from every other event, not merely the external conditions of date and place, but the manner in which it occurred, and its immediate causes. The following are the items of information which the formula should contain. One or more men, in such and such mental states (conceptions, motives of the action), working under such and such material conditions (locality, instrument), performed such and such actions, which had for their result such and such a modification. For the determination of the motives of the actions, the only method is to compare the actions, firstly, with the declarations of those who performed them; secondly, with the interpretation of those who witnessed their performance. There is often a doubt remaining: this is the field of party polemics; every one attributes noble motives to the actions of his own party and discreditable motives to those of the opposite party. But actions described without any indication of motive would be unintelligible.

(2) The extension of the event will be indicated both in space (the place where it happened, and the region in which its immediate effects were felt) and in time, the moment when its realisation began, and the moment when the result was brought about.

V. Descriptive formulæ relating to characters, being merely qualitative, only give an abstract idea of the facts; in order to realise the place they occupied in reality, quantity is necessary. It is not a matter of indifference whether a given usage was practised by a hundred men or by millions.

For the purpose of introducing quantity into formulæ we have at our disposal several methods, of various degrees of imperfection, which help us to attain the end in view with various degrees of precision. Arranged in descending order of precision they are as follows:—

(1) *Measurement* is a perfectly scientific procedure, for equal numbers represent absolutely identical values. But a common unit is necessary, and that can only be had for time and for physical phenomena (lengths, surfaces, weights). Figures relating to production and sums of money are the essential elements in the statement of economic and financial facts. But facts of the psychological order remain inaccessible to measurement.

(2) *Enumeration*, which is the process employed in statistics,[1] is applicable to all the facts which

[1] On the subject of statistics, a method which is now perfected, a good summary with a bibliography will be found in the *Handwörterbuch der Staatswissenschaften*, Jena, 1890–94, la. 8vo. and two good methodical treatises, J. von. Mayr, *Theoretische Statistik* and *Bevölkerungsstatistik*, in the collection of Marquardsen and Seydel, Freiburg, 1895 and 1897, la. 8vo.

have in common a definite characteristic which can be made use of for counting them. The facts which are thus comprehended under a single number do not all belong to the same species, they may have in common but a single characteristic, abstract (crime, lawsuit) or conventional (workman, lodging); the figures merely indicate the number of cases in which a given characteristic is met with; they do not represent a homogeneous whole. A natural tendency is to confuse number with measurement, and to suppose that facts are known with scientific precision because it has been possible to apply number to them; this is an illusion to be guarded against, we must not take the figures which give the number of a population or an army for the measure of its importance.[1] Still, enumeration yields results which are necessary for the construction of formulæ relating to groups. But the operation is restricted to those cases in which it is possible to know all the units of a given species lying within given limits, for it is performed by first ticking off, then adding. Before undertaking a retrospective enumeration, therefore, it will be well to make sure that the documents are complete enough to exhibit all the units which are to be enumerated. As to figures given in documents, they are to be distrusted.

(3) *Valuation* is a kind of incomplete enumeration applying to a portion of the field, and made on the supposition that the same proportions hold good through the whole of the field. It is an expedient to

[1] As is done by Boardeau (*l'Histoire et les Historiens*, Paris, 1888, 8vo), who proposes to reduce the whole of history to a series of statistics.

which, in history, it is often necessary to have recourse when documents are unequally abundant for the different divisions of the subject. The result is open to doubt, unless we are sure that the portion to which enumeration was applied was exactly similar to the remainder.

(4) *Sampling* is a process of enumeration restricted to a few units taken at different points in the field of investigation; we calculate the proportion of cases (say 90 per cent.) where a given characteristic occurs, we assume that the same proportion holds throughout, and if there are several categories we obtain the proportion between them. In history this procedure is applicable to facts of every kind, for the purpose of determining either the proportion between the different forms or usages which occur within a given region or period, or the proportion which obtains, within a heterogeneous group, between members belonging to different classes. This procedure gives us an approximate idea of the frequency of facts and the proportion between the different elements of a society; it can even show what species of facts are most commonly found together, and are therefore probably connected. But in order that the method may be employed correctly it is necessary that the samples should be representative of the whole, and not of a part which might possibly be exceptional in character. They should therefore be chosen at very different points, and under very different conditions, in order that the exceptions may compensate each other. It is not enough to take them at points which are *distant* from each other; for example, on the different frontiers of a country,

for the very circumstance of situation on a frontier is an exceptional condition. Verification may be had by following the methods by which anthropologists obtain averages.

(5) *Generalisation* is only an instinctive process of simplification. As soon as we perceive a certain characteristic in an object, we extend this characteristic to all other objects which at all resemble it. In all human concerns, where the facts are always complex, we make generalisations unconsciously; we attribute to a whole people the habits of a few individuals, or those of the first group forming part of the people which comes within our knowledge; we extend to a whole period habits which are ascertained to have existed at a given moment. This is the most active of all the causes of historical error, and one whose influence is felt in every department, in the study of usages and of institutions, even in the appreciation of the morality of a people.[1] Generalisation rests on a vague idea that all facts which are contiguous to each other, or which resemble each other in some point, are similar at all points. It is an unconscious and ill-performed process of sampling. It may therefore be made correct by being subjected to the conditions of a well-performed process of sampling. We must examine the cases on which we propose to found a generalisation and ask ourselves, What right have we to generalise? That is, what reason have we for assuming that the characteristic discovered in these cases will occur in the remaining thousands of cases? that the cases chosen

[1] A good example will be found in Lacombe, *De l'Histoire Considérée Comme Science*, p. 146.

resemble the average? The only valid reason would be that these cases are representative of the whole. We are thus brought back to the process of methodical sampling.

The right method of conducting the operation is as follows: (1) We must fix the precise limits of the field within which we intend to generalise (that is, to assume the similarity of all the cases), we must determine the country, the group, the class, the period as to which we are to generalise. Care must be taken not to make the field too large by confusing a part with the whole (a Greek or Germanic people with the whole Greek or Germanic race). (2) We must make sure that the facts lying within the field resemble each other in the points on which we wish to generalise, and therefore we have to distrust those vague names under which are comprehended groups of very different character (Christians, French, Aryans, Romans). (3) We must make sure that the facts from which we propose to generalise are representative samples, that they really belong to the field of investigation, for it does happen sometimes that men or facts are taken as specimens of one group when they really belong to another. Nor must they be exceptional, as is to be presumed in all cases when the conditions are exceptional; authors of documents tend to record by preference those facts which surprise them, hence exceptional cases occupy in documents a space which is out of proportion to their real number; this is one of the chief sources of error. (4) The number of samples necessary to support a generalisation is the greater the less ground there is for supposing a resemblance between all the cases occurring within the field of investigation. A small number may suffice in treating of points in which men tend to bear a strong resemblance to each other, either by imitation and convention (language, rites, ceremonies), or from the influence of custom and obligatory regulations (social institutions, political institutions in countries where the authorities are obeyed). A large number is requisite for facts where individual initiative plays a more important part (art, science, morality), and sometimes, as in respect of private conduct, all generalisation is as a rule impossible.

VI. Descriptive formulæ are in no science the final result of the work. It still remains to group the facts in such a way as to bring out their collective import, it still remains to search for their mutual relations; these are the general conclusions. History, by reason of the imperfection of its mode of acquiring knowledge, needs, in addition, a preliminary operation for determining the bearing of the knowledge acquired.[1]

The work of criticism has supplied us with

[1] We have thought it useless to discuss here the question whether history ought, in accordance with the ancient tradition, to fulfil yet another function, whether it ought to pass judgment on men and events, that is to supplement the description of facts by expressions of approbation or censure, either from the point of view of a moral ideal, general or particular (the ideal of a sect, a party, or a nation), or from the practical point of view, by examining, as Polybius did, whether historical actions were well or ill adapted to their purpose. An addition of this kind could be made to any descriptive study: the naturalist might express his sympathy with or his admiration for an animal, he might condemn the ferocity of the tiger, and praise the devotion of the hen to her chickens. But it is obvious that in history, as in every other subject, judgments of this kind are foreign to science.

nothing but a number of isolated remarks on the value of the knowledge which the documents have permitted us to acquire. These must be combined. We shall therefore take a whole group of facts entered under a common heading—a particular class of facts, a country, a period, an event—and we shall summarise the results yielded by the criticism of particular facts so as to obtain a general formula. We shall have to take into consideration: (1) the extent, (2) the value of our knowledge.

(1) We shall ask ourselves what are the blanks left by the documents. By working through the scheme used for the grouping of facts it is easy to discover what are the classes of facts on which we lack information. In the case of evolution, we notice which links are missing in the chain of successive modifications; in the case of events, what episodes, what groups of actors are still unknown to us; what facts enter or disappear from the field of our knowledge without our being able to trace their beginning or end. We ought to construct, mentally at any rate, a tabulated scheme of the points on which we are ignorant, in order to keep before our minds the distance separating the knowledge we have from a perfect knowledge.

(2) The value of our knowledge depends on the value of our documents. Criticism has given us indications on this point in each separate case, these indications, so far as relating to a given body of facts, must be summarised under a few heads. Does our knowledge come originally from direct observation, from written tradition, or from oral tradition?

Do we possess several traditions of different bias, or a single tradition? Do we possess documents of different classes or of one single class? Is our information vague or precise, detailed or summary, literary or positive, official or confidential?

The natural tendency is to forget, in construction, the results yielded by criticism, to forget the incompleteness of our knowledge and the elements of doubt in it. An eager desire to increase to the greatest possible extent the amount of our information and the number of our conclusions impels us to seek emancipation from all negative restrictions. We thus run a great risk of using fragmentary and suspicious sources of information for the purpose of forming general impressions, just as if we were in possession of a complete record. It is easy to forget the existence of those facts which the documents do not describe (economic facts, slaves in antiquity), it is easy to exaggerate the space occupied by facts which are known to us (Greek art, Roman inscriptions, mediæval monasteries). We instinctively estimate the importance of facts by the number of the documents which mention them. We forget the peculiar character of the documents, and, when they all have a common origin, we forget that they have all subjected the facts to the same distortions, and that their community of origin renders verification impossible; we submissively reproduce the bias of the tradition (Roman, orthodox, aristocratic).

In order to resist these natural tendencies, it is enough to pass in review the whole body of facts and the whole body of tradition, before attempting to draw any general conclusion.

VII. Descriptive formulæ give the particular character of each small group of facts. In order to obtain a general conclusion, we must combine these detailed results into a general formula. We must not compare together isolated details or secondary characteristics,[1] but groups of facts which resemble each other in a whole set of characteristics.

We thus form an aggregate (of institutions, of groups of men, of events). Following the method indicated above, we determine its distinguishing characteristics, its extent, its duration, its quantity or importance.

As we form groups of greater and greater generality we drop, with each new degree of generality, those characteristics which vary, and retain those which are common to all the members of the new group. We must stop at the point where nothing is left except the characteristics common to the whole of humanity. The result is the condensation into a single formula of the general character of an order of facts, of a language, a religion, an art, an economic organisation, a society, a government, a complex event (such as the Invasion or the Reformation).

As long as these comprehensive formulæ remain isolated the conclusion is incomplete. And as it is no longer possible to fuse them into higher gene-

[1] Comparison between two facts of detail belonging to very different aggregates (for example the comparison of Abd-el-Kader with Jagurtha, of Napoleon with Sforza) is a striking method of exposition, but not a means of reaching a scientific conclusion.

ralisations, we feel the need of comparing them for the purpose of classification. This classification may be attempted by two methods.

(1) We may compare together similar categories of special facts, language, religions, arts, governments, taking them from the whole of humanity, and classifying together those which most resemble each other. We obtain families of languages, religions, and governments, which we may again classify and arrange among themselves. This is an abstract kind of classification; it isolates one species of facts from all the others, and thus renounces all claim to exhibit causes. It has the advantage of being rapidly performed and of yielding a technical vocabulary which is useful for designating facts.

(2) We may compare real groups of real individuals, we may take societies which figure in history and classify them according to their similarities. This is a concrete classification analogous to that of zoology, in which, not functions, but whole animals are classified. It is true that the groups are less clearly marked than in zoology; nor is there a general agreement as to the characteristics in respect of which we are to look for resemblances. Are we to choose the economic or the political organisation of the groups, or their intellectual condition? No principle of choice has as yet become obligatory.

History has not yet succeeded in establishing a scientific system of comprehensive classification. Possibly human groups are not sufficiently homogeneous to furnish a solid basis of comparison, and not sharply enough divided to be treated as comparable units.

VIII. The study of the relations between simultaneous facts consists in a search for the connections between all the facts of different species which occur in a given society. We have a vague consciousness that the different habits which are separated by abstraction and ranged under different categories (art, religion, political institutions), are not isolated in reality, that they have common characteristics, and that they are closely enough connected for a change in one of them to bring about a change in another. This is a fundamental idea of the *Esprit des Lois* of Montesquieu. This bond of connection, sometimes called *consensus*, has received the name of *Zusammenhang* from the German school. From this conception has arisen the theory of the *Volksgeist* (the mind of a people), a counterfeit of which has within the last few years been introduced into France under the name of "âme nationale." This conception is also at the bottom of the theory regarding the soul of society which Lamprecht has expounded.

After the rejection of these mystical conceptions there remains a vague but incontrovertible fact, the "solidarity" which exists between the different habits of one and the same people. In order to study it with precision it would be necessary to analyse it, and a connecting bond cannot be analysed. It is thus quite natural that this part of social science should have remained a refuge for mystery and obscurity.

By the comparison of different societies which resemble or differ from each other in a given department (religion or government), with the object of discovering in what other departments they resemble or differ from each other, it is possible that interesting empirical results might be obtained. But, in order to *explain* the *consensus*, it is necessary to work back to the facts which have produced it, the common causes of the various habits. We are thus obliged to undertake the investigation of causes, and we enter the province of what is called *philosophical* history, because it investigates what was formerly called the *philosophy* of facts—that is to say, their permanent relations.

IX. The necessity of rising above the simple determination of facts in order to *explain* them by their *causes*, a necessity which has governed the development of all the sciences, has at length been felt even in the study of history. Hence have arisen systematic philosophies of history, and attempts to discover historical laws and causes. We cannot here enter into a critical examination of these attempts, which the nineteenth century has produced in so great number; we shall merely indicate what are the ways in which the problem has been attacked, and what obstacles have prevented a scientific solution from being reached.

The most natural method of explanation consists in the assumption that a transcendental cause, Providence, guides the whole course of events towards an end which is known to God.[1] This explanation can be but a metaphysical doctrine, crowning the work of science; for the distinguishing feature of

[1] This system is still followed by several contemporary authors, the Belgian jurist Laurent in his *Études sur l'histoire de l'humanité*, the German Rocholl, and even Flint, the English historian of the philosophy of history.

science is that it only studies efficient causes. The historian is not called upon to investigate the first cause or final causes any more than the chemist or the naturalist. And, in fact, few writers on history nowadays stop to discuss the theory of Providence in its theological form.

But the tendency to explain historical facts by transcendental causes survives in more modern theories in which metaphysic is disguised under scientific forms. The historians of the nineteenth century have been so strongly influenced by their philosophical education that most of them, sometimes unconsciously, introduce metaphysical formulæ into the construction of history. It will be enough to enumerate these systems, and point out their metaphysical character, so that reflecting historians may be warned to distrust them.

The theory of the rational character of history rests on the notion that every real historical fact is at the same time "rational"—that is, in conformity with an intelligible comprehensive plan; ordinarily it is tacitly assumed that every social fact has its *raison d'être* in the development of society—that is, that it ends by turning to the advantage of society; hence the cause of every institution is sought for in the social need it was originally meant to supply.[1] This is the fundamental idea of Hegelianism, if not with Hegel, at least with the historians who have been his disciples (Ranke, Mommsen, Droysen, in France Cousin, Taine, and Michelet). This is a lay

[1] Thus Taine, in *Les origines de la France Contemporaine*, explains the origin of the privileges of the *ancien régime* by the services formerly rendered by the privileged classes.

disguise of the old theological theory of final causes which assumes the existence of a Providence occupied in guiding humanity in the direction of its interests. This is a consoling, but not a scientific *a priori* hypothesis; for the observation of historical facts does not indicate that things have always happened in the most rational way, or in the way most advantageous to men, nor that institutions have had any other cause than the interest of those who established them; the facts, indeed, point rather to the opposite conclusion.

From the same metaphysical source has also sprung the Hegelian theory of the *ideas* which are successively realised in history through the medium of successive peoples. This theory, which has been popularised in France by Cousin and Michelet, has had its day, even in Germany, but it has been revived, especially in Germany, in the form of the historical mission (*Beruf*) which is attributed to peoples and persons. It will here be enough to observe that the very metaphors of "idea" and "mission" imply a transcendental anthropomorphic cause.

From the same optimistic conception of a rational guidance of the world is derived the theory of the continuous and necessary *progress* of humanity. Although it has been adopted by the positivists, this is merely a metaphysical hypothesis. In the ordinary sense of the word, "progress" is merely a subjective expression denoting those changes which follow the direction of our preferences. But, even taking the word in the objective sense given to it by Spencer (an increase in the variety and coordination of social phenomena), the study of historical facts does not point to a *single* universal and continuous progress of humanity, it brings before us a *number* of partial and intermittent progressive movements, and it gives us no reason to attribute them to a permanent cause inherent in humanity as a whole rather than to a series of local accidents.[1]

Attempts at a more scientific form of explanation have had their origin in the special branches of history (of languages, religion, law). By the separate study of the succession of facts of a single species, specialists have been enabled to ascertain the regular recurrence of the same successions of facts, and these results have been expressed in formulæ which are sometimes called laws (for example, the law of the tonic accent); these are never more than empirical laws which merely indicate successions of facts without explaining them, for they do not reveal the efficient cause. But specialists, influenced by a natural metaphor, and struck by the regularity of these successions, have regarded the evolution of usages (of a word, a rite, a dogma, a rule of law), as if it were an organic development analogous to the growth of a plant; we hear of the "life of words," of the "death of dogmas," of the "growth of myths." Then, in forgetfulness of the fact that all these things are pure abstractions, it has been tacitly assumed that there is a force inhering in the word, the rite, the rule, which produces its evolution. This is the theory of the development (*Entwickelung*) of usages and institutions; it was started in Ger-

[1] A good criticism of the theory of progress will be found in P. Lacombe, *De l'histoire Considérée Comme Science.*

many by the "historical" school, and has dominated all the special branches of history. The history of languages alone has succeeded in shaking off its influence.[1] Just as usages have been treated as if they were existences possessing a separate life of their own, so the succession of individuals composing the various bodies within a society (royalty, church, senate, parliament) has been personified by the attribution to it of a will, which is treated as an active cause. A world of imaginary beings has thus been created behind the historical facts, and has replaced Providence in the explanation of them. For our defence against this deceptive mythology a single rule will suffice: Never seek the causes of an historical fact without having first expressed it concretely in terms of acting and thinking individuals. If abstractions are used, every metaphor must be avoided which would make them play the part of living beings.

By a comparison of the evolutions of the different species of facts which coexist in one and the same society, the "historical" school was led to the discovery of solidarity (*Zusammenhang*).[2] But, before attempting to discover its causes by analysis, the adherents of this school assumed the existence of a permanent general cause residing in the society itself. And, as it was customary to personify society, a special temperament was attributed to it, the peculiar genius of the nation or the race, manifesting itself.

[1] See the very clear declarations of one of the principal representatives of linguistic science in France, V. Henry, *Antinomies linguistiques*, Paris, 1896, 8vo.

[2] See above, p. 284.

in the different social activities and explaining their solidarity.[1] This was simply an hypothesis suggested by the animal world, in which each species has permanent characteristics. It would have been inadequate, for in order to explain how a given society comes to change its character from one epoch to another (the Greeks between the seventh and the fourth centuries, the English between the fifteenth and the nineteenth), it would have been necessary to invoke the aid of external causes. And the theory is untenable, for all the societies known to history are groups of men without anthropological unity and without common hereditary characteristics.

In addition to these metaphysical or metaphorical explanations, attempts have been made to apply to the investigation of causes in history the classical procedure of the natural sciences: the comparison of parallel series of successive phenomena in order to discover those which always appear together. The "comparative method" has assumed several different forms. Sometimes the subject of study has been a detail of social life (a usage, an institution, a belief, a rule), defined in abstract terms; its evolutions in different societies have been compared with a view to determine the common evolution which is to be attributed to one and the same general cause. Thus have arisen comparative philology, mythology, and

[1] Lamprecht, in the article quoted, p. 247, after having compared the artistic, religious, and economic evolutions of mediæval Germany, and after having shown that they can all be divided into periods of the same duration, explains the simultaneous transformations of the different usages and institutions of a given society by the transformations of the collective "social soul." This is only another form of the same hypothesis.

law. It has been proposed (in England) to give precision to the comparative method by applying "statistics"; this would mean the systematic comparison of all known societies and the enumeration of all the cases where two usages are found together. This is the principle of Bacon's tables of agreement; it is to be feared that it will be no more fertile in results. The defect of all such methods is that they apply to abstract and partly arbitrary notions, sometimes merely to verbal resemblances, and do not rest on a knowledge of the whole of the conditions under which the facts occur.

We can conceive a more concrete method which, instead of comparing fragments, should compare wholes, that is entire societies, either the same society at different stages of its evolution (England in the sixteenth, and again in the nineteenth century), or else the general evolution of several societies, contemporary with each other (England and France), or existing at different epochs (Rome and England). Such a method might be useful negatively, for the purpose of ascertaining that a given fact is not the necessary effect of another, since they are not always found together (for example, the emancipation of women and Christianity). But positive results are hardly to be expected of it, for the concomitance of two facts in several series does not show whether one is the cause of the other, or whether both are joint effects of a single cause.

The methodical investigation of the causes of a fact requires an analysis of the conditions under which the fact occurs, performed so as to isolate the necessary condition which is its cause; it presupposes, therefore, the complete knowledge of these conditions. But this is precisely what we never have in history. We must therefore renounce the idea of arriving at causes by direct methods such as are used in the other sciences.

As a matter of fact, however, historians often do employ the notion of cause, which, as we have shown above, is indispensable for the purpose of formulating events and constructing periods. They know causes partly from the authors of documents who observed the facts, partly from the analogy of the causes which we all observe at the present day. The whole history of events is a chain of obviously and incontrovertibly connected incidents, each one of which is the determining cause of another. The lance-thrust of Montgomery is the cause of the death of Henry II.; this death is the cause of the accession to power of the Guises, which again is the cause of the rising of the Protestants.

The observation of causes by the authors of documents is limited to the interconnection of the accidental facts observed by them; these are, in truth, the causes which are known with the greatest certainty. Thus history, unlike the other sciences, is better able to ascertain the causes of particular incidents than those of general transformations, for the work is found already done in the documents.

In the investigation of the causes of general facts, historical construction is reduced to the analogy between the past and the present. Whatever chance there is of finding the causes which explain the evolution of past societies must lie in the direct observation of the transformations of present societies.

This is a branch of study which is not yet firmly established; here we can only state the principles of it.

(1) In order to ascertain the causes of the solidarity between the different habits of one and the same society, it is necessary to look beyond the abstract and conventional form which the facts assume in language (dogma, rule, rite, institution), and attend to the real concrete centres, which are always thinking and acting men. Here only are found together the different species of activity which language separates by abstraction. Their solidarity is to be sought for in some dominating feature in the character or the environment of the men which influences all the different manifestations of their activity. We must not expect the same degrees of solidarity in all the species of activity; there will be most of it in those species where each individual is in close dependence on the actions of the mass (economic, social, political life); there will be less of it in the intellectual activities (arts, sciences), where individual initiative has freer play.[1] Documents mention most habits (beliefs, customs, institutions) in the lump, without distinguishing individuals; and yet, in one and the same society, habits vary considerably from one man to another. It is necessary to take account of these differences, otherwise there is a danger of

[1] The historians of literature, who began by searching for the connection between the arts and the rest of social life, thus gave the first place to the most difficult question.

explaining the actions of artists and men of science by the beliefs and the habits of their prince or their tradesmen.

(2) In order to ascertain the causes of an evolution, it is necessary to study the only beings which can evolve—men. Every evolution has for its cause a change in the material conditions or in the habits of certain men. Observation shows us two kinds of change. In the one case, the men remain the same, but change their manner of acting or thinking, either voluntarily through imitation, or by compulsion. In the other, the men who practised the old usage disappear and are replaced by others who do not practise it; these may be strangers, or they may be the descendants of the first set of men, but educated in a different manner. This renewing of the generations seems, in our day, to be the most active cause of evolution. It is natural to suppose that the same holds good of the past; evolution has been slower, the more exclusively each generation has been formed by the imitation of its forerunners.

There is still one more question to ask. Are men all alike, differing merely in the *conditions* under which they live (education, resources, government), and is evolution produced solely by changes in these *conditions?* Or are there groups of men with *hereditary differences*, born with tendencies to different activities and with aptitudes leading to different evolutions, so that evolution may be the product, in part at least, of the increase, the diminution, and the displacement of these groups? Taking the extreme cases, the white, black, and yellow races of mankind, the differences in aptitude are obvious; no black people has ever developed a civilisation. It is thus probable that smaller hereditary differences may have had their share in the determination of events. If so, historical evolution would be partly produced by physiological and anthropological causes. But history provides us with no sure means of determining the action of these hereditary differences between men; it goes no further than the conditions of their existence. The last question of history remains insoluble by historical methods.

CHAPTER V

EXPOSITION

We have still to study a question whose practical interest is obvious: What are the forms in which historical works present themselves? These forms are, in fact, very numerous. Some of them are antiquated; not all are legitimate; the best have their drawbacks. We should ask, therefore, not only what are the forms in which historical works appear, but also which of these represent truly rational types of exposition.

By "historical works" we mean here all those which are intended to communicate results obtained by the labour of historical construction, whatever may be the nature, the extent, and the bearing of these results. The critical elaboration of documents, which is treated of in Book II., and which is preparatory to historical construction, is naturally excluded.

Historians may differ, and up to the present have differed, on several essential points. They have not always had, nor have they all now, the same conception of the end aimed at by historical work; hence arise differences in the nature of the facts chosen, the manner of dividing the subject, that is, of co-ordinating the facts, the manner of presenting them, the manner of proving them. This would be the place to indicate how "the mode of writing history" has evolved from the beginning. But as the history of the modes of writing history has not yet been written well,[1] we shall here content ourselves with some very general remarks on the period prior to the second half of the nineteenth century, confining ourselves to what is strictly necessary for the understanding of the present situation.

I. History was first conceived as the narration of memorable events. To preserve the memory and propagate the knowledge of glorious deeds, or of events which were of importance to a man, a family, or a people; such was the aim of history in the time of Thucydides and Livy. In addition, history was early considered as a collection of precedents, and the knowledge of history as a practical preparation for life, especially political life (military and civil). Polybius and Plutarch wrote to instruct, they claimed to give recipes for action. Hence in classical antiquity the subject-matter of history consisted chiefly of political incidents, wars, and revolutions. The ordinary framework of historical exposition (within which the facts were usually arranged in chronological order) was the life of

[1] For the earlier epochs, consult good histories of Greek, Roman, and mediæval literature which contain chapters devoted to "historians." For the modern period, consult the Introduction of M. G. Monod to vol. i. of the *Revue historique;* the work by F. X. v. Wegde, *Geschichte der deutschen Historiographie* (1885), relates only to Germany, and is mediocre. Some "Notes on History in France in the Nineteenth Century" have been published by C. Jullian as an Introduction to his *Extraits des historiens français du xixe siècle* (Paris, 1897, 12mo). The history of modern historiography has still to be written. See the partial attempt by E. Bernheim, *Lehrbuch,* pp. 13 *sqq.*

a person, the whole life of a people, or a particular period in it; there were in antiquity but few essays in general history. As the aim of the historian was to please or to instruct, or to please and instruct at the same time, history was a branch of literature: there were not too many scruples on the score of proofs; those who worked from written documents took no care to distinguish the text of such documents from their own text; in reproducing the narratives of their predecessors they adorned them with details, and sometimes (under pretext of being precise) with numbers, with speeches, with reflections, and elegances. We can in a manner see them at work in every instance where it is possible to compare Greek and Roman historians, Ephorus and Livy, for example, with their sources.

The writers of the Renaissance directly imitated the ancients. For them, too, history was a literary art with apologetic aims or didactic pretensions. In Italy it was too often a means of gaining the favour of princes, or a theme for declamations. This state of affairs lasted a long time. Even in the seventeenth century we find, in Mézeray, an historian of the ancient classical pattern.

However, in the historical literature of the Renaissance, two novelties claim our attention, in which the mediæval influence is incontrovertibly manifest. On the one hand we see the retention of a form of exposition which was unusual in antiquity, which was created by the Catholic historians of the later ages (Eusebius, Orosius), and which enjoyed great favour in the Middle Ages,—that which, instead of embracing only the history of a single man, family, or people, embraces universal history. On the other hand there was introduced a mechanical artifice of exposition, having its origin in a practice common in the mediæval schools (the gloss), which had far-reaching consequences. The custom arose of adding notes to printed books of history.[1] Notes have made it possible to distinguish between the historical narrative and the documents which support it, to give references to sources, to disencumber and illustrate the text. It was in collections of documents, and in critical dissertations, that the artifice of annotation was first employed; thence it penetrated, slowly, into historical works of other classes.

A second period begins in the eighteenth century. The "philosophers" then began to conceive history as the study, not of events for their own sakes, but of the habits of men. They were thus led to take an interest, not only in facts of a political order, but in the evolution of the arts, the sciences, of industry, and in manners. Montesquieu and Voltaire personified these tendencies. The *Essai sur les mœurs* is the first sketch, and, in some respects, the masterpiece of history thus conceived. The detailed narration of political and military events was still regarded as the main work of history, but to this it now became customary to add, generally by way of supplement or appendix, a sketch of the "progress of the human mind." The expression "history of

[1] It would be interesting to find out what are the earliest printed books furnished with notes in the modern fashion. Bibliophiles whom we have consulted are unable to say, their attention never having been drawn to the point.

civilisation" appears before the end of the eighteenth century. At the same time German university professors, especially at Göttingen, were creating, in order to supply educational needs, the new form of the historical "manual," a methodical collection of carefully justified facts, with no literary or other pretensions. Collections of historical facts, made with a view to aid in the interpretation of literary texts, or out of mere curiosity in regard to the things of the past, had existed from ancient times; but the medleys of Athenæus and Aulus Gellius, or the vaster and better arranged compilations of the Middle Ages and the Renaissance, are by no means to be compared with the "scientific manuals" of which the German professors then gave the models. These professors, moreover, contributed towards the clearing up of the vague, general notion which the philosophers had of "civilisation," for they applied themselves to the organisation of the history of languages, of literatures, of the arts, of religions, of law, of economic phenomena, and so on, as so many separate branches of study. Thus the domain of history was greatly enlarged, and scientific, that is, simple and objective, exposition began to compete with the rhetorical or sententious, patriotic or philosophical ideals of antiquity.

This competition was at first timid and obscure, for the beginning of the nineteenth century was marked by a literary renaissance which renovated historical literature. Under the influence of the romantic movement historians sought for more vivid methods of exposition than those employed by their predecessors, methods better adapted to strike the imagination and rouse the emotions of the public, by filling the mind with poetical images of vanished realities. Some endeavoured to preserve the peculiar colouring of the original documents, which they adapted: "Charmed with the contemporary narratives," says Barante, "I have endeavoured to write a consecutive account which should borrow from them their animation and interest." This leads directly to the neglect of criticism, and to the reproduction of whatever is effective from the literary point of view. Others declared that the facts of the past ought to be recounted with all the emotions of a spectator. "Thierry," says Michelet, praising him, "in telling us the story of Klodowig, breathes the spirit and shows the emotion of recently invaded France . . ." Michelet "stated the problem of history as the resuscitation of integral life in the inmost parts of the organism." With the romantic historians the choice of subject, of plan, of the proofs, of the style, is dominated by an engrossing desire to produce an effect—a literary, not a scientific ambition. Some romantic historians have slid down this inclined plane to the level of the "historical novel." We know the nature of this species of literature, which flourished so vigorously from the Abbé Barthélemy and Chateaubriand down to Mérimée and Ebers, and which some are now vainly attempting to rejuvenate. The object is to "make the scenes of the past live again" in dramatic pictures artistically constructed with "true" colours and details. The obvious object of the method is that it does not provide the reader with any means of distinguishing between the elements borrowed from the documents and the imaginary elements, not to mention the fact that generally the documents used are not all of the same origin, so that while the colour of each stone may be "true" that of the mosaic is false. Dezobry's *Rome au siècle d'Auguste*, Augustin Thierry's *Récits mérovingiens*, and other "pictures" produced at the same epoch were constructed on the same principle, and are subject to the same drawbacks as the historical novels properly so-called.[1]

We may summarise what precedes by saying that, up to about 1850, history continued to be, both for historians and the public, a branch of literature. An excellent proof of this lies in the fact that up till then historians were accustomed to publish new editions of their works, at intervals of several years, without making any change in them, and that the public tolerated the practice. Now every scientific work needs to be continually recast, revised, brought up to date. Scientific workers do not claim to give their works an immutable form, they do not expect to be read by posterity or to achieve personal immortality; it is enough for them if the results of their researches, corrected, it may be, and possibly transformed by subsequent researches, should be incorporated in the fund of knowledge which forms the scientific heritage of mankind. No one reads Newton or Lavoisier; it is enough for their glory that their labours should have contributed to the production

[1] It is clear that the romantic methods which are used for the purpose of obtaining effects of local colour and "revising" the past, often puerile in the hands of the ablest writers, are altogether intolerable when they are employed by any others. See a good example (criticism of a book of M. Mourin by M. Monod) in the *Revue Critique*, 1874, ii. pp. 163 *sqq*.

of works by which their own have been superseded, and which will be, sooner or later, superseded in their turn. It is only works of art that enjoy perpetual youth. And the public is well aware of the fact; no one would ever think of studying natural history in Buffon, whatever his opinion might be of the merits of this stylist. But the same public is quite ready to study history in Augustin Thierry, in Macaulay, in Carlyle, in Michelet, and the books of the great writers who have treated historical subjects are reprinted, fifty years after the author's death, in their original form, though they are manifestly no longer on a level with current knowledge. It is clear that, for many, form counts before matter in history, and that an historical work is primarily, if not exclusively, a work of art.[1]

II. It is within the last fifty years that the scientific forms of historical exposition have been evolved and settled, in accordance with the general principle that the aim of history is not to please, nor to give practical maxims of conduct, nor to arouse the emotions, but knowledge pure and simple.

We begin by distinguishing between (1) monographs and (2) works of a general character.

[1] It is a commonplace, and an error all the same, to maintain the exact opposite of the above, namely, that the works of critical scholars live, while the works of historians grow antiquated, so that scholars gain a more solid reputation than historians do: "Père Daniel is now read no longer, and Père Anselme is always read." But the works of scholars become antiquated too, and the fact that not all the parts of the work of Père Anselme have yet been superseded (that is why he is still read), ought not to deceive us: the great majority of the works written by scholars, like those of researchers in the sciences proper, are provisional and doomed to oblivion.

(1) A man writes a monograph when he proposes to elucidate a special point, a single fact, or a limited body of facts, for example the whole or a portion of the life of an individual, a single event or a series of events between two dates lying near together. The types of possible subjects of a monograph cannot be enumerated, for the subject-matter of history can be divided indefinitely, and in an infinite number of ways. But all modes of division are not equally judicious, and, though the reverse has been maintained, there are, in history as in all the sciences, subjects which it would be stupid to treat in monographs, and monographs which, though well executed, represent so much useless labour,[1] Persons of moderate ability and no great mental range, devoted to what is called "curious" learning, are very ready to occupy themselves with insignificant questions;[2] indeed, for the purpose of making a first estimate of an historian's intellectual power, a fairly good criterion may be had in the list of the monographs he has written.[3] It is the gift of seeing the

[1] "It is in vain that those professionally concerned try to deceive themselves on this point; not everything in the past is interesting. "Supposing we were to write the Life of the Duke of Angoulême," says Pécuchet. "But he was an imbecile!" answers Bouvard; "Never mind; personages of the second order often have an enormous influence, and perhaps he was able to control the march of events."—G. Flaubert, *Bouvard et Pécuchet*, p. 157.

[2] As persons of moderate ability have a tendency to prefer insignificant subjects, there is active competition in the treatment of such subjects. We often have occasion to note the simultaneous appearance of several monographs on the same subject. It is not rare for the subject to be altogether devoid of importance.

[3] Interesting subjects for monographs are not always capable of being treated: there are some which the state of the sources puts out of the question. This is why beginners, even those

important problems, and the taste for their treatment, as well as the power of solving them, which, in all the sciences, raise men to the first rank. But let us suppose the subject has been rationally chosen. Every monograph, in order to be useful—that is, capable of being fully turned to account—should conform to three rules: (1) in a monograph every historical fact derived from documents should only be presented accompanied by a reference to the documents from which it is taken, and an estimate of the value of these documents;[1] (2) chronological order should be followed as far as possible, because this is the order in which we know that the facts occurred, and by which we are guided in searching for causes and effects; (3) the title of the monograph must enable its subject to be known with exacti-

who have ability, experience so much embarrassment in choosing subjects for their first monographs, when they are not aided by good advice or good fortune, and often lose themselves in attempting the impossible. It would be very severe, and very unjust, to judge any one from the list of his *first* monographs.

[1] In practice it is proper to give at the beginning a list of the sources used in the whole of the monograph (with appropriate bibliographical information as to the printed works, and in the case of manuscripts, a mention of the nature of the documents and their shelf-marks); besides, each special statement should be accompanied by its proof: the exact text of the supporting document should be quoted, if possible, so that the reader may be in a position to verify the interpretation; otherwise an analysis of it should be given in a note, or, at the least, the title of the document, with its shelf-mark, or with a precise indication of the place where it was published. The general rule is to put the reader in a position to know the exact reasons for which such and such conclusions have been adopted at each stage of the analysis.

Beginners, resembling ancient authors in this respect, naturally do not observe all these rules. Frequently, instead of quoting the text or the titles of documents, they refer to these by their shelf-mark, or by the title of the general collection in which they are printed, from which the reader can learn nothing as to the nature

tude: we cannot protest too strongly against those incomplete or fancy titles which so unnecessarily complicate bibliographical searches. A fourth rule has been laid down; it has been said "a monograph is useful only when it exhausts the subject"; but it is quite legitimate to do temporary work with documents which one has at one's disposal, even when there is reason to believe that others exist, provided always that precise notice is given as to what documents have been employed.

Any one who has tact will see that, in a monograph, the apparatus of demonstration, while needing to be complete, ought to be reduced to what is strictly necessary. Sobriety is imperative; all parading of erudition which might have been spared without inconvenience is odious.[1] In history it often happens that the best executed monographs furnish no other result than the proof that knowledge is impossible. It is necessary to resist the desire which leads some to round off with subjective, ambitious, and vague conclusions monographs which will not

of the text adduced. The following is another mistake of the crudest kind, and yet of frequent occurrence: Beginners, and persons of little experience, do not always understand why the custom has been introduced of inserting footnotes; at the bottom of the pages of the books they have they see a fringe of notes; they think themselves bound to fringe their own books in the same way, but their notes are adventitious and purely ornamental; they do not serve either to exhibit the proof or to enable the reader to verify the statements. All these methods are inadmissible, and should be vigorously denounced.

[1] Almost all beginners have an unfortunate tendency to wander off into superfluous digressions, to amass reflections and pieces of information which have no relevance to the main subject; they would recognise, if they reflected, that the causes of this tendency are bad taste, a kind of naïve vanity, sometimes mental confusion.

bear them.[1] The proper conclusion of a good monograph is the balance-sheet of the results obtained by it and the points left doubtful. A monograph made on these principles may grow antiquated, but it will not fall to pieces, and its author will never need to blush for it.

(2) Works of a general character are addressed either to students or to the general public.

A. General works intended principally for students and specialists now appear in the form of "repertories," "manuals," and "scientific histories." In a repertory a number of verified facts belonging to a given class are collected and arranged in an order which makes it easy to refer to them. If the facts thus collected have precise dates, chronological order is adopted: thus the task has been undertaken of compiling "Annals" of German history, in which the summary entry of the events, arranged by dates, is accompanied by the texts from which the events are known, with accurate references to the sources and the works of critics; the collection of the *Jahrbücher der deutschen Geschichte* has for its object the elucidation, as far as is possible, of the facts of German history, including all that is susceptible of scientific discussion and proof, but omitting all that belongs to the domain of appreciation and general views. When the facts are badly dated, or

[1] We meet with declarations like the following: "I have been long familiar with the documents of this period and this class. I have an impression that such and such conclusions, which I cannot prove, are true." Of two things one: either the author can give the reasons for his impression, and then we can judge them, or he cannot give them, and we may assume that he has none of serious value.

are simultaneous, alphabetical arrangement must be employed; thus we have Dictionaries: dictionaries of institutions, biographical dictionaries, historical encyclopædias, such as the *Realencyclopædie* of Pauly-Wissowa. These alphabetical repertories are, in theory, just as the *Jahrbücher*, collections of proved facts; if, in practice, the references in them are less rigorous, if the apparatus of texts supporting the statements is less complete, the difference is without justification.[1] *Scientific manuals* are also, properly speaking, repertories, since they are collections in which established facts are arranged in systematic order, and are exhibited objectively, with their proofs, and without any literary adornment. The authors of these "manuals," of which the most numerous and the most perfect specimens have been composed in our days in the German universities, have no object in view except to draw up minute inventories of the acquisitions made by knowledge, in order that workers may be enabled to assimilate the results of criticism with greater ease and rapidity, and may be furnished with starting-points for new researches. Manuals of this kind now exist for most of the special branches of the history of civilisation (languages, literature, religion, law, *Alterthümer*, and so on), for the history of institutions, for the different parts of

[1] This difference has a tendency to disappear. The most recent alphabetical collections of historical facts (the *Realencyclopædie der classischen Alterthumswissenschaft* of Pauly-Wissowa, the *Dictionnaire des antiquités* of Daremberg and Saglio, the *Dictionary of National Biography* of Leslie Stephen and Sidney Lee) are furnished with a sufficiently ample apparatus. It is principally in biographical dictionaries that the custom of giving no proofs tends to persist; see the *Allgemeine deutsche Biographie*, &c.

ecclesiastical history. It will suffice to mention the names of Schœmann, of Marquardt and Mommsen, of Gilbert, of Krumbacher, of Harnack, of Möller. These works are not marked by the dryness of the majority of the primitive "manuals," which were published in Germany a hundred years ago, and which were little more than tables of subjects, with references to the books and documents to be consulted; in the modern type the exposition and discussion are no doubt terse and compact, but yet not abbreviated beyond a point at which they may be tolerated, even preferred by cultivated readers. They take away the taste for other books, as G. Paris very well says:[1] "When one has feasted on these substantial pages, so full of facts, which, with all their appearance of impersonality, yet contain, and above all suggest, so many thoughts, it is difficult to read books, even books of distinction, in which the subject is cut up symmetrically to fit in with a preconceived system, is coloured by fancy, and is, so to speak, presented to us in disguise, books in which the author continually comes between us and the spectacle which he claims to make intelligible to us, but which he never allows us to see." The great historical "manuals," uniform with the treatises and manuals of the other sciences (with the added complication of authorities and proofs), ought to be, and are, continually improved, emended, corrected, brought up to date: they are, by definition, works of science and not of art.

The earliest repertories and the earliest scientific "manuals" were composed by isolated individuals.

[1] *Revue Critique*, 1874, i. p. 327.

But it was soon recognised that a single man cannot correctly arrange, or have the proper mastery over a vast collection of facts. The task has been divided. Repertories are executed, in our days, by collaborators in association (who are sometimes of different nationalities and write in different languages). The great manuals (of I. von Müller, of G. Gröber, of H. Paul, and others) are collections of special treatises each written by a specialist. The principle of collaboration is excellent, but on condition (1) that the collective work is of a nature to be resolved into great independent, though co-ordinated, monographs; (2) that the section entrusted to each collaborator has a certain extent; if the number of collaborators is too great and the part of each too limited, the liberty and the responsibility of each are diminished or disappear.

Histories, intended to give a narrative of events which happened but once, and to state the general facts which dominate the whole course of special evolutions, still have a reason for existence, even after the multiplication of methodical manuals. But scientific methods of exposition have been introduced into them, as into monographs and manuals, and that by imitation. The reform has consisted, in every case, in the renunciation of literary ornaments and of statements without proof. Grote produced the first model of a "history" thus defined. At the same time certain forms which once had a vogue have now fallen into disuse: this is the case with the "Universal Histories" with continuous narrative, which were so much liked, for different reasons, in the Middle Ages and in the eighteenth century; in the present century Schlosser and Weber in Germany, Cantù in Italy, have produced the last specimens of them. This type has been abandoned for historical reasons, because we have ceased to regard humanity as a whole, bound together by a single evolution; and for practical reasons, because we have recognised the impossibility of collecting so overwhelming a mass of facts in a single work. The Universal Histories which are still published in collaboration (the Oncken collection is the best type of them), are, like the great manuals, composed of independent sections, each treated by a different author; they are publishers' combinations. Historians have in our days been led to adopt the division by states (national histories) and by epochs.[1]

B. There is in theory no reason why historical works intended principally for the public should not be conceived in the same spirit as works designed for students and specialists, nor why they should not be composed in the same manner, apart from simplifications and omissions which readily suggest themselves. And, in fact, there are in existence succinct, substantial, and readable summaries, in which no statement is advanced which is not tacitly supported by solid references, in which the acquisitions

[1] The custom of appending to "histories," that is to narratives of political events, summaries of the results obtained by the special historians of art, literature, &c., still persists. A "History of France" would not be considered complete if it did not contain chapters on the history of art, literature, manners, &c., in France. However, it is not the summary account of special evolutions, described at second hand from the works of specialists, which is in its proper place in a scientific "History"; it is the study of those general facts which have dominated the special evolutions in their entirety.

of science are precisely stated, judiciously explained, their significance and value clearly brought out. The French, thanks to their natural gifts of tact, dexterity, and accuracy of mind, excel, as a rule, in this department. There have been published in our country review-articles and works of higher popularisation in which the results of a number of original works have been cleverly condensed, in a way that has won the admiration of the very specialists who, by their heavy monographs, have rendered these works possible. Nothing, however, is more dangerous than popularisation. As a matter of fact, most works of popularisation do not conform to the modern ideal of historical exposition; we frequently find in them survivals of the ancient ideal, that of antiquity, the Renaissance, and the romantic school.

The explanation is easy. The defects of the historical works designed for the general public—defects which are sometimes enormous, and have, with many able minds, discredited popular works as a class—are the consequences of the insufficient preparation or of the inferior literary education of the "popularisers."

A populariser is excused from original research; but he ought to know everything of importance that has been published on his subject, he ought to be up to date, and to have thought out for himself the conclusions reached by the specialists. If he has not personally made a special study of the subject he proposes to treat, he must obviously read it up, and the task is long. For the professional populariser there is a strong temptation to study superficially a few recent monographs, to hastily string together or combine extracts from them, and, in order to render this medley more attractive, to deck it out, as far as is possible, with "general ideas" and external graces. The temptation is all the stronger from the circumstance that most specialists take no interest in works of popularisation, that these works are, in general, lucrative, and that the public at large is not in a position to distinguish clearly between honest and sham popularisation. In short, there are some, absurd as it may seem, who do not hesitate to summarise for others what they have not taken the trouble to learn for themselves, and to teach that of which they are ignorant. Hence, in most works of historical popularisation, there inevitably appear blemishes of every kind, which the well-informed always note with pleasure, but with a pleasure in which there is some touch of bitterness, because they alone can see these faults: unacknowledged borrowings, inexact references, mutilated names and texts, second-hand quotations, worthless hypotheses, imprudent assertions, puerile generalisations, and, in the enunciation of the most false or the most debatable opinions, an air of tranquil anthority.[1]

On the other hand, men whose information is all that could be desired, whose monographs intended

[1] It is hard to imagine what it is possible for the most interesting and best established results of modern criticism to become, in the hands of negligent and unskilful popularisers. The persons who know most of these possibilities are those who have occasion to read the improvised "compositions" of candidates in history examinations: the ordinary defects of inferior popularisation are here pushed sometimes to an absurd length.

for specialists are full of merit, sometimes show themselves capable, when they write for the public, of grave offences against scientific method. The Germans are habitual offenders: consider Mommsen, Droysen, Curtius, and Lamprecht. The reason is that these authors, when they address the public, wish to produce an effect upon it. Their desire to make a strong impression leads them to a certain relaxation of scientific rigour, and to the old rejected habits of ancient historiography. These men, scrupulous and minute as they are when they are engaged in establishing details, abandon themselves, in their exposition of general questions, to their natural impulses, like the common run of men. They take sides, they censure, they extol; they colour, they embellish; they allow themselves to be influenced by personal, patriotic, moral, or metaphysical considerations. And, over and above all this, they apply themselves, with their several degrees of talent, to the task of producing works of art; in this endeavour those who have no talent make themselves ridiculous, and the talent of those who have any is spoilt by their preoccupation with the effect they wish to produce.

Not, let it be well understood, that "form" is of no importance, or that, provided he makes himself intelligible, the historian has a right to employ incorrect, vulgar, slovenly, or clumsy language. A contempt for rhetoric, for paste diamonds and paper flowers, does not exclude a taste for a pure and strong, a terse and pregnant style. Fustel de Coulanges was a good writer, although throughout his life he recommended and practised the avoidance of metaphor. On the contrary we see no harm in repeating[1] that the historian, considering the extreme complexity of the phenomena he undertakes to describe, is under an obligation not to write badly. But he should write *consistently* well, and never bedeck himself with finery.

[1] Cf. *supra*, p. 266.

CONCLUSION

I. History is only the utilisation of documents. But it is a matter of chance whether documents are preserved or lost. Hencé the predominant part played by chance in the formation of history.

The quantity of documents in existence, if not of known documents, is given; time, in spite of all the precautions which are taken nowadays, is continually diminishing it; it will never increase. History has at its disposal a limited stock of documents; this very circumstance limits the possible progress of historical science. When all the documents are known, and have gone through the operations which fit them for use, the work of critical scholarship will be finished. In the case of some ancient periods, for which documents are rare, we can now see that in a generation or two it will be time to stop. Historians will then be obliged to take refuge more and more in modern periods. Thus history will not fufil the dream which, in the nineteenth century, inspired the romantic school with so much enthusiasm for the study of history: it will not penetrate the mystery of the origin of societies; and, for want of documents, the beginnings of the evolution of humanity will always remain obscure.

The historian does not collect by his own observation the materials necessary for history as is done in the other sciences: he works on facts the knowledge of which has been transmitted by former observers. In history knowledge is not obtained, as in the other sciences, by direct methods, it is indirect. History is not, as has been said, a science of observation, but a science of reasoning.

In order to use facts which have been observed under unknown conditions, it is necessary to apply criticism to them, and criticism consists in a series of reasonings by analogy. The facts as furnished by criticism are isolated and scattered; in order to organise them into a structure it is necessary to imagine and group them in accordance with their resemblances to facts of the present day, an operation which also depends on the use of analogies. This necessity compels history to use an exceptional method. In order to frame its arguments from analogy, it must always combine the knowledge of the particular conditions under which the facts of the past occurred with an understanding of the general conditions under which the facts of humanity occur. Its method is to draw up special *tables* of the facts of an epoch in the past, and to apply to them sets of *questions* founded on the study of the present.

The operations which must necessarily be performed in order to pass from the inspection of documents to the knowledge of the facts and evolutions of the past are very numerous. Hence the necessity of the division and organisation of labour in history. It is requisite, on the one hand, that those specialists who occupy themselves with the search for documents, their restoration and preliminary classification, should co-ordinate their efforts, in order that the preparatory work of critical scholarship may be finished as soon as possible, under the best conditions as to accuracy and economy of labour. On the other hand, authors of partial syntheses (monographs) designed to serve as materials for more comprehensive syntheses ought to agree among themselves to work on a common method, in order that the results of each may be used by the others without preliminary investigations. Lastly, workers of experience should be found to renounce personal research and devote their whole time to the study of these partial syntheses, in order to combine them scientifically in comprehensive works of historical construction. And if the result of these labours were to bring out clear and certain conclusions as to the nature and the causes of social evolution, a truly scientific "philosophy of history" would have been created, which historians might acknowledge as legitimately crowning historical science.

Conceivably a day may come when, thanks to the organisation of labour, all existing documents will have been discovered, emended, arranged, and all the facts established of which the traces have not been destroyed. When that day comes, history will be established, but it will not be fixed: it will continue to be gradually modified in proportion as the direct study of existing societies becomes more scientific and permits a better understanding of social phenomena and their evolution; for the new ideas which will doubtless be acquired on the nature, the causes, and the relative importance of social facts will continue to transform the ideas which will be formed of the societies and events of the past.[1]

II. It is an obsolete illusion to suppose that history supplies information of practical utility in the conduct of life (*Historia magistra vitæ*), lessons directly profitable to individuals and peoples; the conditions under which human actions are performed are rarely sufficiently similar at two different moments for the "lessons of history" to be directly applicable. But it is an error to say, by way of reaction, that "the distinguishing feature of history is to be good for nothing."[2] It has an indirect utility.

History enables us to understand the present in so far as it explains the origin of the existing state of things. Here we must admit that history does not offer an equal interest through the whole extent of time which it covers; there are remote genera-

[1] We have spoken above of the element of subjectivity which it is impossible to eliminate from historical construction, and which has been misinterpreted to the extent of denying history the character of a science: this element of subjectivity which troubled Pécuchet (G. Flaubert, *Bouvard et Pécuchet*, p. 157) and Sylvestre Bonnard (A. France, *Le crime de Silvestre Bonnard*, p. 310), and which causes Faust to say:

> "Die Zeiten der Vergangenheit
> Sind uns ein Buch mit sieben Siegeln.
> Was ihr den Geist der Zeiten heisst,
> Das ist im Grund der Herren eigner Geist,
> In dem die Zeiten sich bespiegeln."

["Past times are to us a book with seven seals. What you call the spirit of the times is at bottom your own spirit, in which the times are mirrored."—Goethe, *Faust*, i. 3.]

[2] A saying attributed to a "Sorbonne professor" by M. de la Blanchère (*Revue Critique*, 1895, i. p. 176). Others have declaimed on the theme that the knowledge of history is mischievous and paralyses. See F. Nietzsche, *Unzeitgemässe Betrachtungen*, II. *Nutzen und Nachtheil der Historie für das Leben*, Leipzig, 1874, 8vo.

tions whose traces are no longer visible in the world as it now is; for the purpose of explaining the political constitution of contemporary England, for example, the study of the Anglo-Saxon witangemot is without value, that of the events of the eighteenth and nineteenth centuries is all-important. The evolution of the civilised societies has within the last hundred years been accelerated to such a degree that, for the understanding of their present form, the history of these hundred years is more important than that of the ten preceding centuries. As an explanation of the present, history would almost reduce to the study of the contemporary period.

History is also indispensable for the completion of the political and social sciences, which are still in process of formation; for the direct observation of social phenomena (in a state of rest) is not a sufficient foundation for these sciences—there must be added a study of the development of these phenomena in time, that is, their history.[1] This is why all the sciences which deal with man (linguistic, law, science of religions, political economy, and so on) have in this century assumed the form of historical sciences.

But the chief merit of history is that of being an instrument of intellectual culture; it is so in several

[1] History and the social sciences are mutually dependent on each other; they progress in parallel lines by a continual interchange of services. The social sciences furnish a knowledge of the present, required by history for the purpose of making representations of the facts and reasoning from documents. History gives the information about evolutions which is necessary in order to understand the present.

ways. Firstly, the practice of the historical method of investigation, of which the principles have been sketched in the present volume, is very hygienic for the mind, which it cures of credulity. Secondly, history, by exhibiting to us a great number of differing societies, prepares us to understand and tolerate a variety of usages; by showing us that societies have often been transformed, it familiarises us with variation in social forms, and cures us of a morbid dread of change. Lastly, the contemplation of past evolutions, which enables us to understand how the transformations of humanity are brought about by changes of habits and the renewal of generations, saves us from the temptation of applying biological analogies (selection, struggle for existence, inherited habits, and so on) to the explanation of social evolution, which is not produced by the operation of the same causes as animal evolution.

APPENDICES

APPENDIX I

THE SECONDARY TEACHING OF HISTORY IN FRANCE

I. The teaching of history is a recent addition to secondary education. Formerly history was taught to the sons of kings and great persons, in order to give them a preparation in the art of governing, according to the ancient tradition, but it was a sacred science reserved for the future rulers of states, a science for princes, not for subjects. The secondary schools which have been organised since the sixteenth century, ecclesiastical or secular, Catholic or Protestant, did not admit history into their plan of study, or only admitted it as an appendage to the study of the ancient languages. This was the tradition of the Jesuits in France; it was adopted by the University of Napoleon.

History was only introduced into secondary education in the nineteenth century, under the pressure of public opinion; and although it has been allotted more space in France than in England, or even in Germany, it has continued to be a subsidiary subject, not taught in a special class (as philosophy is), nor always by a special professor, and counting for very little in examinations.

Historical instruction has for a long time felt the effects of the manner in which it was introduced. The subject was imposed by the authorities on teachers trained exclusively in the study of literature, and could find no suitable place in a system of classical education based on the study of forms, and indifferent to the knowledge of social phenomena. History was taught because it was prescribed by the programme; but this programme, the sole motive and guide of the instruction, was always an accident, and varied with the preferences, or even the personal studies of those who framed it. History formed part of the social conventions; there are, it was said, names and facts "of which it is not permissible to be ignorant"; but the things of which ignorance was not permitted varied greatly, from the names of the Merovingian kings and the battles of the Seven Years' War to the Salic Law and the work of Saint Vincent de Paul.

The improvised staffs which, in order to carry out the programme, had to furnish impromptu instruction in history, had no clear idea either of the reasons for such instruction, or of its place in general education, or of the technical methods necessary for giving it. With this lack of tradition, of pedagogic preparation, and even of mechanical aids, the professor of history found himself carried back to the ages before printing, when the teacher had to supply the pupil with all the facts which formed the subject-matter of instruction, and he adopted the mediæval procedure. Armed with a note-book in which he had written down the list of facts to be taught, he read it out to the pupils, sometimes making a pretence of extemporising; this was the "lesson," the corner-stone of historical instruction. The whole series of lessons, determined by the programme, formed the "course." The pupil was expected to write as he listened (this was called "taking notes") and to compose a written account of what he had heard (this was the *rédaction*). But as the pupils were not taught how to take notes, nearly all of them were content to write very rapidly, from the professor's dictation, a rough draft, which they copied out at home in the form of a *rédaction*, without any endeavour to grasp the meaning either of what they heard or what they transcribed. To this mechanical labour the most zealous added extracts copied from books, generally with just as little reflection.

Appendix I

In order to get the facts judged essential into the pupils' heads, the professor used to make a very short version of the lesson, the "summary" or "abstract," which he dictated openly, and caused to be learnt by heart. Thus of the two written exercises which occupied nearly the whole time of the class, one (the summary) was an overt dictation, the other (the *rédaction*) an unavowed dictation.

The only means adopted to check the pupils' work was to make them repeat the summary word for word, and to question them on the *rédaction*, that is to make them repeat approximately the words of the professor. Of the two oral exercises one was an overt, the other an unavowed repetition.

It is true the pupil was given a book, the *Précis d'histoire*,[1] but this book had the same form as the professor's course, and instead of serving as a basis for the oral instruction, merely duplicated it, and, as a rule, duplicated it badly, for it was not intelligible to the pupil. The authors of these text-books,[2] adopting the traditional methods of "abridgments," endeavoured to accumulate the greatest possible number of facts by omitting all their characteristic details and summarising them in the most general, and therefore vague, expressions. In the elementary books nothing was left but a residue of proper names and dates connected by formulæ of a uniform type; history appeared as a series of wars, treaties, reforms, revolutions, which only differed in the names of peoples, sovereigns, fields of battle, and in the figures giving the years.[3]

Such, down to the end of the Second Empire, was histori-

[1] The same institution has been adopted in German-speaking countries under the name of *Leitfaden* (guiding-thread), and in English-speaking countries under the name of *Text-book.*

[2] We must make an exception of Michelet's *Précis de l'histoire moderne*, and do Duruy the justice to acknowledge that in his school-books, even in the first editions, he has endeavoured, often successfully, to make his narratives both interesting and instructive.

[3] For a criticism of this method, see above, p. 265.

cal instruction in all French institutions, both secular and ecclesiastical—with a few exceptions, whose merit is measured by their rarity, for in those days a professor of history needed a more than common share of energy and initiative to rise above the routine of *rédaction* and summary.

II. In recent times the general movement of educational reform, which began in the Department and the Faculties, has at last extended to secondary instruction. The professors of history have been emancipated from the jealous supervision which weighed on their teaching under the government of the Empire, and have taken the opportunity to make trial of new methods. A system of historical pedagogy has been devised. It has been revealed with the approbation of the Department in the discussions of the society for the study of questions of secondary education, in the *Revue de l'enseignement secondaire*, and in the *Revue universitaire*. It has received official sanction in the *Instructions* appended to the programme of 1890; the report on history, the work of M. Lavisse, has become the charter which protects the professors who favour reform in their struggle against tradition.[1]

Historical instruction will no doubt issue from this crisis of renovation organised and provided with a rational pedagogic and technical system, such as is possessed by the older branches of instruction in languages, literature, and philosophy. But it is only to be expected that the reform should be much slower than in the case of the higher instruction. The *personnel* is much more numerous, and takes longer to train or to renew; the pupils are less zealous and less intelligent: the routine of the parents opposes to the new methods a force of inertia which is unknown to the Faculties; and the Baccalaureate, that general obstacle to all reform, is

[1] The most complete, and probably the most accurate, account of the state of the secondary teaching of history after the reforms has been given by a Spaniard, R. Altamira, *La Enseñanza de la historia*, 2nd edition, Madrid, 1895, 8vo.

particularly mischievous in its effect on historical instruction, which it reduces to a set of questions and answers.

III. It is now possible, however, to indicate what is the direction in which historical instruction is likely to develop in France [1] and the questions which will need to be solved for the purpose of introducing a rational technical system. Here we shall endeavour to formulate these questions in a methodical table.

(1) *General Organisation.*—What object should historical instruction aim at? What services can it render to the culture of the pupil? What influence can it have upon his conduct? What facts ought it to enable him to understand? And, consequently, what principles ought to guide the choice of subjects and methods? Ought the instruction to be spread over the whole duration of the classes, or should it be concentrated in a special class? Should it be given in one-hour or two-hour classes? Should history be distributed into several cycles, as in Germany, so as to cause the pupil to return several times to the same subject at different periods of his studies? Or should it be expounded in a single continuous course, beginning with the commencement of study, as in France? Should the professor give a complete course, or should he select a few questions and leave the pupil to study the others by himself? Should he expound the facts orally, or should he require the pupils to learn them in the first instance from a book, so as to make the course a series of explanations?

(2) *Choice of Subjects.*—What proportion should be observed between home and foreign history? between ancient and contemporary history? between the special branches of history (art, religion, customs, economics) and general his-

[1] We are here treating only of France. But, in order to dispel an illusion of the French public, we may remark that historical pedagogy is still less advanced in English-speaking countries, where the methods used are still mechanical, and even in German-speaking countries, where it is hampered by the conception of patriotic teaching.

tory? between institutions or usages, and events? between the evolution of material usages, intellectual history, social life, political life? between the study of particular incidents, of biography, of dramatic episodes, and the study of the interconnection of events and general evolutions? What place should be assigned to proper names and dates? Should we profit by the opportunities afforded by legends to arouse the critical spirit? or should we avoid legends?

(3) *Order.*—In what order should the subjects be attacked? Should instruction begin with the most ancient periods and the countries with the most ancient civilisations in order to follow chronological order and the order of evolution? or should it begin with the periods and the countries which are nearest to us so as to proceed from the better known to the less known? In the exposition of each period, should the chronological, geographical, or logical order be followed? Should the teacher begin by describing conditions or by narrating events?

(4) *Methods of Instruction.*—Should the pupil be given general formulæ first or particular images? Should the professor state the formulæ himself or require the pupil to search for them? Should formulæ be learnt by heart? In what cases? How are images of historical facts to be produced in the pupils' minds? What use is to be made of engravings? of reproductions and restorations? of imaginary scenes? What use is to be made of narratives and descriptions? of authors' texts? of historical novels? To what extent ought words and formulæ to be quoted? How are facts to be localised? What use is to be made of chronological tables? of synchronical tables? of geographical sketches? of statistical and graphic tables? What is the way to make comprehensible the character of events and customs? the motives of actions? the conditions of customs? How are the episodes of an event to be chosen? and the examples of a custom? How is the interconnection of facts and the process of evolution to be made intelligible? What use is to

be made of comparison? What style of language is to be employed? To what extent should concrete, abstract, and technical terms be used? How is it to be verified that the pupil has understood the terms and assimilated the facts? Can exercises be organised in which the pupil may do original work on the facts? What instruments of study should the pupil have? How should school-books be compiled, with a view to giving the pupil practice in original work?

For the purpose of stating and justifying the solutions of all these problems, a special treatise would not be too much.[1] Here we shall merely indicate the general principles on which a tolerable agreement seems to have been now reached in France.

We no longer go to history for lessons in morals, nor for good examples of conduct, nor yet for dramatic or picturesque scenes. We understand that for all these purposes legend would be preferable to history, for it presents a chain of causes and effects more in accordance with our ideas of justice, more perfect and heroic characters, finer and more affecting scenes. Nor do we seek to use history, as is done in Germany, for the purpose of promoting patriotism and loyalty; we feel that it would be illogical for different persons to draw opposite conclusions from the same science according to their country or party; it would be an invitation to every people to mutilate, if not to alter, history in the direction of its preferences. We understand that the value of every science consists in its being true, and we ask from history truth and nothing more.[2]

[1] I have endeavoured, in a course of lectures at the Sorbonne, to do a part of this work.—[Ch. S.]

[2] Let it be noted, however, that to the question put to the candidates for the modern Baccalaureate in July 1897, "What purpose is served by the teaching of history?" eighty per cent. of the candidates answered, in effect, either because they believed it, or because they thought it would please, "To promote patriotism."—[C. V. L.]

APPENDIX I

The function of history in education is perhaps not yet clearly apparent to all those who teach it. But all those who reflect are agreed to regard it as being principally an instrument of social culture. The study of the societies of the past causes the pupil to understand, by the help of actual instances, what a society is; it familiarises him with the principal social phenomena and the different species of usages, their variety and their resemblances. The study of events and evolutions familiarises him with the idea of the continual transformation which human affairs undergo, it secures him against an unreasoning dread of social changes; it rectifies his notion of progress. All these acquisitions render the pupil fitter for public life; history thus appears as an indispensable branch of instruction in a democratic society.

The guiding principle of historical pedagogy will therefore be to seek for those subjects and those methods which are best calculated to exhibit social phenomena and give an understanding of their evolution. Before admitting a fact into the plan of instruction, it should be asked first of all what educational influence it can exercise; secondly, whether there are adequate means of bringing the pupil to see and understand it. Every fact should be discarded which is instructive only in a low degree, or which is too complicated to be understood, or in regard to which we do not possess details enough to make it intelligible.

IV. To make rational instruction a reality it is not enough to develop a theory of historical pedagogy. It is necessary to renew the material aids and the methods.

History necessarily involves the knowledge of a great number of facts. The professor of history, with no resources but his voice, a blackboard, and abridgments which are little better than chronological tables, is in much the same situation as a professor of Latin without texts or dictionary. The pupil in history needs a repertory of historical facts as the Latin pupil needs a repertory of Latin words; he needs collections of *facts*, and the school text-books are mostly collections of *words*.

There are two vehicles of facts, engravings and books. Engravings exhibit material objects and external aspects, they are useful principally for the study of material civilisation. It is some time since the attempt was first made in Germany to put in the hands of the pupil a collection of engravings arranged for the purposes of historical instruction. The same need has, in France, produced the *Album historique*, which is published under the direction of M. Lavisse.

The book is the chief instrument. It ought to contain all the characteristic features necessary for forming mental representations of the events, the motives, the habits, the institutions studied; it will consist principally in narratives and descriptions, to which characteristic sayings and formulæ may be appended. For a long time it was endeavoured to construct those books out of extracts selected from ancient authors; they were compiled in the form of collections of texts.[1] Experience seems to indicate that this method must be abandoned; it has a scientific appearance, it is true, but is not intelligible to children. It is better to address pupils in contemporary language. It is in this spirit that, pursuant to the *Instructions* of 1890,[2] collections of *Historical Readings* have been compiled, of which the most important has been published by the firm of Hachette.

The pupils' methods of work still bear witness to the late introduction of historical teaching. In most historical classes methods still prevail which only exercise the pupils' receptivity: the course of lectures, the summary, reading, questioning, the *rédaction*, the reproduction of maps. It is as

[1] This is what has been produced in Germany under the name of *Quellenbuch*.

[2] The same pedagogic theory will be found in the preface to my *Histoire narrative et descriptive des anciens peuples de l'Orient*, Supplement for the use of professors, Paris, 1890, 8vo.—[Ch. S.]

if a Latin pupil were to confine himself to repeating grammar-lessons and extracts from authors, without ever doing translation or composition.

In order that the teaching may make an adequate impression, it is necessary, if not to discard all these passive methods, at least to supplement them by exercises which call out the activity of the pupil. Some such exercises have already been experimented with, and others might be devised.[1] The pupil may be set to analyse engravings, narratives, and descriptions in such a way as to bring out the character of the facts: the short written or oral analysis will guarantee that he has seen and understood, it will be an opportunity to inculcate the habit of using only precise terms. Or the pupil may be asked to furnish a drawing, a geographical sketch, a synchronical table. He may be required to draw up tables of comparison between different societies, and tables showing the interconnection of facts.

A book is needed to supply the pupil with the materials for these exercises. Thus the reform of methods is connected with the reform of the instruments of work. Both reforms will progress according as the professors and the public perceive more clearly the part played by historical instruction in social education.

[1] I have treated this question in the *Revue universitaire*, 1896, vol. i. —[Ch. S.]

APPENDIX II

THE HIGHER TEACHING OF HISTORY IN FRANCE

The higher teaching of history has been in a great measure transformed, in our country, within the last thirty years. The process has been gradual, as it ought to have been, and has consisted in a succession of slight modifications. But although a rational continuity has been observed in the steps taken, the great number of these steps has not failed, in these last days, to astonish, and even to offend, the public. Public opinion, to which appeal has been made in favour of reforms, has been somewhat surprised by being appealed to so often, and perhaps it is not superfluous to indicate here, once more, the general significance and the inner logic of the movement which we are witnessing.

I. Before the last years of the Second Empire, the higher teaching of the historical sciences was organised in France on no coherent system.[1]

There were chairs of history in different institutions, of different types: at the Collège de France, in the Faculties of Letters, and in the "special schools," such as the École normale supérieure and the École des chartes.

The Collège de France was a relic of the institutions of the *ancien régime*. It was founded in the sixteenth century

[1] On the organisation of higher education in France at this epoch and on the first reforms, see the excellent work of M. L. Liard, *l'Enseignement supérieur en France*, Paris, 1888-94, 2 vols. 8vo.

in opposition to the scholastic Sorbonne, to be a refuge for the new sciences, and had the glorious privilege of representing historically the higher speculative studies, the spirit of free inquiry, and the interests of pure science. Unfortunately, in the domain of the historical sciences, the Collège de France had allowed its traditions to be obliterated up to a certain point. The great men who taught history in this illustrious institution (J. Michelet, for example), were not technical experts, nor even men of learning, in the proper sense of the word. The audiences which they swayed by their eloquence were not composed of students of history.

The Faculties of Letters formed part of a system established by the Napoleonic legislator. This legislator, in creating the Faculties, by no means entertained the design of encouraging scientific research. He had no great love for science. The Faculties of Law, of Medicine, and so on, were intended by him to be professional schools supplying society with the lawyers, physicians, and so on, which it needs. But three of the five Faculties were unable, from the beginning, to perform the part allotted them, while the other two, Law and Medicine, successfully performed theirs. The Faculties of Catholic Theology did not train the priests needed by society, because the State consented to the education of the priests being conducted in the diocesan seminaries. The Faculties of Sciences and of Letters did not train the professors for secondary education, the engineers, and so on, needed by society, because they were here met by the triumphant competition of "special schools" previously instituted: the École normale, the École polytechnique. The Faculties of Catholic Theology, of Sciences, and of Letters were therefore obliged to justify their existence by other modes of activity. In particular, the professors of history in the Faculties of Letters could not undertake the instruction of the young men who were destined to teach history in the *lycées*. Deprived of these special pupils, they found themselves in a situation analogous to that of those charged with historical instruction at the Collège de France. They too were not, as a rule, technical experts. For half a century they carried on the work of higher popularisation in lectures delivered to large audiences of leisured persons (since much abused), who were attracted by the force, the elegance, and the pleasing style of their diction.

The function of training the future teachers for secondary education was reserved for the École normale supérieure. Now at this epoch it was an admitted principle that to be a good secondary teacher it is necessary for a man to know, and sufficient to know perfectly, the subject he is charged to teach. The one is certainly necessary, but the other is not sufficient: knowledge of a different, of a higher, order is no less indispensable than the regular "scholastic" equipment. At the École there was never any question of such higher knowledge, but, in accordance with the prevailing theory, preparation was made for secondary teaching simply by imparting it. However, as the École normale has always been excellently recruited, the system in vogue has not prevented it from numbering among its former pupils men of the first order, not only as professors, thinkers, or writers, but even as critical scholars. But it must be recognised that they made their way for themselves, in spite of the system, not thanks to it, after, not during, their pupilage, and principally when they had the advantage, during a stay at the French School at Athens, of the wholesome contact with documents which they had not enjoyed at the Rue d'Ulm. "Does it not seem strange," it has been said, "that so many generations of professors should have been turned out by the École normale incapable of utilising documents? . . . Formerly, in short, students of history, on leaving the École, were not prepared either to teach history, which they had learned in a great hurry, or to investigate difficult questions."[1]

As for the École des chartes, which was founded under

[1] E. Lavisse, *Questions d'enseignement national*, p. 12.

the Restoration, it was, from a certain point of view, a special school like the others, designed in theory to train those useful functionaries, archivists and librarians. But professional instruction was early reduced to a strict minimum, and the École des chartes was organised on a very original plan, with a view to provide a rational and complete apprenticeship for the young men who proposed to study mediæval French history. The pupils of the École des chartes did not follow any course of "mediæval history," but they learnt all that is necessary for doing work on the solution of the still open questions of mediæval history. Here alone, in virtue of an accidental anomaly, the subjects which are preliminary and auxiliary to historical research were systematically taught. We have already had occasion to note the effects of this circumstance. [1]

This was the state of affairs when, towards the end of the Second Empire, a vigorous reform movement set in. Some young Frenchmen had visited Germany; they had been struck by the superiority of the German university system over the Napoleonic system of Faculties and special schools. Certainly France, with its defective organisation, had produced many men and many works, but it now began to be held that "in all kinds of enterprises the least possible part should be left to chance," and that "when an institution proposes to train professors of history and historians, it ought to supply them with the means of becoming what it intends them to be."

M. V. Duruy, minister of Public Education, supported the partisans of a renaissance of the higher studies. But he did not think it practicable to interfere, for the purpose either of remodelling, of fusing, or of suppressing them, with the existing institutions,—the Collège de France, the Faculties of Letters, the École normale supérieure, the École des chartes, all of which were consecrated by the services they had rendered, and by the lustre they received from the

[1] Cf. *supra*, p. 55.

eminent men who had been, or were, connected with them. He changed nothing, he added. He crowned the somewhat heterogeneous edifice of existing institutions by the creation of an "École pratique des hautes études," which was established at the Sorbonne in 1868.

The École pratique des hautes études (historical and philological section) was intended by those who founded it to prepare young men for research of a scientific character. It was not meant to be subservient to the interests of the professions, and there was to be no popularisation. Students were not to go there to learn the results obtained by science, but, for the same purpose which takes the chemical student to the laboratory, to be initiated into the technical methods by which new results can be obtained. Thus the spirit of the new institution was not without some analogy to that of the primitive tradition of the Collège de France. It was endeavoured to do there, for all the branches of universal history and philology, what had long been done at the École des chartes for the limited domain of French mediæval history.

II. As long as the Faculties of Letters were satisfied to be as they were (that is, without students), and as long as their ambition did not go beyond their traditional functions (the holding of public lectures, the conferring of degrees), the organisation of the higher teaching of the historical sciences in France remained in the condition which we have described. When the Faculties of Letters began to seek a new justification for their existence and new functions, changes became inevitable.

This is not the place to explain why and how the Faculties of Letters were led to desire to work more actively, or rather in other ways than in the past, for the promotion of the historical sciences. M. V. Duruy, in inaugurating the École des hautes études at the Sorbonne, had declared that this young and vigorous plant would thrust asunder the old stones; and, without a doubt, the

spectacle of the fruitful activity of the École des hautes études has contributed not a little to awaken the conscience of the Faculties. On the other hand the liberality of the public authorities, which have increased the *personnel* of the Faculties, which have built palaces for them, and liberally endowed them with the materials required by their work, has imposed new duties on these privileged institutions.

It is about twenty-five years since the Faculties of Letters began to transform themselves, and during this period their progressive transformation has occasioned changes in the whole fabric of the higher teaching of historical science in France, which up to that time had remained unshaken, even by the ingenious addition of 1868.

III. The first care of the Faculties was to provide themselves with students. This was not, to be sure, the main difficulty, for the École normale supérieure (in which twenty pupils are admitted every year, chosen from among hundreds of candidates) was no longer sufficient for the recruiting of the now numerous body of professors engaged in secondary education. Many young men who had been candidates (along with the pupils of the École normale supérieure) for the degrees which give access to the scholastic profession, were thrown on their own resources. Here was an assured supply of students. At the same time the military laws, by attaching much-prized immunities to the title of *licencié ès lettres*, were calculated to attract to the Faculties, if they prepared students for the licentiate, a large and very interesting class of young men. Lastly, the foreigners (so numerous at the École des hautes études), who come to France to complete their scientific education, and who up to that time were surprised to have no opportunity of profiting by the Faculties, were sure to go to them as soon as they found there something analogous to what they had been accustomed to find in the German universities, and the kind of instruction they wanted.

Before students in any great number could be taught the

way to the Faculties, great efforts were necessary and several years passed; but it was after the Faculties obtained the students they desired that the real problems presented themselves for solution.

The great majority of the students in the Faculties of Letters have been originally candidates for degrees, for the licentiate, and for *agrégation*, who entered with the avowed intention of "preparing" for the licentiate and for *agrégation*. The Faculties have not been able to escape the obligation of helping them in this "preparation." But, twenty years ago, examinations were still conceived in accordance with ancient formulæ. The licentiate was an attestation of advanced secondary study, a kind of "higher baccalaureate"; for the *agrégation* in the classes of history and geography (which became the real *licentia docendi*), the candidates were required to show that they "had a very good knowledge of the subjects they would be charged to teach." Henceforth there was a danger lest the teaching of the Faculties, which must, like that of the École normale supérieure, be preparatory for the examinations for the licentiate and for *agrégation*, should be compelled by the force of circumstances to assume the same character. Note that a certain emulation could not fail to arise between the pupils of the École normale and those of the Faculties in the competitions for *agrégation*. The *agrégation* programmes being what they were, this emulation seemed likely to have the result of engaging the rival teachers and students more and more in school work, not of a scientific kind, equally devoid of dignity and real utility.

The danger was very serious. It was perceived from the first by those clear-sighted promoters of the reform of the Faculties, MM. A. Dumont, L. Liard, E. Lavisse. M. Lavisse wrote in 1884: "To maintain that the Faculties have for their chief object the preparation for examinations is to substitute drill for scientific culture: this is the serious grievance which able men have against the partisans of innovation. . . . The partisans of innovation reply that they have seen the drawbacks of the new departure from the beginning, but that they are convinced that a modification of the examination-system will follow the reform of higher education; that a reconciliation will be found between scientific work and the preparation for examinations; and that thus the only grievance their opponents have against them will fall to the ground." It is only doing justice to the foremost champion of reform to acknowledge that he was never tired of insisting on the weak point; and in order to convince oneself that the *examination question* has always been considered the key-stone of the problem of the organisation of higher education in France, it is only necessary to look through the speeches and the articles entitled "Education and Examinations," "Examinations and Study," "Study and Examinations," &c., which M. Lavisse has collected in his three volumes published at intervals of five years from 1885 onwards: *Questions d'enseignement national, Études et étudiants, A propos de nos écoles.*

Thus the question of the reform of the examinations connected with higher education (licentiate, *agrégation*, doctorate) has been placed on the order of the day. It was there in 1884; it is still there in 1897. But, during the interval, visible progress has been made in the direction which we consider the right one, and now a solution seems near.

IV. The old examination-system required candidates for degrees to show that they had received an excellent secondary education. As it condemned those candidates, students receiving higher instruction, to exercises of the same kind as those of which they had already had their fill in the *lycées*, it was a simple matter to attack it. It was defended feebly, and has been demolished.

But how was it to be replaced? The problem was very complex. Is it any wonder that it was not solved at a stroke?

First of all, it was important to come to an agreement on

this preliminary question: What are the capacities and what is the knowledge students should be required to give proof of possessing? General knowledge? Technical knowledge and the capacity of doing original research (as at the École des chartes and the École des hautes études)? Pedagogic capacity? It came gradually to be recognised that, considering the great extent and variety of the class from which the students are drawn, it is necessary to draw distinctions.

From candidates for the licentiate it is enough to require that they should give proof of good general culture, permitting them at the same time, if they wish, to show that they have a taste for, and some experience in, original research.

From the candidates for *agrégation* (*licentia docendi*) who have already obtained the licentiate, there will be required (1) formal proof that they know, by experience, what it is to study an historical problem, and that they have the technical knowledge necessary for such studies; (2) proof of pedagogic capacity, which is a professional necessity for this class.

The students who are not candidates for anything, neither for the licentiate nor for *agrégation*, and who are simply seeking to obtain scientific initiation—the old programmes did not contemplate the existence of such a class of students—will merely be required to prove that they have profited by the tuition and the advice they have received.

This settled, a great stride has been made. For programmes, as we know, regulate study. By virtue of the authority of the programmes historical studies in the Faculties will now have the threefold character which it is desirable that they should have. General culture will not cease to be held in honour. Technical exercises in criticism and research will have their legitimate place. Lastly, pedagogy (theoretical and practical) will not be neglected.

The difficulties begin when it is attempted to determine

the tests which, in each department, are the best, that is, the most conclusive. On this subject opinions differ. Though no one now contests the principles, the modes of application which have hitherto been tried or suggested do not meet with unanimous approval. The organisation of the licentiate has been revised three times; the statute relating to the *agrégation* in history has been reformed or amended five times. And this is not the end. New simplifications are imperative. But what is the importance of this instability—of which, however, complaints begin to be heard[1]—if it is established, as we believe it is, that progress towards a better state of things has been continuous through all these changes, without any notable retrogression?

There is no need to explain here in detail the different transitory systems which have been put into practice. We have had occasion to criticise them elsewhere.[2] Now that most of what we objected to has been abolished, what is the use of reviving old controversies? We shall not even mention the points in which the present system seems to us to be still capable of improvement, for there is reason to hope that it will soon be modified, and in a very satisfactory manner. Let it suffice to say that the Faculties now confer a new diploma, the *Diplôme d'études supérieures*, which all the students have a right to seek, but which the candidates for *agrégation* are obliged to obtain. This diploma of higher studies, analogous to that of the École des hautes études, the *brevet* of the École des chartes, and the doctorate in philosophy at the German universities, is given to those students of history who, qualified by a certain academical standing, have passed an examination in which the principal tests are, besides questions on the "sciences" auxiliary to historical research, the composition and the defence of an

[1] *Revue historique*, lxiii. (1897), p. 96.

[2] See the *Revue internationale d'enseignement*, Feb. 1893; the *Revue universitaire*, June 1892, Oct. and Nov. 1894, July 1895; and the *Political Science Quarterly*, Sept. 1894.

original monograph. Every one now recognises that "the examination for the diploma of studies will yield excellent fruit, if the vigilance and conscientiousness of examiners maintain it at its proper value."[1]

V. To sum up, the attractions of preparation for degrees have brought the Faculties a host of students. But, under the old system of examinations for the licentiate and for *agrégation*, preparation for degrees was a task which did not harmonise very well with the work which the Faculties deemed suitable for themselves, useful to their pupils, and advantageous to science. The examination-system has therefore been perseveringly reformed, not without difficulty, into conformity with a certain ideal of what the higher teaching of history ought to be. The result is that the Faculties have taken rank among the institutions which contribute to the positive progress of the historical sciences. An enumeration of the works which have appeared under their auspices during the last few years would, if necessary, bear witness to the fact.

This evolution has already produced satisfactory results, and will produce more if it goes on as well as it has begun. To begin with, the transformation of historical instruction in the Faculties has brought about a corresponding transformation at the École normale supérieure. The École normale has also, for two years, been awarding a "*Diplôme d'études*"; original researches, pedagogic exercises, and general culture are encouraged there in the same degree as by the new Faculties. It now differs from the Faculties only in being a close institution, recruited under certain precautions; practically it is a Faculty like the others, but with a small number of select students. Secondly, the École des hautes études and the École des chartes, both of which will be installed at the end of 1897, in the renovated

[1] *Revue historique*, l.c. p. 98. I have developed elsewhere what I have here contented myself with stating. See the *Revue internationale de l'enseignement*, Nov. 1897.—[C. V. L.]

Sorbonne, have still their justification for existence ; for many specialists are represented at the École des hautes études which are not, and doubtless never will be, represented in the Faculties; and, in the case of the studies bearing on mediæval history, the body of converging instruction given at the École des chartes will always be incomparable. But the old antagonism between the École des hautes études and the École des chartes on the one hand, and the Faculties on the other, has disappeared. All these institutions, lately so dissimilar, will henceforth co-operate for the purpose of carrying on a common work in a common spirit. Each of these retains its name, its autonomy, and its traditions; but together they form a whole: the historical section of an ideal University of Paris, much vaster than the one which was sanctioned by the law in 1896. Of this "greater" University, the École des chartes, the École des hautes études, the École normale supérieure, and the whole body of historical instruction given by the Faculty of Letters, are now practically so many independent "*instituts.*"

INDEX OF PROPER NAMES

Index of Proper Names

Index of Proper Names